W9-CZO-488

THE WAY TO GO

The Coming Revival of
U.S. Rail Passenger Service

THOMAS C. SOUTHERLAND, JR.
AND WILLIAM McCLEERY

Simon and Schuster / *New York*

SBN 671-21585-X
Library of Congress Catalog Card Number: 73-13119
Designed by Irving Perkins
Manufactured in the United States of America

1   2   3   4   5   6   7   8   9   10

CONTENTS

5

Contents

Some people see things as they are and say, "Why?"
I see things as they ought to be and say, "Why not?"
— ROBERT F. KENNEDY

PART ONE

UGLY PROBLEM, ATTRACTIVE SOLUTION

A Prize for Slaying the Traffic Dragon

AMERICANS TODAY are beset by a multitude of large, sticky problems—from urban crime to a looming power shortage—to which the solutions are unclear; or, if clear, unattractive, and fantastically expensive. But we have one major problem whose solution is not only clear but attractive and, in the long run, relatively inexpensive.

The problem: how to control the intolerable pollution, congestion, and depletion of resources caused by the automobile and its ever-spreading highways, and to a lesser degree by the airplane and its ever-spreading airports.

The solution: provide a balanced transportation system in which railroad passenger service is made so good that many people who now travel by automobile or plane will freely choose to go by rail. Then, when travel by automobile or plane becomes impossibly difficult, or is restricted by law in defense of our environment and our resources, the rail lines will be there.

But *is* the automobile a major problem? Have we not been promised virtually emission-free automobile engines by 1975 or 1980, and, soon after, engines that will use far less fuel? Yes. But even if those promises are kept—even if automobiles can be made to run on used bathwater and emit pure mountain air— their proliferation still must be checked because of the space they occupy; the way they overrun our cities and swarm over our countryside, demanding a constantly expanding highway system that scars field and forest and neighborhood and disrupts our ecology. And, to repeat, what is true of the automobile and its highways is true in lesser degree of the airplane and its airports.

The case against the automobile as our principal means of transportation has been made so often and so well that we assume most of our readers need no further convincing. For those who do, we recommend an immediate reading of this book's Appendix— "Frightening Facts and Figures about Automobiles and Airplanes" —and of one or more of the good, angry books briefly reviewed in Chapter VI.

But given the problem of automobile and airplane over-proliferation, how certain is it that a modernized rail passenger service is the only or best solution? Locomotives, after all, burn fuel; rail lines and their stations or depots occupy space; tracks and railroad equipment use metals. True. But the highways that railroads travel on already exist, linking coast with coast, city with city, threading through towns and suburbs and into metropolitan centers. Even where track has been ripped up, the rights-of-way often remain clear, and even when roadbed and tracks need upgrading—which most of ours urgently do—this can be done at a fraction of the cost of building a highway, and does not involve the violation of fresh countryside or neighborhoods.

Nearly all of the relevant statistics favor rail travel.

A one-lane highway, for example, can handle 2,000 persons an hour; a six-lane highway, 9,000 persons an hour: but a single set of railroad tracks can carry between 40,000 and 60,000 persons an hour.

In pollution terms, only the bicycle is a cleaner vehicle than the train, whose fuel mileage (.36 gallons per 100 passenger-miles) is 12 times that of the automobile (4.4 gallons per 100 passenger-miles), 15 times that of the airplane (5.5 gallons per 100 passenger-miles), and twice that of the bus. The train uses lead-free fuel—or electricity—and compared with the bus emits only small quantities of sulfur oxides.

Travel by rail, according to one study, is 23 times as safe as by automobile, 2½ times as safe as by plane, 1½ times as safe as by bus; it is more dependable than any of its competitors (being nearly immune to bad weather and less subject to mechanical failure when kept in top condition—as it will be in the new railroad age with the aid of computers, automatic sensory devices, and even laser beams for track alignment); and it is more relaxing, allowing the traveler to work, read, eat, sleep, or even think while moving at high speed toward his destination. (An automobile commuter was stopped one morning on the New Jersey Turnpike for driving with his elbows while eating a bowl of cereal.)

This is not to say that the train is superior in every way to the automobile, plane, or bus; but a balanced transportation system will not eliminate those means of travel. Giving rails their proper and sensible place in the transportation scheme will actually help to keep the other choices open, because the highways and air lanes will be freed up a bit when people who hate to drive in traffic and people who are scared to death of flying are no longer compelled to do so—as they now are—by the almost complete absence of a rail option or by its insuperable difficulty and inconvenience and its unreasonable expensiveness.

Well, then: If modernizing our passenger rail service is so clearly the solution to the automobile and airplane problem, is it not inevitable that America *will* modernize—and, being America, will soon have the world's finest rail service? And is this not, then, one problem we can afford not to worry about?

Yes and no. Yes, it is inevitable that we will one day have if not the finest then a very fine rail service. But no, it is *not* something we can feel relaxed about, because it is not inevitable that we will have it *soon*: soon enough to head off another great spasm of superhighway and airport building already in the planning stage or beyond. We will certainly not have our new rail service soon unless great pressure in its behalf is brought to bear by

worried citizens upon elected officials at every level, and particularly at the topmost levels.

The unarguable fact that we *must* revive our railroads does not
insure us against incredibly expensive foot-dragging. It was
evident to some Americans fifty years ago that the country would
one day regret allowing itself to become so dependent on the
automobile—but it happened. The number of U.S. intercity
passenger trains dwindled from 20,000 in 1929 to fewer than 240
in 1972. In 1950 we had 37,360 passenger rail cars in service; today
there are fewer than 8,500—and this in a period in which our
population rose by 60 million.

But is citizen pressure the only force that can speed the coming
of good rail service?

The most obvious answer to that question is that in a capitalist
democracy, neither business nor government ever gets far out in
front of public demand—unless there is financial or political
profit to be made in *arousing* public demand.

Some, but not many, politicians are farsighted enough to recognize the likelihood that good rail service will become a popular
cause in the future, and have already enlisted in it. Most will wait
until the popular demand has begun to build up.

The financial profit motive, which one might expect to move the
railroad companies to push for great new passenger service, is
largely absent because, for reasons explored later in this book,
the rail companies have always made their big money on freight,
not passengers, and most of them are locked into a posture of trying to get rid of passenger service rather than trying to increase
and improve it.

Most large companies that stand to profit, in the new railway
age, from building locomotives and railroad cars, improving rights-
of-way, and so on are now deeply involved in building automobiles
and planes, and highways and airports. They can and will shift
some of their enormous productive capacity when someone else
has created a new demand. But they are by nature market-

conscious and will not take the lead in creating a new demand when the old one is still so profitable.

So, though the new age is clearly coming, we are still moving down the old wrong road with tremendous momentum, and there is great profit to many people in our continuing to do so as long as possible. Only private citizens, motivated by concern for the national welfare, can be counted upon to lead the movement for better rail service *soon*.

(If the authors of this book are optimists, we are of the long- and not the short-range variety, a long-range optimist being one who expects things to get worse before they get better and is therefore not disheartened when they do get worse. And U.S. rail passenger service—particularly intercity service—*is* getting worse. It is worse at this writing than when we began this book two years ago. True, the Highway Trust Fund described in Chapter V is being opened up somewhat to finance mass transit, including commuter rail service; but the second Nixon administration is not seeking as much additional funding as Amtrak needs, is urging further curtailment of Amtrak service, and is cutting back funds for research into new modes of rail travel described in Chapter IX. The *Metroliner* and many other intercity trains are on "go slow" orders because of poor roadbed and track conditions; the Penn Central has turned out to be in even worse shape than was earlier supposed; and—though a nationwide rail labor pact has been agreed upon—local rail strikes have been occurring with the usual regularity. A rash of mostly minor train wrecks is casting doubt on the safety of train travel when in reality what they show is the almost criminal neglect of roadbeds, tracks, and rolling stock. The question is *how much worse* things will be allowed to get before aroused citizens move to make them better.)

But if the new railroad age is surely coming, does it matter so much whether it comes soon or late?

It matters to the land that will be destroyed by the new highways and airports that will be built unless the new rail service

comes soon. It matters to the quality of life everywhere in
America, for the bulldozing and paving of land is virtually irreversible. Moreover, the building of new highways and airports,
or the enlarging of old ones, serves to mask the magnitude of our
transportation problem while it grows rapidly, dangerously worse.
That is, the congestion of present highways and airports is a
graphic reminder, persuasive even to the unimaginative, that
something is very wrong. Enlarging and multiplying highways
and airports lessens the congestion, postpones the day of reckon-
ing, encourages the building and buying of more cars and planes
—requiring more freeways and landing strips.

Second—and this is a sentimental or, if you will, patriotic
reason: if we start moving now to balance our transportation
system, using the democratic devices our forefathers willed us,
we can accomplish the partial transition from autos and planes to
rails with a minimum of fuss, as free men and women. If we
procrastinate like spoiled children, the federal government eventually will have to yank us out of our cars and shove us onto trains,
with an inevitable loss of freedom and dignity.

The authors of this book are confident that Americans *will*
generate the citizen pressure needed to start the move now; but
this will not come about as easily as one might expect, for a
number of reasons—some obvious, some fairly subtle.

Among obvious reasons is the passionate psychosexual attach-
ment many Americans have for their very own automobiles. It is
possible to love both good automobiles and good trains, but it
takes an emotional versatility not universally possessed. Many
Americans would rather adjust to those ills they have—sitting
stalled in their air-conditioned cars spewing exhaust into the
atmosphere—than work for a real change.

Those who love their automobiles single-heartedly, those who
lack imagination and foresight, and those who have a personal
financial stake in perpetuating the present overpopulation of
autos and planes add up to a goodly number of citizens who will

not soon join, much less lead, a drive to bring U.S. rail service into the twentieth century.

All right. No good cause ever had everybody's support. Surely there is no dearth of people who *would* lead or support such a drive: concerned environmentalists, for one group; and commuters whose noses are rubbed almost daily in the urban traffic mess, whether they come to work by clotted freeways or by antiquated, strike-prone commuter rail lines. Commuter fury alone should be enough to fuel a transportation revolution.

The truth is, though, that many who ought to be, whom one would expect to be, prorailroad activists, and who must be if the movement is to get out of the roundhouse soon, are slow to show enthusiasm for it. We suggest that these people, whose enthusiasm is so essential, fall into three groups.

First, those who know that automobiles and planes are becoming awesome enemies of the environment, but who can't get excited about railroads as an alternative because *they have never seen or ridden a really good train* and so are unconvinced that such trains really exist. This group includes particularly the young, whose energies have proved so valuable to other environmental causes. It also includes some older people who know there were once good railroads in America but who have been subjected in recent years to such unspeakable equipment and service that they cannot believe salvation will ever come down that track.

It is understandable why anyone would be diffident about leading or joining a prorail movement if he thought it would bring many more trains like those now running on most American lines. The truth is that the good trains now running in other countries are a new breed: not merely a practical alternative to auto and plane, but a glamorous and exciting alternative. But those who have never been exposed to really modern railroads can hardly be expected to understand that, and they are therefore denied a legitimate and potent motive for being prorail enthusiasts.

A second group that ought to be actively involved in the fight for better rail service, but isn't, consists of those who assume over-optimistically that a great American rail-modernization program, because it is so urgently and obviously needed, will come about soon without a great upsurge of citizen pressure. That group underestimates the forces working against rails in America: the traditional, deeply entrenched mutual antagonism between rail managements and rail passengers; the complex network of old rail unions with their stored-up enmity toward management and their willingness to use passengers as pawns in their periodic battles to protect themselves against exploitation or progress; and the incredible political clout of the automobile-highway-petroleum lobby in Washington, now joined by the aircraft-airline-airport lobby, both of which are by their nature antirailroad.

A third group fails to work for the railroads it knows are needed because it overpessimistically assumes—from a firsthand knowledge of the obstacles mentioned in the preceding paragraph—that nothing short of a series of catastrophes will ever move America to stop overproducing automobiles, highways, planes, and airports and turn to railroads. So they are fatalistically willing to sit by and let the transportation crisis run its devastating course.

It is to those three groups that this book is especially directed, and for whom it has been arranged as it has. We begin, in the chapter following this one, with descriptions of great foreign trains, taking the reader to Japan and Europe and other foreign places for a taste of the kind of trains and service we ought to have in America. We know of no better way—short of their actually riding on those outstanding trains—to persuade the uninitiated and the disillusioned that the passenger train is, to repeat, a glamorous and exciting alternative to the automobile and the plane.

Next, we offer a short course in railroad history and economics and politics to sober up the optimist who presumes the rail revival will occur soon without knockdown, dragout fights.

And finally, for the pessimist, we report some encouraging developments: first, on the political front, and on the environmental barricades; second, in various parts of this country where some good new trains are now running; third, we describe some cruise trains now available in the United States; fourth, we report on the scientific research being done in this country to develop fantastic new trains for the future; and finally, we round up the news about projected improvements in commuter rail service.

We anticipate three criticisms of this book which we would like to answer in advance.

One—to be expected from conscientious environmentalists and furious commuters—will be that the book is not angry enough, not militant enough; that, in tone if not in words, it minimizes the threat to our environment and the dastardy of railroad and highway and other interests by being too hopeful, too upbeat, too good-humored.

Our answer is that while most transportation-reform books are indeed harder-hitting, it is because they star a villain that needs to be knocked down: automobiles, highways, airports, railroad managements. This book stars a hero that needs to be built up: the good passenger train. This book is positive in tone because it deals primarily with the solution, not the problem.

There is much to be angry about in the transportation situation today. But there is so much to be angry about in *every* area today that we suspect the average good citizen's capacity for anger is beginning to run low. And anger is not the only or always the best emotion to bring to a cause.

In olden times, if we can believe the storybooks, when a king wanted a dragon slain, he offered his beautiful daughter as a prize to the one who would slay it. The dragon might have gobbled up entire villages and done untold other damage with his fiery breath and all, but hatred or fear of the dragon did not seem to be enough to motivate the kind of knight who could do the job. He needed to know what the prize would be. He had to fall a little in love with the prize.

We believe that if Americans would fall out of love a little with their sleek new motorcars and planes, and in love a little with sleek new trains, the rail revival would take a great leap forward, and Mother Nature would be grateful.

A second criticism—which we would expect from those a little to the left of political and economic center—is that we have not come out for nationalization of the railroads.

Our reply is that precisely *how* fine passenger rail service is to be brought to the United States is not the concern of this book, nor do we think it should be the primary concern of those who, having read the book, will charge out to attack the traffic dragon. Maybe the lines *will* have to be nationalized. They already are in nearly every one of the developed countries whose railroads we praise in the next chapter. Certainly ours will have to be more heavily subsidized. *The Wall Street Journal* has said, "The federal government continues to move toward a takeover of the nation's railroads, and it's hard to see how the trend is going to be stopped or reversed."

Our attitude is that the highway-and-airport juggernaut must be stopped and a balanced transportation system achieved through development of a spectacular new rail system. If railroad managements will work up some enthusiasm for their own commodity and push for great passenger service through privately owned lines, heavily subsidized by the federal government, fine. Let it come about that way. If the antipassenger attitude of rail management is so deeply ingrained (and you will find evidence in this book that it does go very deep) that private ownership simply cannot do the job, then let there be nationalization.

But however it is achieved, let there be railroads. That is the result that all friends of the environment and of national sanity need to concentrate on achieving. Premature debate over nationalization can be a great concentration-breaker.

A third possible criticism is that we have not differentiated sufficiently between commuter rail service, which few oppose, and intercity rail service, which many consider outdated and impractical.

Our view is that the two are not really separable. They only seem so because they are on different timetables. That is, the automobile has already uglified many of our cities and choked them half to death; it is only beginning on our towns and suburbs and parks (fairly well along there, actually) and other places that attract travelers and tourists. It is not too late to save the cities, but saving them will be many times more costly than it would have been if we had acted sooner. We ought to learn a lesson from the cities about putting too much reliance on auto and plane, and apply that lesson to the rest of the country.

All aboard, then, for a trip into America's transportation future, through some fascinating physical, scientific, economic, political, historical, and psychological scenery. Much that was colorful and romantic in our past can—and should—never be revived, or even glimpsed outside a museum. But the railroad as a means of moving passengers is a great, romantic old idea whose time has come again. In fighting for the coming rail revival, one can be motivated by both a love of the past and a love of the future. We have come to a junction where nostalgia and science fiction intersect.

"On the face of it, a passenger instrument which can propel 200 to 300 people at eighty miles an hour with only 1500 horsepower and a crew of three or four men is not bound for the museum for the same reason that the stage coach landed there. Man has yet to invent an overland passenger mode of transport with the train's unique combination of speed, safety, comfort, dependability, and economy."

—The editor of *Trains* Magazine, quoted in *The Interstate Commerce Omission*

"The Port Authority's New York City Trade Center has the fastest vertical transport in the world [i.e., elevators] and the slowest horizontal transport in the world [autos and trains] for getting there."
—THEODORE KHEEL, labor mediator and transportation gadfly

"To save American capitalism as well as the environment, I propose that President Nixon negotiate the sale of all of America's automobile production to Russia—which is foolishly following our lead and moving into the private automobile age. Such a pact would tremendously improve our economy and environment, promote physical fitness and destroy Communism just as surely as cars have been threatening to destroy us."
—DAVID W. LEVINE, Scarsdale, N. Y., Jan. 14, 1973
(Letter to *The New York Times*)

"A sizable majority of the American public favors continuing intercity passenger trains even if it means Federal subsidies, according to a nationwide poll made public yesterday.

"The survey showed a 64-to-22 per cent margin for this policy, while at the same time showing a distinctly unfavorable rating of the performance of the railroad industry.

"The survey was taken last May by Louis Harris and Associates for Amtrak . . ."
—*The New York Times*, October 4, 1972

CHAPTER 〔〕

The Way It Ought to Be: Great Trains Abroad

IT IS HARD to believe, but true, that the United States of America—
the world's number one technological nation, winner of the race
to the moon, leading consumer of the world's natural resources,
and the world's biggest spender on scientific research—has the
worst rail passenger service of all the world's developed nations.
As a Mobil Oil Corporation advertisement remarked recently,
"Intercity trains in other countries make ours look pitiful."

The statistics are startling. In early 1971 we had fewer than 200
intercity trains; Britain had 1,000, France 850, and West Germany
527. Since then, these nations have increased theirs, and ours have
declined further. Obviously it would be a mistake to conclude
from these figures that Americans are less enterprising and up-to-
date than their foreign cousins. Given our wealth, our technology,
our fuel resources, and our wide-open spaces, they too would
probably have converted largely to automobile and plane travel.
Since they could not afford to do that, they have developed their
passenger trains—as we might have, had we been less affluent.
But now that there are, once more, railroads in our future, we can
learn about modern railroading from nations that in many other
respects are less advanced than we are.

If everyone in America could take a ride on Japan's New
Tokaido Line—in Japanese, Tokaido Shin Kansen—between To-

kyo and Osaka, it might set American railroading ahead twenty
years. (*Tokaido* in Japanese means literally "east seaway" and is
the name of an ancient—long before railroads—road between Tokyo and Osaka; *shin* means "new superfast"; and *kansen* means
"main line.") The combination of high speed, good service, immaculate cars, and an incredibly smooth ride has made the "bullet
trains," as they are called outside Japan, the front-runner among
all modern high-speed rail lines.

Built by the government-owned Japanese National Railways
(JNR) to whisk people along Japan's heavily industrialized Pacific
coast—Japan's major urban corridor—these trains impress visitors
almost as much as Mount Fujiyama, visible from the train. A
Tokaido Shin Kansen train made its first commercial run on
October 1, 1964 (in time for the 1964 Tokyo Olympic Games), and
today there are more than 100 of them operating each way every
day. These sparkling blue-and-white, bullet-nosed trains come in
two categories: The superexpress *Hikari* ("Lightning"), with 16
cars, and the limited-express *Kodama* ("Echo"), with 12 cars. The
longer "Lightning" makes two stops en route and covers the Tokyo–Osaka distance of 320 miles (about the rail distance between
New York and Richmond, Virginia) in three hours and ten
minutes. The "Echo" stops eleven times en route and makes it in
exactly four hours and ten minutes.

Trains depart on the dot, at twenty-minute intervals during
peak operating periods. Electronic computers provide instant con-
firmation of reservations—and there are redcaps in the station!

For those who like to know what makes things go, the train is
powered by 60-cycle—and, through certain areas, 50-cycle—electric current received via an on-board pantograph (the upthrust
arm that links an electric engine with its power line) from an overhead catenary structure over the tracks, much like most American
electrical trains. Because current feeds into each pair of cars in
the train, the bullet is classified as a multiple-unit train. (Throughout the world, haulage by electric trains often employs the

multiple-unit system, in which several motor coaches are distributed throughout the train, each matched to a varying number of trailers, or conventional coaches. On multiple-unit trains, motor coaches are virtually identical to trailers except that they receive the motive power.) Control cables linking all the motor coaches allow the train to be driven from the front or rear, so that no time need be spent in turning around at terminals.

The trains are bullet-nosed at both front and rear to reduce air resistance, and have controls at either end; seats throughout the train can be flipped over to face in the opposite direction—as they can be, of course, in conventional American coaches.

The Shin Kansen has two modern operational features for improving safety and efficiency. One is automatic train control which automatically keeps the train within proper speeds. The other is a centralized traffic-control system which permits surveillance of each train's position by officials at central control in Tokyo. The system receives signals from the trains which are fed into elaborate instrument panels, display boards, and computers.

The cars are air-conditioned, and equipment includes buffet and bar cars, business compartments, and telephones for calls to major cities along the line. A "no tipping" system is strictly enforced.

The "bullets" knock off for a six-hour period every evening so that maintenance crews can inspect the roadbed and keep it in top condition for smoothness of ride. At its running speed of 131 mph (a speedometer is clearly visible in the two buffet cars), this train vibrates so little that a full glass of water on a table in the train will not slosh a drop. There is no rattle, sway, or lurching.

The smoothness of a train ride depends on several factors: roadbed construction, type of track, the resiliency of the car, and the wheels. The Japanese constructed special new roadbeds for the "bullet," using prestressed-concrete ties and a continuous welded rail. Prestressed concrete is more stable and requires less maintenance than a roadbed of earth and crushed stone, and

welded tracks are more efficient and there is no clickety-clack
sound. (Welded tracks are more efficient because there are no
discontinuities in the track, therefore less vibration; i.e., every time
a "click" is heard on a conventional train, metal is grinding against
metal, and this causes wear.) The Japanese rails, mounted on
rubber track pads and springs to absorb lateral thrust and impact,
are held by double-elastic–type fastenings. The track gauge is the
same standard width used in this country. To ensure the train's
consistent high speed as well as to make it safe, there are no grade
crossings; the entire route is either elevated or fenced off. Airtight
cars ensure that the quiet ride will not be disturbed by sudden
changes in air pressure as the train passes through tunnels.
Insulated safety glass in the windows also helps to minimize noise
and prevent condensation, and protects against flying particles
that might strike windows as the train races along.

Another Shin Kansen safety feature, which would be of little
use along our northeast coast but might be welcomed in California, is a seismoscope: when earthquake tremors reach a certain
intensity, the train's power is automatically cut off. Similarly, the
trains are slowed or stopped when rain or wind becomes excessive.

Other nations have studied the Tokaido line because of its
conspicuous success. The trains are 92 percent occupied; they
average over 150,000 passengers a day, and on some days have
carried over 350,000. It took our Metroliners two and a half years
to carry 3 million passengers, a feat the Tokaido line accomplishes
every two weeks. The fare is half that of airline travel between the
same points. During the first five years of "bullet" operation, air
travel in this Japanese corridor remained at ten percent of rail
travel. One of the effects of such high-density rail service is that
congestion on the auto route between Tokyo and Osaka has been
reduced considerably. Though Japan still has a mammoth auto
congestion and pollution problem, think what it would be without
the trains. The magazine *Railway Gazette International* says the
"bullets" prove that "a fast passenger train service running several

times an hour between large cities can run rings around the competition on a 500 km [311-mile] journey."

The Tokaido Shin Kansen has been such a success—it was making money within two years, including interest on the invested capital, and in five years earned nearly $1.6 billion—that JNR made plans to extend the line in several stages. The first stage, 103 miles from Osaka to Okayama, opened in April 1972, having been constructed at the rate of one-fourth to one-third of a mile per day. Called either the San-Yo Shin Kansen or New San-Yo Line, it was built to even higher standards than the Tokaido Line in order to handle speeds of 155 miles per hour.

Building the New San-Yo Line involved much tunneling. For the first stage, thirty-four tunnels were built, five of which are longer than 1.8 miles each. Of the entire first-stage extension, 35 percent is tunneled—that is, some 36 miles. Rokko, one of the tunnels, is the world's third-longest, at 10 miles. The train at its designated operating speed of 155 mph clears it in less than four minutes.

The second stage of the New San-Yo Line, now under construction, should be in service by 1975. It will extend the line another 247 miles down the southern tip of Honshu to Fukuoka, on the island of Kyushu. (Japan is made up of four main islands: Kyushu, Shikoku, Honshu, and Hokkaido. Kyushu is the southernmost; Hokkaido is the northernmost; Honshu is the longest and biggest; and Shikoku is adjacent to both Kyushu and Honshu.)

That second stage, Okayama to Fukuoka, will involve tunneling about 128 miles, or at least 52 percent of the total distance. The longest tunnel will be the 11.6-mile New Kanmon tunnel, which will supplant Rokko as the longest in Japan. New Kanmon will be the second undersea tunnel linking Honshu with the island of Kyushu across the Shimonoseki Strait, but the first uses a narrow-gauge track and is not as long. (In contrast to the ultramodern Tokaido Line, a 13,000-mile narrow-gauge track makes up the balance of the JNR system.)

Much new construction is planned for the future. Obviously, all this is costing a great deal—partly because new rights-of-way have had to be acquired and new depots built, whereas most nations building such lines can use existing rights-of-way and depots to keep costs down. But the results are dramatic and will be more so.

When all the projected new construction is completed, passengers will be able to streak the whole length of the Japanese archipelago, a track distance of 1,340 miles, at speeds that by 1978 are expected to reach 185 mph.

In the Tokyo metropolitan area, JNR carries over 14 million passengers daily, about four times the number moved by rail in New York City. To handle the great volume of people on its intercity trains, JNR since 1964 has used a computerized reservation system. By 1970, from 410,000 to 460,000 seats a day were being processed. A 700,000-seat-a-day computer system went into effect in 1972, and a 1.4-million-seat-per-day system will follow.

Japan is also looking to the future in other ways. Three-car trains with an unusual suspension system are being tested. One is electric; the other is powered by gas turbines. The most exciting project, however, is the program announced by the Japanese Ministry of Transport to develop, by stages, rails using magnetic levitation and linear-induction motors to reach speeds as high as 250 to 300 mph by 1985. Even at the lower figure, the Tokyo–Osaka run would take only eighty minutes. (Incidentally, visitors to Expo '72 at Osaka were able to transfer from intercity trains to rapid-transit lines on a network of silent moving pavements over a mile long. These "Travelators" have also been installed to connect intercity French trains with the Paris Métro.)

When the U.S. Senate in March 1971 voted down the supersonic transport (SST), there was immediate speculation that the Japanese might want to take over our equipment, materials, and plans and manufacture this aircraft themselves. ABC-TV's Harry Reasoner commented that "instead of selling our SST to the

Japanese, why don't we ask them over here to show us how to run our railroads?"

Like the Japanese, the Europeans have some crack passenger trains, some just as exciting to ride as the "bullets." The twenty-three Trans-Europe Express trains, easily recognized by their red-and-beige colors and the "TEE" emblazoned on their engines, speed passengers across Europe at half the price of air travel, meanwhile treating them to oversized windows for viewing the landscape, delicious food, excellent wines. The trains are clean, comfortable, quiet, smooth, and air-conditioned, with hostesses, telephones, public-address systems, and sometimes free breakfast.

Countries participating in TEE include the members of the European Economic Community ("Common Market" or the "Inner Six") plus Austria and Switzerland, but not including Great Britain. Each nationality contributes its own service and flavor.

TEE trains carry customs and immigration officials to avoid delays at border crossings, and their electrical engines can adapt to the four different methods of feeding electrical current in Western Europe. A computer network and an international teleprinter enable passengers to make reservations easily and confirm them up to two months in advance of a trip.

Growing numbers of Americans are traveling Europe by train, many by the Eurailpass, which must be bought in advance outside Europe. This entitles the purchaser to travel first class in thirteen European countries at a rate that ranges from $150 for three weeks to $300 for three months, as of 1973. The trains exceed 100 mph; some have vista domes and are on the luxurious side. A Eurailpass holder in West Germany, for example, may have his luggage picked up at his hotel in one city and delivered to his hotel in the next one for 50 cents. A Student-Railpass provides students with unlimited second-class travel for two months for

$165, but as the Eurailpass ads state: ". . . there's very little second class about second class in Europe." And for the economy-minded traveler there are clean cafeterias and bar cars. That Americans approve of Eurailpass is evidenced by the fact that over 132,500 of them took advantage of it in 1972.

European railroad stations come in many sizes and shapes. Some are antique monumental, some ultramodern, all are architecturally eye-catching and seem to care about the traveler. Good restaurants, helpful information booths, baggage rooms, quaint shops can be found in most of them.

Riding the train for Europeans is a way of life and is far more popular than flying for distances up to 500 miles, since many trains hit speeds of 100 mph and some go even faster. The train systems are largely nationalized and partially subsidized, and are cheap by U.S. standards. The taxpayer pays some of the cost, but he gets good, relatively cheap transportation in return—and he pays less for highway construction and suffers less from auto pollution and congestion than the American taxpayer does.

Mussolini gave the on-time train a bad name temporarily, but there is much to be said for it. In France when a train enters the Paris terminal, the engineer reportedly adjusts his speed so that the train comes to a halt within ten seconds of its timetable listing. And West German trains are just as meticulous. American trains simply do not compare.

It is debatable which European train is number one, but it is probably France's *Mistral*, which runs between Paris and the Riviera at Nice, a distance of 680 miles—the equivalent of, say, Chicago to Baltimore. Noted for conveniences, the fourteen-car, shiny aluminum train has: a beauty/barber salon; a bar car equipped with a long counter where simple dishes are served along with various French wines, champagnes, and imported beer; the *Mistral* boutique, selling books, magazines, newspapers, and such exotic items as Hermès scarves, French perfumes, and Mikimoto pearls; bilingual secretaries available for typing and dictation via tape recorder; a lavish dining room where chefs still take pride in their cooking. (A several-course dinner reminds one of the heyday of first-class American trains, described in Chapter III. On *Le Mistral,* the good life still exists, according to John Roberson in an article in *Holiday.* "The goal of the French railroads is to have passengers get off their trains more rested than when they got on. I was relaxed, nourished, neither tired nor stiff and my hair was cut.")

France's Paris–Toulouse *Capitole* goes even faster than *Le Mistral,* reaching a top speed of 125 mph. It is also a glamorous TEE member.

On a par with *Le Mistral* for convenience and luxury is the celebrated TEE deluxe *Train Bleu,* which runs from Paris to Monte Carlo (700 miles) with stops at Lyon, Marseille, and Toulon before entering Italy at Ventimiglia. It is not as fast as some of France's fastest, but makes up for this lack in nostalgia, distinction, and refinement. It is still the pride of the International Sleeping Car and Great European Express Company (Compagnie Internationale des Wagon-Lits et des Grands Exprès Européens), and like the *Orient Express* in its heyday is a glamorous train with a tradition of mystery and intrigue. The royal blue train with its gold-lettered inscriptions may no longer carry royalty and connoisseurs as it once did, but it still has much to offer, including the early-1900s atmosphere of dining, bar, and salon cars with their dark-paneled walls and soft leather seats. The service is excellent, the ride smooth, the cost moderate. For about $5 one can get the popular *assiette Train Bleu* consisting of salmon, caviar, herring, smoked eel, and Polish Vyborova vodka. A meal of beef, veal, and lamb en brochette costs only $4.60, at this writing.

The Gallic temperament admires not only timetable reliability, comfort, and service, but also speed. As far back as 1955 the French, using conventional electric engines like that of *Le Mistral,* established a world's speed record of 207 mph. (In 1964 the French had almost 5,000 miles of electrified line, compared with 1,500 miles in the United States.) The electric *Aquitaine* between Paris and Bordeaux makes the best time, at this writing, of any intercity train outside Japan, but the way Europeans are concentrating on trains, the record may be short-lived. At any rate, it makes the 359.8 miles in four hours, and in doing so it hits speeds of over 120 mph. It averages 90 mph—a very respectable average considering the distance involved and the stops made.

The French National Railways (SNCF—Société Nationale des Chemins de Fer Français) has gas-turbine trains running between Paris and Cherbourg, and in late 1970 put in orders for six five-car trains with even more powerful locomotion for services across the country. SNCF also would like to add a high-speed (130-mph average) route from Paris to Lyon. Ultimately, the planned maximum speed will be 186 mph, with an average of 150—at which speed a train could go from New York to Washington, D.C., in an hour and a half.

France excels in other ways. A French turbotrain placed in service during the spring of 1970 was the first in Europe. France, like Japan, is installing some 126-mph trains that demand less reduction of speed on curves. In 1972 a French turbotrain was clocked at a quiet 190 mph. The French have also developed a number of diversified new ground transportation systems, including a silent, linear-induction-motor (LIM) elevated monorail, a linear-motor rail jet, and the tracked air-cushion vehicle (TACV) known as the "Aerotrain." (The reader will learn more about LIM and TACV in Chapter IX.) Now in service, the Aerotrain zips along at 150 mph along its 15-mile route from Paris to the new town of Cergy-Pontoise. A full-size model powered by an aircraft jet engine had been tested earlier, but abandoned because of noise. The completely noiseless linear-electric-motor system is now being used on the Aerotrain.

West Germany's crack *Rheingold,* a TEE member, is that country's most popular train for businessmen. It covers the 682 miles from Amsterdam to Geneva in only 11¼ hours despite fifteen stops. As on *Le Mistral*, the passenger can spend all his travel time in a mini-office or dictating to a multilingual secretary at $3 per hour. The train has dome cars, elegant dining and bar facilities, wall-to-wall carpeting, and soundproof construction. The German Federal Railway (the Deutsche Bundesbahn, or DB) runs 20,000 passenger trains daily. One all-sleeper, the *Comet* (Basel–Hamburg) remains full even though its capacity has been doubled.

Electric trains running from Munich to Augsburg at speeds as high as 125 mph during the International Transport Exhibition encouraged the DB to institute an 1,800-mile line connecting 72 German cities, part of which was ready for the 1972 Olympic Games in Munich.

The DB has also been conducting some unusual operational tests in Munich with a new Series 210 gas-turbine–diesel locomotive. A 2,500-hp diesel engine was given a supplementary boost by a 1,150-hp gas-turbine engine (combined total of 3,650-hp), enabling trains on nonelectric routes to achieve speeds of 100 mph.

Although their current rail service is fast and efficient, the West Germans are planning still faster service. In 1972 their largest aerospace company—Messerschmitt-Bolkow-Blohrm, famous for its World War II Messerschmitt planes—successfully completed the initial test of a prototype train that "floats" below its overhead "rail" supported by the attraction of a magnetic field. It is powered by a noiseless, frictionless, nonpolluting linear-induction motor. Two other German manufacturers developing such a system are Krauss-Maffei—magnetic attraction—and Krupp—magnetic repulsion.

To make clear, or clearer, the difference between the two: In the attraction system, the train, like a nail drawn to a magnet, is drawn to an overhead magnetic track. Its own weight keeps it from going all the way up and locking onto the magnetic track above, so it "floats." In the repulsion system, the magnet is below the train and the train itself is magnetized, so that the two repulse each other—as two magnets do—and the train "floats" *above* its track. (See sketches.)

As we were saying, we will review in Chapter IX U.S. experiments with linear-induction motors. But whereas our work on a magnetic-suspension system (we, like the Japanese, are directing our research to the magnetic-repulsion system) is still in the study stage, with no actual LIM-powered magnetic trains expected to be in operation until near the end of this century, the West German Transport Minister talks of having a Munich–Hamburg commuter train using magnetic suspension, with speeds up to 350 mph, in service early in the 1980s. *The New York Times* took the occasion of the initial testing of the German magnetic-field prototype to chide the Nixon Administration for its "obsession with the SST" and for not following Europe's example in aggressively pushing for high-speed rail service.

Business Week quoted DB's president, Heinz Maria Oeftering, on the advantages of obtaining an average rail speed of between 250 and 300 mph: "When the high speed train is here, who'd want

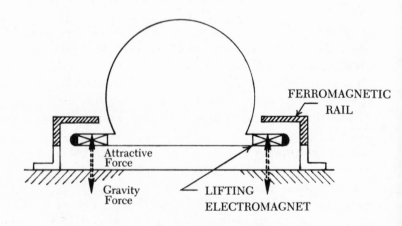

ATTRACTION

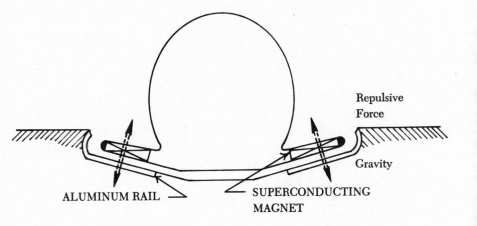

ALUMINUM RAIL → ← SUPERCONDUCTING
MAGNET

Repulsive
Force

Gravity

REPULSION

to fly 500 miles from Hamburg to Munich when the rail trip mid-city to mid-city would take only an hour and 40 minutes?" At these speeds one could go from New York City to Cleveland by rail in less than two hours, or Los Angeles to San Francisco in an even shorter time—regardless of weather or traffic conditions.

Speaking of Munich, and of repulsion, when Munich's popular mayor, Hans-Jocken Vogel, visited Los Angeles in 1970 he was shown the immense expressways of the region and they so repelled him that upon his return to Munich, according to an issue of *Deutsche Welle* (The Voice of Germany), he announced that "every additional billion marks invested in city street and highway planning would lead the community one step further on the road to urban decay." He had earlier been partly responsible for expanding the highways in his own area by 23 percent.

A *New York Times* correspondent in Germany, Hans J. Stueck, wrote in the *Saturday Review* that Hamburg's urban transit, operating since 1966, has attracted transportation experts from all over the world. Hamburg, like many American cities, suffers from what one might call the "doughnut effect": the inner city is being emptied while the suburbs expand and thrive.

Hamburg's system is coordinated so that all transportation methods complement one another, and congestion has been spectacularly reduced. Between 10,000 and 20,000 suburban commuters have returned to mass transport, and commuting time has been nicely cut. A commuter is offered three types of tickets (single, zonal, and seasonal) and can have the ticket price deducted automatically from his bank account without having to make monthly purchases at a ticket counter.

A single ticket is good for all types of transit—buses, trains, subways, and ferries—and the boarding process has been simplified by the elimination of barriers and turnstiles. Under an honor system, the commuter need show his ticket only when subjected to a spot check. Losses from freeloading are assumed to be more than offset by the saving on conductors and ticket takers.

The switch of commuters away from automobiles has lessened air pollution, and Streeck reports a Hamburg announcement that "by 1985 no citizen ought to have to walk more than five minutes to the nearest subway or railway station." Construction is proceeding to back up the statement.

In addition, DB is now creating high-performance S-Bahn (high-speed ground rail) mass transit or intracity trains in Munich, Frankfurt, Stuttgart, and the Ruhr similar to existing ones in Hamburg and Berlin, but there will be many improvements and refinements over the latter. In Munich, the fast section of a U-Bahn (subway) opened in late 1971. This one crosses beneath and links with one section of the new S-Bahn that reaches to the site of the 1972 Olympics. Incidentally, most major European cities have new subway rail lines.

In Great Britain, home of famous crack trains such as *The Flying Scotsman*, 100-mph trains are becoming common, and as a result there was a 60-percent increase in passengers between 1966 and 1969, while airline travel dropped 20 percent in the same period. (Britain being a small country, more than half of all British rail revenues come from passenger service. There is not much long-distance freight hauling, as there is in the United States.) Plans are being made to extend electrification to those sections of the British system still dependent on diesel power. Completion as far north as Glasgow is scheduled for 1974, by which time 125-mph trains will be operating between London and Glasgow.

Britain has 1,000 daily intercity trains (in addition to 15,000 commuter trains), and most are handsome, relaxing to ride, and punctual. They reach to almost every point in the closely knit island. One official description of a first-class compartment was that "it was designed to offer passengers a standard of comfort in seating and space far above that possible in a private car or aircraft."

For $7.80 (as of mid-1973), between any two points in Great Britain, the passenger receives a first-class berth and a free breakfast. And carrying one's automobile has become so popular, Britain is presently adding 10,000 spaces to its auto-and-passenger trains. (See Chapter VIII for a report on U.S. auto-carrying passenger trains.)

According to *Railway Age* Magazine, a businessman can go by train from central London to downtown Manchester—a distance of 189 miles—in two hours and forty minutes. By air, using the airlines' own estimate and adding city-to-airport time, it would take three hours and cost $25 more than going first class on the rails. Obviously, the train in England is the way to go.

It appears that the on-again, off-again, much-talked-about and long-dreamed-of Channel Tunnel connecting England and France may at last be on its way to reality. When this *tunnel sous la Manche*, the inspiration of French engineer Mathieu-Favier in 1802, is built, it will be some 22 miles long and may be restricted to rail transportation.

The Channel Tunnel is being spurred on by several factors: by Britain's entry into the Common Market; by studies that show the tunnel will be a profit-making venture; and, perhaps, by the Japanese Government's decision to build the Seikan Tunnel across the Tsugaru Strait. *Railway Gazette International* reports the possibility that the Channel Tunnel will be open by 1980.

The tunnel trip made at bullet-train speeds will take only 15 minutes, maybe less, allowing Frenchmen to commute daily to work in England, and vice versa, since the entire London–Paris run could be made in 2½ hours or less. Chances are that Britain would then become a TEE member.

A magazine ad by British Railways (BR) makes clear its view of the future of transportation: "The Superhighways of the future are already built," it says of high-speed rail lines, and it describes them as "10,000 miles of rapid, uncongested, non-polluting, high capacity, load carrying steel arteries."

Farsighted Britons are developing a sleek train with a wedge-shaped nose, called the Advanced Passenger Train, or APT. One APT prototype, now being built, will have gas-turbine propulsion; the other, electric propulsion. Designers claim these will provide "the fastest, quietest and smoothest riding in the world" and will be the first to be able to run at very high speed—up to 155 mph—on existing rail routes "with little or no alteration to the track and signaling." This is made possible through lightweight construction and an advanced suspension system similar to those being tested in Japan, France, and Canada (and not too unlike that of the American TurboTrain described in Chapter VII). This system enables the cars to lean inward when going around curves, eliminating the centrifugal force that pushes a passenger against the window—or against a seatmate.

The APT is scheduled to enter service in 1975, and British Rail chairman Richard Marsh told *Railway Age* that if the United States should decide to stay in the passenger-railway business, "I think they will find themselves purchasing the APT." He admitted that the APT will be in competition with the American Turbo and Canada's LRC, the latter to be discussed later in this chapter. Meanwhile, the British have had talks with Israeli officials about using the APT along a 30-mile route between Tel Aviv and Jerusalem. (The United States is acquiring two five-car French turbotrains for high-speed service in the Midwest.)

To round out the passenger rail picture in Europe, some miscellaneous items:

Trains of the Danish State Railways (DSB) board giant ferries to travel between Copenhagen and a number of other major Danish cities. Ferries also provide the link with trains in Norway and Sweden. An electronic seat-reservation system is used, and Americans who travel within these Scandinavian countries speak of the cleanliness and regularity of the ferries. The Danes have a celebrated first-rate train in bright red-orange named "Lightning"— in Danish, *Lyntog.*

Sweden has a new suspension system on 125-mph trains that permits them to go faster on curves than they otherwise could. On-board features include fashion shows, showers, libraries, and a "Mother's Compartment" for baby care—including free diapers.

In Norway, the *Bergen–Oslo Express* passes through two hundred tunnels and winds its way through breathtaking fiords and up steep slopes, a camera buff's delight.

Netherlands Railways is continuing to expand and modernize its service and by 1975 will have seventy-five new stations. (New transit and subway lines are also planned for Amsterdam, Rotterdam, and The Hague.)

In Austria, all domestic air service has been discontinued as uneconomical, leaving travel within the country to trains, buses, and autos.

One of the most famous Swiss trains is the TEE *Ticino,* noted for its efficient service, 100-mph speeds, modern bars and restaurants, and, of course, its trip through breathtaking scenery from Zurich to Milan. A tunnel is being cut through the Alps to avoid the steep climb at the St. Gotthard Pass.

The train in Spain is mainly fast and modern. Spain has a number of deluxe "Talgo III" trains with rotating armchairs and buffet bars, and the Spanish National Railway has recently completed a ten-year modernization scheme. The latest Talgos come equipped with special axle assemblies so that they can make the shift from Spanish broad-gauge track to standard-gauge, common throughout Europe, thus enabling them to go beyond Spain's borders.

In Italy, many intercity trains now exceed 100 mph and run frequently. Although not a TEE train, the luxury Rome–Milan *Settebello* ("Beautiful Seven"—it has seven coaches) comes equipped with observation decks, gift shops, and, of course, high-caloric meals, in dining areas noted for their atmosphere. Train exteriors of Italian State Railways are always flashy in appearance, and this particular one comes in green and silver. Its present speed is 100 mph, but preparations are being made for higher speeds. Refinements in suspension, braking, and signaling; the use of automatic speed control; the addition of new rolling stock; and the realignment and improvement of track and roadbed eventually will enable *Il Settebello* to streak along at 155 or 160 mph. By 1975 the *Super Rapido* is expected to run at equally high speeds between Rome and Milan (389 miles), the world's longest nonstop route.

Rome, noted for its auto congestion and intermittently critical air pollution, offered free transit rides for an eight-day period at the start of 1972. The results at this writing are being collated and analyzed. At present Rome has no real subway system, but one is under construction.

The Soviet Union is also busily building new railroad lines or expanding present ones. In 1971, Russian trains alone ran 174 billion passenger miles over 85,000 miles of main line, while the United States ran only 10 billion passenger miles over 205,000 miles of track. (This is not to suggest that if the Russians had been affluent enough to build great highways and millions of automobiles they would have resisted the temptation any better than we have.) In 1970 Soviet Railways purchased from East Germany a number of new sleeping cars of very high standards designed to run at 100 mph. If society is classless in the Soviet Union, the trains are not; there are first- and second-class cars. First-class cars are air-conditioned and well insulated against noise. An attendant provides refreshments and light meals. Individual first-class compartments are reported to be luxuriously outfitted with folding tables, comfortable armchairs, teak paneling, reading lamps, carpeting, and even showers. In second class, private compartments are arranged more compactly but are said to be neat and comfortable.

The modern, all-sleeper *Red Arrow Express* makes an overnight run between Moscow and Leningrad that is said to be one of the world's smoothest rides. The world's longest train ride, incidentally, which would seem to demand endurance of passenger as well as train, is over the famous Trans-Siberian Railroad from Moscow to Vladivostok, a distance of 5,780 miles. The trip takes seven days and seven nights.

The Russians also have a less celebrated but more unusual long-distance train. Once a week it departs (on time) from Moscow, and six days and 4,890 miles later it arrives in Peking, China. Chris Mullin, a British journalist, took this train and, in *The New York Times Magazine*, described its passage through the Ural Mountains; through endless forests of birches; along portions of Lake Baikal, the world's deepest lake; and across the vast Gobi Desert in the Mongolian People's Republic. He reported that the train continued its run faithfully during the period when Sino-Soviet diplomatic relations had been broken off. (Because the Mongolian and Chinese rail gauges differ by six inches, not only do locomo-

tives have to be changed at the border, but each coach is lifted
from its undercarriage by a crane and a different set of wheels
installed.)

South of the Equator, passenger rail service is thriving. South
African Railways every year replaces more steam locomotives
with diesels and electrics. Concrete crossties and continuous
welded track—now approximately 3,000 miles of it—provide a
smoother ride than Americans usually get.

The comfortable *Blue Train* makes a 980-mile run (the distance
from New York to Jacksonville, Florida) across the magnificent
South African veld and through spectacular mountains from
Johannesburg to Cape Town and is still a first-class railroad despite narrow-gauge track. Its thirty-year-old polished blue cars
have wood paneling and leather seats. The dining car has its own
silver service to complement the excellent cuisine. In fact, the
Blue Train is so luxurious it attracts more business than it can
handle. But South African Railways has on order a whole new set
of luxury cars which will gradually replace the old. The first re-
placements, consisting of two sixteen-car trains, were introduced
in 1972. They are exceedingly quiet, air-conditioned, and equipped
with cocktail bars, dining cars with sumptuous food, lounge cars,
wall-to-wall carpeting, and tinted heat-absorbing glass windows.
There are also luxurious bedroom suites, with a separate lounge,
bathroom, refrigerator, and wine rack. Because of the splendid
scenery the train journeys through, passengers seem not to mind
the trip's taking twenty-five hours. The new trains could make it in
several hours less.

While U.S. cross-country trains are nearly extinct, Australia in
March 1970 initiated a new twice-weekly transcontinental *Indian–
Pacific Express* between Sydney and Perth, a run of 2,460 miles.

In order to cross that continent in the past, one had to make a number of train changes (at one time as many as six) because of the variety of track gauges that existed through the different continental states. But the Trans-Australian Railway track standardization was completed on November 29, 1969, when a gold spike was driven at official ceremonies at Broken Hill, New South Wales, a noted lead-, silver-, and zinc-mining town. This was a little over a hundred years after a golden spike was driven to link our country (May 10, 1869). This seemed fitting, for as the Australians sometimes say, in terms of settlement their outback, or wilderness, is roughly 100 years behind our own West. The single-track Trans-Australian route across the southern portion of the continent would correspond roughly to a trip from Los Angeles to Savannah, Georgia, both in mileage and in relative placement within the two countries.

Railroad buffs may be interested in some other facts. At one place along that route there is 29 miles of continuously welded track, at this writing the longest such stretch in the world. The ride on this curveless portion is broken only by a slight undulating motion caused by gentle slopes. Part of this long straightaway is through a dry limestone plain called the Nullarbor Plain, a monotonous, flat, treeless (Latin *nulla arbor*—"no tree") area that in prehistoric times was a seabed. A good stretch to read through.

Almost the whole trip is through wild, remote frontier land the Australians refer to as "never-never," and encompasses some of the most desolate and waterless areas in the world. The complete trip, however, passes through various habitats including forests; rich, red sandy-soil regions; spear grass plains; wheat fields; brushlands; and a 3,584-foot summit of the Blue Mountains (via ten tunnels) outside Sydney. From the train can be seen such plant and animal life as salmon gum trees, salt and blue bushes, myall and mallee gums, many wild flowers, foxes, and, of course, kangaroos. There is nothing frontierlike about the train. It is luxurious and air-conditioned, and its first-class sleeping quarters are spacious and softly carpeted, with curtains, indirect lighting, lounge chairs, showers. One can have breakfast in bed or berth. Lounge cars, a cafeteria, and a dining room encourage people to walk about and socialize. The train is so popular that space must be booked well ahead.

Less luxurious than the newer *Indian–Pacific Express* but still a good Australian train is the *Southern Auroras,* which goes overnight from Sydney to Melbourne. Here too the vacationer can have breakfast in bed and can take a shower in his own private compartment.

In New Zealand, the government is stepping up passenger rail service. On the South Island a new train has replaced the present *South Island Limited* and is called the *Southerner.* It cuts the 367-mile run (between Christchurch and Invercargill) by one hour and forty minutes. This is still not a top-speed train, but it passes through unexcelled scenery and is a delight to take.

A traveler who went from Christchurch to Dunedin commented on the unspoiled terrain as the train sped down the east coast. He told us that for many uninterrupted hours you could look out one side and see nothing but big white breakers from the Pacific and out the other you viewed the impressive snow-capped peaks of the Southern Alps—sixteen of which tower above 10,000 feet—extending down the west coast.

On the North Island, thirty-one new sleeping cars purchased from Japan are now in service on the new *Silver Star* running the 300 miles between Auckland in the north and Wellington in the south.

Our next-door neighbors Canada and Mexico seem also to appreciate the many advantages of rail travel, having been spared the wealth that permitted and encouraged us to go overboard for automobiles and highways. Good Mexican trains are said to be clean, well maintained, and likely to be on schedule.

When a new 22.5-mile subway line, the "Metro," was completed in Mexico City in 1970, Bernardo Tuintana, Mexico's leading construction engineer, remarked that "for a long time we went in for freeways, thinking they would speed up traffic, and all we did was congest the center of the city, through which buses now barely crawl." The Metro is highly automated and carries one million passengers daily in its 537 bright orange cars. They operate at a frequency of about one every three minutes, and more cars planned for the future should reduce the interval to every ninety seconds.

The Metro is the world's newest subway, and probably the handsomest. Built with the help of a substantial loan from France, the $400-million Metro initially faced a number of knotty construction problems, including the fact that tunneling often had to be done at a minimum depth, since Mexico City has many ancient lake bottoms and is noted for earthquake tremors. Another rather unusual and unexpected construction delay occurred when major archaeological discoveries were made during excavation. One of the most spectacular stone pieces found was placed in one of the main stations. On the subject of the Metro stations, *Railway Age* reports that archaeological reproductions, Mexican mosaics, marble platforms, brilliant colors, piped-in music, and constant cleaning have given the Mexicans civic pride in them.

These French-built trains are not only clean but punctual and comfortable and are controlled by computer. They are cheap to ride, too—standard fare is 8 cents. They are unusual in another respect. Instead of steel wheels on steel rails, these cars have rubber wheels to reduce vibration and noise. All in all, the Metro subway, according to *The New York Times,* is widely recognized as the most modern and beautiful in the world.

The Mexicans now operate a *Mexico Winter Fun Train* which carries visitors, mostly Americans, in an eight-car special from

Nuevo Laredo to Mexico City, Guadalajara, Sufragio, and Pre-
sidio. One full day is spent on the *Chihuahua–Pacific* through
rugged mountains. The track in this vicinity took sixty years to
build.

Canadians view their TurboTrain as only a preliminary to their
newest high-speed rail train, the LRC—"Light, Rapid, Comfortable" (or "Léger, Rapide, Confortable" in French). The Canadian
Government is supporting one-half of the cost, an industrial con-
sortium the other. As we write, experimental test runs have
started. Very similar to the British APT, this train has a 2,900-hp
diesel-electric locomotive that operates in push-pull fashion
(pushes in one direction, pulls in the other, to avoid turning
around). Control cables run the length of the train, allowing the
engineer up front to command the train when the locomotive is in
the rear. When a pair of locomotives is used, they are at either
end, and the train so powered can accelerate to 120 mph in four
minutes. (Actually, only 2,000 hp is available for power; the remainder is for auxiliaries.)

According to *Railway Age*, the LRC was designed primarily,
like the British APT, to operate over "existing rail routes at substantially higher speeds without excessive rebuilding of curves or
the necessity for maintaining track surface to uneconomical standards." An active—and complicated—tilt suspension system also
similar to the APT's allows it to bank on the curves at high speeds.
Railway Gazette International estimates the speed on curves to be
"35 to 40 per cent higher than would otherwise be possible."

A waiting passenger in the Montreal Central Station can deposit
a quarter and view a small television set with seven channels for
half an hour. The set is attached to the armrest of a comfortable
chair. (In San Francisco, the bus depot also has pay TV for waiting passengers.) Television watching in Montreal's terminal is not
as popular as it might be in most U.S. stations, because sometimes

as many as six crack trains leave Montreal per hour for such large cities as Quebec and Toronto.

An unusual Canadian passenger train is the *Polar Bear Express* from Cochrane, Ontario, overnight to Moosonee, near James Bay, home of the Cree Indians. Here there are no roads, only the track and the wilderness consisting of scrub brush and musk. There are no timetables, and no stations along the route. Hunters, trappers, and fishermen use the train partly because it stops anywhere at any time and partly because of the remote area it covers.

Another colorful trip is on the Canadian National's nonstop *Rapido* (Montreal to Toronto), which has a ragtime piano and Gay Nineties decor in the "bistro car"—and scenery for those who prefer to stay in their seats and look out the window. There is an even faster train along this route: Canada's seven-car, 100-mph Turbo.

Evidence that Canadians have kicked the highway habit within urban areas was demonstrated in Toronto when a controversial $237-million expressway was halted in June 1971 and a subway built instead. "Toronto does not belong to the automobile," Ontario Premier William Davis said. "If we are building a transportation system to serve the automobile, the Spadina Expressway would be a good place to stop."

"In Los Angeles . . . I went to the downtown Santa Fe ticket office to pick up a reservation which had been made for me on the City of San Francisco Amtrak service east to Iowa. The clerk couldn't have been more helpful in phoning around for details. But when he got it sorted out, it still took him 20 minutes to type up an accordion of ticket stubs involving a Pullman roomette and Amtrak conveyance east via Southern Pacific, Union Pacific and the Burlington. In Europe you buy one little piece of paper for a trip from Paris to Istanbul across seven countries—two of them Communist. Your ticket is then duly inspected, punched and returned to you all along the way."
        —REPORTER DON COOK, *Los Angeles Times,* February 22, 1972

PART TWO

WHY WHAT OUGHT TO BE ISN'T

CHAPTER Ⅲ

A Legacy of Ill Will

Now THAT IT has become necessary to sell Americans again on the advantages of rail travel, it is unfortunate that so many of them have unhappy memories or unpleasant impressions of what it is to travel by rail.

For a variety of reasons, U.S. railroad management since World War II has shown the opposite of enterprise in dealing with passengers: has provided antique equipment, skimpy schedules, and surly service at a time when exciting technological advances were taking place in other fields and in other modes of transportation; and this has earned railroads a reputation for being musty and fusty. It can be overcome, as the success of the *Metroliner* and other new trains has demonstrated, but it will take some doing. This chapter will cite historic reasons for recent passenger neglect, and will make clearer what must be overcome in the way of accumulated ill will and lack of respect for railroads as a way to go.

Given the growing affluence of Americans and the appeal and availability of automobiles and airliners, there was no way the railroads could have stopped the stampede of travelers away from day coach and parlor car and Pullman onto the ever-extending highways and into the sky. But the stampede might have been slowed somewhat, and railroads might have come out better in the competition for commuters at least, and might be held in more esteem by the American public today, if they had *tried harder* to compete. The basic reason they didn't is that the big money in American railroading was always in freight—and in free land— rather than in passenger service, and so with few exceptions rail tycoons through the years have been only too glad to see passenger business on any line dwindle to the point at which that line could be dropped.

It would be wrong to suggest that the rail lines at no time tried to win passenger business, or that the passenger always and invariably got a bad deal. On the contrary, there once were fabulously good American passenger trains for those who could afford them, and they were numerous until after World War II. To balance the account, and to explain why *some* Americans have *happy* memories of travel by rail, and to show how far rail management would go for passengers when there was money in it, we offer a bit of history.

Luxurious rail passenger service in America began during the years of the coal-burning locomotive, from the early 1870s to the 1920s—a period historians call "the golden age of steam," when the locomotive had lost its large, funnel-shaped stack and when bells, whistles, and headlights were added. Later on, engines became heavier; steel cabs were introduced to protect the engineer; roadbeds were improved; air brakes and automatic couplers were installed.

Elegance was a byword in those days, and the conductor of a crack passenger train, in the words of railroad historian John F. Stover, was "an aristocrat among wage earners in this nation." By the late 1870s, George M. Pullman's cars were giving well-to-do travelers a pampering unequaled anywhere. The rich and powerful (including Presidents of the United States and rail tycoons) rode in their own private cars, and in the competition for passengers one line even whitewashed its coal. The one place to be sure of getting a gourmet meal was a Pullman dining car, where menus boasted such items as *coeur de filet de boeuf*, porterhouse steak, terrapin Maryland, antelope steak, broiled live Maine lobster, and

Scotch grouse. Sparkling wines and expensive champagnes were served on some trains; waiters were courteous, linens immaculate, silver and china of the finest quality.

The Pullman Palace Car Company was an appropriate name for the manufacturer of passenger cars whose interior furnishings equaled those of the very finest hotels and most beautifully decorated mansions.

The late Lucius Beebe, well-known railroad buff and publisher, has written extensively of railroading, and in *Mr. Pullman's Elegant Palace Car* (Doubleday, 1961) he outdid himself with pictures and descriptions of hundreds of fascinating passenger cars during the "golden age of steam."

There were cars finished in satinwood, French or English oak, Circassian walnut, and rare mahoganies; cars with shimmering chandeliers, richly finished lamps, French mirrors, ornate columns and pedestals, decoratively painted ceilings, brocaded velvets, deep fauteuils upholstered in rich terra cotta, plus Wilton carpeting and draperies of exotic materials (India silk damask in green and white, for example). There were drawing rooms of koko wood, spacious smoking rooms in tigerwood, richly adorned vestibules, barbershops with manicurists and valets, cardrooms and well-fitted libraries, and, throughout, cut flowers and ferns.

Some of the more elegant private cars were fit for (and sometimes carried) a king and boasted marble baths, wood-burning fireplaces, king-size beds, pipe organs, solid-gold fixtures, and art masterpieces. The exteriors of these cars were painted in vermilion reds, bronzes, royal blues, or, in one case, creamy white. Lettering was often in blazing gold leaf.

Railroad terminals, from Grand Central and Pennsylvania Station in New York to the friendly small-town depot, were picturesque, some with mansard roofs and gables, pillars, fountains, statues, all reflecting America's affluence and sense of pride in her rail passenger service—and the relatively low wages of workmen. The exteriors of many were of expensive materials: stone, polished

marble, beautiful brick, with massive wooden beams and steel gir-
ders, fancy iron latticework, and bronze plaques. In small towns,
frame buildings, red or cream-colored, were customary.

The 1920s and '30s saw the birth of a new generation of trains,
including the glamorous and sophisticated "Limiteds." Each section of the country had its own distinct train, and each line its
own "spit and polish" train. To name a few, there were the *Broadway Limited* and *Twentieth Century Limited*, out of New York;
the Milwaukee Road's *Pioneer Limited*; and *The Congressional
Limited* out of Washington, D.C. There were the *Dixie Limited,
Florida East Coast Limited*, and *Merchants Limited*.

The steam locomotive, in the '30s, yielded to the 1892 invention
of a German engineer, Rudolf Diesel. Diesel-powered trains were
called streamliners or speedliners, *Zephyr, Meteor*, and *Comet*;
engines went from black to silver or bright colors, became tor-
pedo-shaped, used sealed-beam headlights, and were equipped
with the new dynamic braking, high-capacity cooling systems, and
an earsplitting horn, replacing the old steam whistle.

By the late 1950s, diesels had completely replaced steam locomotives and an era had ended. The automobile and the airliner
were clearly ahead in the fight for passengers. And the railroads
had thrown in the sponge.

Even a railroad system oriented toward passengers, as we said
earlier, would have lost that fight. But it would have been a different kind of fight. The fact that passengers were never first in
the hearts of most American railroad management, even in the
days of luxurious rail travel for some, meant that the surrender
was fast and abject. And, more significant: insofar as today's railroad management has inherited the attitude of its forebears toward passengers—and there is ample evidence, in the Penn Central scandal and elsewhere, that it has—it cannot be depended
upon to help very much in the fight to bring passengers back to
the railroads.

To say that passenger service was always the unwanted stepchild of American railroads is to make only half the point. The other half is that the stepparents—the railroad tycoons—were a particularly unscrupulous and insensitive lot. But frank, at least, toward their stepchild. "A passenger train," said "empire builder" James J. Hill when he was president of the Great Northern, "is like the male teat—neither useful nor ornamental." W. H. Vanderbilt of the New York Central was not talking specifically about passengers when he made his famous remark "The public be damned" aboard his private railroad car in 1881. His granddaughter, Consuelo Vanderbilt Balsan, later claimed he made his statement in response to a reporter's remark that "your public demands an interview"; that he jovially replied "Oh, my public be damned," and was misquoted in the next day's newspapers. Another version is that he was interrupted at dinner by a reporter who said, "The public cannot wait," and that he replied "You and your newspapers be damned; my dinner comes first." Whatever his words, his actions and those of his fellow railroad barons clearly showed contempt for the public. J. Pierpont Morgan, railroad financier, summed it up pretty well when he said, "I owe the public nothing."

In truth, the early railroad owners were dedicated primarily not even to the carrying of freight but to the manipulation of the railroads as pawns in a big financial game. Milton H. Smith, once president of the Louisville and Nashville Railroad, put it this way: "Society as created was for the purpose of one man's getting what the other fellow has, if he can, and keeping out of the penitentiary." During that era (1865–1914), other prominent railroad "robber barons," besides Vanderbilt, Hill, and Morgan, included Jay Gould; James Fisk; Thomas Scott; Leland Stanford; Collis P. Huntington; Edward H. Harriman; Russell Sage; the brothers Oliver and Oakes Ames; W. H. Vanderbilt's father, Cornelius Vanderbilt ("The Commodore"); and Daniel Drew. Books abound about these men and their rate wars, wage slashes, conspiracies, stock manipulations, illegal holding companies, the corruptive free pass, shipping rebates, the Crédit Mobilier scandal, monopoly battles, and the "Erie War." Peter Lyon, in his lively book *To Hell in a Day Coach* (Lippincott, 1968), accuses such men not of building railroads but of stealing them.

The British historian James Bryce in 1888 observed of those American "railway kings" that "they have power, more power—that is, more opportunity of making their will prevail—than perhaps anyone in political life except the President and the Speaker who, after all, hold theirs only for four years and two years, while the railroad monarch may keep his for life."

Those men commanded great empires. Montana, North Dakota, and Nebraska were referred to as James J. Hill's feudal states. When railroad monarch Leland Stanford rode in his private car, railroad workers all along the tracks lined up and stood at attention as he passed by. State legislatures were often subservient to the railroad kings.

An uneasy balance of power existed among railroads, and, as with governments, the balance often shifted, sometimes causing wars. Occasionally a railroad king dealt directly with the President of the United States. For example, when President Theodore Roosevelt, reacting to a public outcry, brought antitrust proceedings against J. P. Morgan's holding company, the Northern Securities Company, an upset Morgan with remarkable candor reportedly told Roosevelt face to face, "If we have done anything wrong, send your man [Attorney General Philander Knox] to see my man, and they can fix it up." In this case, Morgan was rebuffed, but only after a split Supreme Court decision.

There were high risks and high profits in railroading, and the aggressive speculators attracted to it were not motivated by a passion to serve their fellowman. Rather it was the enormous land grants given to the railroads by the federal government that lured them. Such grants were made during the pre– and post–Civil War era, 1850 to 1871, a time when the nation was impatient to open new economic, technological, and territorial frontiers, and the railroads could expect to receive anywhere from 10 to 40 sections of land *per mile* of track constructed, depending on terrain and location. (A section is one square mile, or 640 acres; 40 sections adds up to 25,600 acres.) The land thus granted was in a checkerboard pattern, the government hoping that the non-railroad-held portions would be homesteaded.

In this fashion the federal government gave to some 80 railroads more than 187 million acres, some of it the richest in resource value of any in the world—and grants from states added another 50 million acres. Northern Pacific received the most land of any railroad: 49 million acres. Texas gave away an amount larger than the state of New York. Also, growing communities and established cities offered railroads land, and sometimes cash, as inducements to get rails through their towns—not for the convenience of passengers, but so that livestock and lumber and grain and coal and other products could be hauled to market. Additional land was sometimes offered for depot sites. Not all the federal grants were of western land; chunks of Alabama, Florida, Illinois, Michigan, Mississippi, and Wisconsin were included.

In 1906, in response to a bitter public outcry, the Hepburn Act was passed to strengthen the Interstate Commerce Commission regulation of railroads, and after a number of investigations by Congress, the era of really rapacious railroading was over by 1914. But the public remained distrustful.

The relevance of all this to the subject at hand is threefold: 1) The railroads of the United States, unlike those of most other countries, were never thought of by management as people carriers primarily, and at the higher levels, they have seldom attracted people-serving people. 2) When the United States needed railroads to carry freight, it offered enormous subsidies—which suggests that today and tomorrow, when the United States needs railroads to lure passengers off the highways, it should again offer generous subsidies to get done what must be done. 3) With their great landholdings, the railroads were tempted to get into many

businesses other than railroading—a temptation few resisted, with
the result that when they should have been paying attention to
their railroads, some were off wheeling and dealing in more profitable areas. The suspicion that their hearts are still not in railroading, and certainly not in passenger carrying, was reinforced by a
quite recent occurrence.

The Penn Central, which was created in a 1968 merger (the
largest in our nation's history) of the Pennsylvania Railroad and
the New York Central Railroad, thereupon became the nation's
biggest real estate operator—actually more a giant conglomerate
than a railroad. Before it sent shock waves through the financial
community by going bankrupt (the biggest bankruptcy in our nation's history), it owned or controlled 186 companies. In addition
to a number of companies involved in rail transportation, its non-
rail assets included industrial parks, luxury hotels, coal mines,
amusement parks, warehouses, choice metropolitan waterfront
property, and the Madison Square Garden Corporation. It had extensive and extraordinarily valuable real estate investments in
states as far away as Florida, California, and Texas, and in such
cities as St. Louis; Philadelphia; Cleveland; New York; Pittsburgh;
Columbus, Ohio; and Chicago.

In the heart of Manhattan—the Park Avenue area, near its
Grand Central Terminal—it owned real estate of incredible value,
including many world-famous landmarks: all told, sixteen sky-
scrapers, including the Pan Am Building, Chemical Bank Building, ITT Building, and Manufacturers Hanover Trust Company
Building; five luxury hotels, including the Waldorf Astoria and
the Biltmore; and the Yale Club.

Is it any wonder the Penn Central showed little enthusiasm for
the small pickings—or *no* pickings—of rail passenger service?

Senator Lee Metcalf of Montana spoke for many of us when he
said, "The United States did not grant millions of acres to an oil
company known as Northern Pacific, to a mining company known
as Northern Pacific, to a timber company known as Northern Pa-

cific. The lands were to construct a railroad and to keep it in working order."

The Christian Science Monitor's editorial line has been echoed
by many other newspapers: "One problem with the railroads is
that they lost interest in their very purpose for existing: rail transportation. Managements became more preoccupied with land and
other capital assets which could be turned into short-term profits.
This created an opportunity for self-dealing."

Robert G. Bartlett made a similar observation about Penn Central when he retired as Pennsylvania's Highway Secretary in June
1970:

"If the Penn Central had spent as much time and as much effort
in recent years in improving its passenger service as it has on its
other profit ventures—land development and freight cars—there
is not a question in my mind that passenger service would now be
active, efficient, sparkling and profitable."

Railroaders justify such diversification as an alternative to the
kind of losses that might lead to nationalization.

Joseph R. Daughen and Peter Binzen in their fascinating book
The Wreck of the Penn Central (Little, Brown, 1971) suggest
that in the future "Washington won't appropriate funds to railroads if there's the slightest possibility that the money could be
used for nonrailroad purposes."

As we write, a bill (S.1380) is pending in the Senate Commerce
Committee, introduced by Montana Senators Mike Mansfield and
Lee Metcalf, that would amend the Rail Passenger Act of 1970 so
that no railroad holding title to land (other than rights-of-way)
received from the federal government would be allowed to discontinue passenger service unless it reconveyed such land to the
government at the rate of 100 acres for each mile discontinued.
Mansfield told the Senate that the railroads were given the original land grants as incentives: "If they abandon this intention, I see
no reason why they should benefit from the land grants. It is my
distinct impression that, in many instances, the railroads are more

interested in investments and benefits associated with these lands than they are in the business of running a railroad."

So, for one reason and another, justly or unjustly, the average American probably sees railroad management as fat cats with their minds on something other than running railroads, and their railroads, therefore, as ill run and no way to go. That impression was confirmed for many Americans during World War II by conditions for which railroad management was not really to blame.

Robert S. Carper in *Focus: The Railroad in Transition* (Barnes, 1968) tells how during that war the railroads were called upon to move masses of men to and from induction centers, meanwhile carrying masses of gasoline-rationed civilians. They had to roll out just about every car they had, including antiques providing "cattle car comfort," with moth-eaten and ripped interiors and what often felt like square wheels. In some cases, benches were substituted for seats during mass troop movements. A whole generation, says Carper, would remember "the miles after miles of jolting, grinding, creaking, and groaning as these trains rattled onward to their destinations." When the war was over, the discomfort and delays were remembered, and many with autos said, "Never again." Furthermore, the old railroad cars were still in service years later.

But now that the cities are saturated with automobiles, and the countryside aches from the gouging of superhighways, and the air lanes are filling up, and nobody wants an airport near his home, and the next move is clearly back to the rails, does railroad management see this as the dawning of a great new day? So far, no— with some exceptions noted in later chapters.

Actually, the attitude of railroad management toward passenger service seems too little changed from James Hill's day. A *New York Times* survey of railroad executives taken in June 1969 revealed a general conviction that only commuters want to travel by rail; that rail passenger service no longer serves a public need; and all wanted to reduce it because of money losses.

Louis Menk, chairman of Burlington Northern, in late 1971 was quoted in several periodicals as having said "the long distance passenger train is in the same position now as the stage coach once was to railroading; it is time to let it die an honorable death." And Mr. Menk made the statement while serving as a director of Amtrak, the organization presumably dedicated to saving U.S. passenger service!

A few weeks later, in early 1972, B. F. Biaggini, president of Southern Pacific, interviewed by *U.S. News and World Report,* apparently oblivious to the environmental dangers in continued highway building, predicted that intercity rail passenger service would not amount to anything ten years from now except in the Northeast corridor because "the demand is not there."

He went on to say, "I think Amtrak's function should be to preside over an orderly shrinkage of rail passenger service." Biaggini, incidentally, was one of many railroaders who predicted that the auto-train concept would be a failure even on the East Coast.

Today, as so often in the past, conventional railroaders almost to a man are ready to dump passenger service for the more lucrative freight business. (It may not be significant, but it is interesting that in 1930 the Pennsylvania Railroad spent over $300,000 for Greyhound Bus stock. At that time it also had investments in airlines and trucking facilities. Likewise, the Chicago, Burlington & Quincy in 1930 started its own bus lines serving Chicago, Omaha, Kansas City, Denver, and Billings, Montana. It also owned a trucking division. And Biaggini, in the interview just mentioned, said, "We are in the trucking business as well as the railroad business." Stuart T. Saunders, while chairman of Penn Central, commuted from his Main Line home to his Philadelphia office by chauffeured limousine.)

Freight trains take precedence over passenger trains not only in the hearts of railroad executives but on their tracks as well, often causing delays in passenger schedules in the days before Amtrak. Critics of this procedure point out that control towers don't wave off or hold up a Pan Am passenger flight so that cargo airlines, such as Flying Tiger, can take off or land first.

Because the railroaders essentially gave up on passenger service long ago, no new roadbeds have been built since the 1920s, research-and-development effort initiated by the railroads has almost been nil, much of the rolling stock is worn out, and stations have been allowed to deteriorate. Train safety has also been neglected. According to the National Transportation Board, "there has been no research whatever involving the interaction of train, track and passenger during and after initiation of a derailment or crash. By contrast, most other modes of public transportation are actively engaged in crash testing of safety during system failure."

Authors Daughen and Binzen in *The Wreck of the Penn Central* said of that line's handling of passenger service: "The railroad publicly kept up the fiction that it was truly concerned about the Penn Central's riders long after it became clear that the opposite was true. Equipment broke down, stations fell into disrepair, and the railroad, while making sympathetic pronouncements, did very little about it."

Railroads also virtually quit trying to *sell* passenger service. *Passenger Train Journal* compared advertising and promotion of railroads with that of airlines in 1970 and found that the former spent $1.7 million for passenger and $900,000 more for passenger-freight combined, whereas the airlines spent over $220 million. A brief demonstration program by the Pullman Company to provide incentives for ticket salesmen was rejected by the industry even after it had been proved effective. Travel agents receive commissions for selling airline tickets, but not for selling railroad tickets.

In March 1970, three land-grant railroads—the Great Northern, the Northern Pacific, and the Chicago, Burlington & Quincy—merged with the Spokane, Portland & Seattle Railway to become the Burlington Northern (BN). With 25,000 miles of track, it was the longest privately owned system in the world. Soon after the merger BN distributed a seventeen-page supplement in sixty-eight Sunday newspapers saying among other things that it saw little future for its passenger trains, for which "It can only just be a matter of time."

The Interstate Commerce Commission at one time made it fairly difficult for railroads to drop passenger trains, but the way was made easier in 1958 when Section 13a was inserted (in response to pressure from the railroads) into the Interstate Commerce Act. This authorized the ICC to permit the discontinuance of passenger trains being operated at a loss unless "required by the public convenience and necessity." Thereupon the number of passenger trains began to shrink rapidly—from 1,500 to a low of 176 in 1971. Some trains were being dropped so fast that the Supreme Court ruled that the railroads would have to give the public forty-eight hours' notice of actual terminations. That they had to be ordered to show this minimal courtesy is significant.

Ralph Nader, consumer advocate, in his report *The Interstate Commerce Omission* (Grossman, 1970) accuses the ICC of maintaining a "working economic and personal relationship" with the railroads, frequently involving "insidious possible influence by an industry upon an agency holding the public trust." That report also accuses the ICC of basing its permission to drop trains on exaggerated loss figures on passenger service, and of often failing to take the steps within its power to require the railroads to maintain decent standards. It concludes that the ICC considers the railroads' interest more important than the public's and that the "ICC has done virtually nothing but preside over the funeral." (*Business Week* made the point that when the common carriers—rail, barge, and truck—"leaped to the defense of the ICC" [in response to the report], they simply reinforced the criticism.)

Of course, the railroads have their side of the argument. They have to operate in a restrictive atmosphere characterized by archaic labor laws, large subsidies to their competitors, and an inability to increase rates. When they complain, however, it is in behalf of freight, not passengers.

Whether the railroads have a beef or not, the views expressed in reports such as Nader's, and by certain Congressmen and other critics, reinforce the public's notion that American railroads are inhospitable to passengers.

"An antagonistic public is always hard to deal with. I am afraid the public has little warmth and affection for the railroads."
    —ILLINOIS CENTRAL PRESIDENT ALAN S. BOYD

"All the problems of featherbedding, creaky roadbeds and general decrepitude that contributed to the disappearance of passenger trains are still holding back their return. But the most conspicuous of Amtrak's failures has been its predictable inability to shake railroad management out of its torpor.

"The initial decision to rely on the same managements that had wrecked service to carry out the new corporation's operating responsibilities was itself an invitation to disaster. But any chance for real improvement was removed when Amtrack omitted from its contracts with these managements performance guarantees to spur more efficient and dependable operation. Instead, the contracts offer an open track for waste. Unions and politicians add to the red ink by insistence on unneeded jobs and unneeded runs."
    —The New York Times, May 3, 1972

"But suppose the Telephone Company decided to eliminate telephone service in the Catskills because it was not profitable. Suppose the Post Office said, 'Sorry, we're losing so much on Rural Free Delivery we'll have to cut it out.' Would there be a howl? Well, I am howling now."
    —ERNEST M. BRIMBO, author, reacting to cuts in rail service (quoted in *The New Yorker*)

CHAPTER IV

Old Unions with Long Memories

As THE EVENING rush hour was coming to a close on May 17, 1971, commuters leaving Manhattan Island for New Jersey were startled to see nineteen elephants marching toward them out of the center tube of the Lincoln Tunnel. Was this the latest attempt by the Metropolitan Transit Authority to solve the mass-transit problem? No, the elephants, property of Ringling Brothers and Barnum & Bailey's circus, had been stranded in the railroad yards at South Kearney, New Jersey, by a strike of the Brotherhood of Railroad Signalmen, and were tramping the last few miles into Madison Square Garden.

It was a graphic if unnecessary reminder that elephants and people who travel by rail are subject to strike-caused delays, and that rail labor unions are so rigid that they make U.S. railroads' adaptation to modern times difficult.

Like many other problems faced by the industry today, labor strife is, in part, a legacy of the robber barons. The seeds of ill will sown in an earlier day are still producing bitter fruit. Not only did the Hills, Vanderbilts, and Goulds damn the public; they damned their workers as well; and the labor unions that were formed in self-defense, and united and motivated by an intense hatred for unscrupulous, exploitative employers, are with us today, even though conditions for railroad workers are much improved. The workers and their unions still are not emotionally inclined to sit down quietly with management to solve problems and work out imaginative plans.

One difficulty is that the short-range effect of achieving greater efficiency and economy in railroad operation would be the elimination of some jobs. In the long run, as passenger rail business increased, this loss would be more than offset by more and better jobs. But union leaders and members are apt to be present-oriented and to hold grudges, and the many unions of railway labor, among the oldest in the country, suffer from what C. G. Jung called "tribal memory."

Ironically, the rail unions have come to embody many of the very traits which they despised earlier in management, tending under pressure to be autocratic, combative, stubborn, suspicious, and jealous among themselves. As an old yoga maxim has it, we tend to "become what we hate."

The roots of labor-union antagonism toward rail management run deep. Railroad employees traditionally worked long hours, at difficult or dangerous jobs, for little money. Job security, of course, was virtually unknown, as was medical compensation, though injuries were common. Part of the old-time brakeman's job, for example, was to couple cars by standing between them and—as the locomotive nudged them together—guiding a link into a socket so that a pin could be dropped for locking, and to uncouple cars by doing the reverse. It was dangerous work and could cost a man a finger, a hand, or his life. Eli Hamilton Janney's automatic coupler was perfected in 1875, but brakemen came cheaper than automatic couplers, and rail management did not flock to buy the new device.

An Iowa farmer, Lorenzo Coffin, the Ralph Nader of his day, became obsessed with railroad safety in 1874 when he saw a brakeman lose a finger while operating a link-and-pin coupling, and he led a campaign that pressured the railroads into adopting Janney's couplers and George Westinghouse's air brakes—but not before the seeds for much future bitterness had been sown.

It might be said that railroad labor unions as we know them today were born in 1877. Some had been formed earlier, but 1877 was the year the New York Central, the Pennsylvania, the Erie, and the B&O all agreed to cut workers' already low wages 10 percent. When the first three roads announced the cut, the workers did nothing. Other roads, some as far away as the Northern Pacific and Central Pacific on the West Coast, seeing that no strikes had resulted, were encouraged to follow suit. It was not until the B&O got around to making its cut that the worm turned. The B&O workers, who had taken one pay cut eight months earlier, went out on strike. Soon railroad workers across the country were walking out in what became the first nationwide strike. It set the pattern for many to follow. Public sentiment was clearly on the side of the workers, but government and press, largely controlled by the same interests that controlled the railroads, naturally sided with management. President Rutherford B. Hayes, at the request of the powerful B&O, ordered out federal troops to control strikers. (The government was later billed by the B&O for use of trains to transport those troops.) In cities everywhere there were riots and running battles between strikers and soldiers. In Pittsburgh, a storm center, 24 people were killed, more than 2,000 railroad cars destroyed, some 70 buildings burned, including the depot. In Reading, 10 people were killed.

The strike ended with the jailing of many strikers, and with only a few roads rescinding the wage cuts. Then, instead of improving the lot of labor, management beefed up its police forces, espionage systems, and company blacklists. (Many newspapers and railroad officers blamed the strike on "Communists." About the same time, that charge was being leveled by Collis P. Huntington at those midwestern farmers organized as Grangers, because they dared to initiate state laws to prevent a number of railroad abuses including the free pass, excessive passenger fares, and manipulative freight rates.)

For railroad labor, this was a great awakening. Although it still had a long, hard battle to fight, it learned that it did have the strength to fight. No longer was labor a collection of fraternal groups—the Brotherhood of Locomotive Engineers (1863), the Order of Railway Conductors (1868), the Band of the Brotherhood of Locomotive Firemen (1863), and so on. The strike of 1877 led to the organization or reorganization of brotherhood and craft unions that would cover virtually every job skill related to railroads, and would be hard to push around. Eventually, hard even to reason with.

Today that proliferation of unions is one of the biggest tangles facing those who would straighten out the railroads. Each union now must arrive at a separate agreement with each railroad in the country, and since there are 15 major unions, some 1,800 total contract agreements must be made. The railroads do often present a united front through a single bargaining agent, but even then the difficulties are compounded because of the number of unions. Furthermore, not all contracts have the same effective dates. Thus, if one union negotiates a settlement, the unions following it to the bargaining table may find themselves unable to bargain freely but in effect committed to the terms of the first accord. If rail management gives a succeeding union greater benefits than it gave the first, it can be accused of breaking faith with the first, or be pressed for retroactive pay.

While consolidation of railroad unions would have certain obvious advantages, this is difficult because some of the shop-craft unions—the International Association of Machinists, for example—have a majority of members who are in other than railroad industries. In addition, politics, jealousies, and conflicts between union leaders and members complicate the situation. Despite these hard-to-resolve complications, four of the five operating unions did merge in the late 1960s.

Another big year in the history of railway labor was 1926, when Congress passed the Railway Labor Act, amended and strengthened in 1934, to provide guidelines for the settlement of labor disputes through mediation and voluntary arbitration so that stoppages of interstate commerce could be prevented or greatly reduced. Collective agreements, said the act, would remain in effect unless changed by mutual consent or until thirty days after all possibilities had been exhausted. Should negotiations fail, the President was given power to appoint an emergency board to investigate and make recommendations. Responsibility for administering the act was given to the National Mediation Board.

By the end of 1971, the emergency provisions of the act had been invoked 190 times, or an average of four times yearly. By the end of 1969 there had been 425 major strikes (excluding transit strikes). However, as Donald E. Cullen points out in his book *National Emergency Strikes* (Humphrey Press, 1968), "the proportion of work time lost has been even lower in this industry than in the private economy as a whole," because many of the strikes lasted only a few days.

Today railroad unions, like other trade unions, are among the most powerful forces in the nation, and insofar as they tend to block modernization of the railroads, they rank among the passengers' "enemies in high places" dealt with in Chapter V. Most politicians are reluctant to tangle with powerful unions which—as a *Fortune* Magazine article once pointed out—are seldom incorporated yet "enjoy in tax matters the immunities of a private club, though they spend lavishly for political purposes." Union bosses often rule the rank and file with autocratic authority, and enjoy the advantages of the "closed shop," or compulsory unionization, whereby all employees must join the union.

The complexities of the railroad labor problem were dramatized during the eight-month period from late 1970 through the summer of 1971 when all contracts between the railroads and the fifteen major rail unions came up for renegotiation. The result was three nationwide strikes, or a total of twenty-two days virtually without rail service for either intercity passengers or freight. It also brought about shutdowns or cutbacks in some railroad-dependent industries, including auto manufacturing and food shipping. Twice, Congress had to pass back-to-work legislation before the strikes ended.

One reason railroad labor disputes are hard to resolve is that the unions are old, and some of their work rules are inherited from a period when railroading was quite different from what it is today.

For example, in the early days, with more frequent stops, manual switching and coupling, and a relatively slow steam locomotive, a typical freight train could travel only about 100 miles in an eight-hour day. So the unions and management wrote up a rule that set 100 miles or so as the distance a train could travel without changing crews. Today, moved by a diesel locomotive and with many other improvements, a freight train can travel 100 miles in two and a half hours. But under the old rules it must still stop and change crews every 100 miles, the retiring crew getting a full day's pay for little more than a quarter day's work. In a contract settlement on May 13, 1971, the Brotherhood of Locomotive Engineers finally agreed to allow the railroads to scrap the old "divisional rule" that called 100 miles a day's work.

One union-inspired practice that has made it difficult for the railroads to compete economically with other forms of transportation is—to use the management term—"featherbedding": that is, requiring more crew members than are needed to run a modern train, or requiring an unnecessarily long time to perform a given piece of work. A classic example of this practice was the requirement that there be a fireman on a diesel engine. With no fire to control, the fireman could snooze through his run and still collect his pay. Similarly, air brakes have made the brakeman's job mostly obsolete.

The fireman featherbedding problem began to be resolved in the 1960s after rail management mounted a full-fledged attack. In 1962, a Presidential railroad commission agreed with management that firemen were nonessential on freight and yard diesels. The unions took the matter to court, and a district court, then the Circuit Court of Appeals, and finally, in March 1963, the U.S. Supreme Court all upheld the railroads' position. But when the railroads announced their intention of acting on the court decision, they were threatened with a strike. It was prevented by President Kennedy's creation of a temporary emergency board, and the following year a seven-man tripartite arbitration board representing labor, management, and the public was appointed to resolve the issue. This board's "Award 282" was upheld by the Supreme Court, and by 1966 firemen's jobs had begun to be gradually eliminated except in states whose full-crew laws still required them. Nevertheless, there were still 3,500 firemen joyriding Penn Central's diesel-drawn freight trains in the spring of 1972. (Rail management does not challenge labor's contention that firemen should continue to ride on big intercity *passenger* trains in the interest of passenger safety.)

In July 1972, the nation's railroads and the United Transportation Union (which some time ago absorbed the Brotherhood of Locomotive Firemen and Enginemen) agreed to a plan for eventual elimination of firemen on freights. To get this agreement, the railroads made so many concessions on the rate of phasing out that a *New York Times* editorial called it "a costly buy-out by the railroads," and one that would probably call for more federal help to ailing roads such as the Penn Central. "The real question," said the *Times,* "is whether both sides have finally run up a green light for modernizing all the other archaic labor-management practices that continue to plague this benighted industry."

The *Times* was referring to the fact that in this electronic age, many devices once used for signaling, communication, and operational control have been superseded by modern ones. The signal lantern, for example, has yielded to the two-way radio or walkie-talkie. Aware that such efficient devices would eliminate jobs and reduce working hours, the unions have pressured management through the years to pay workers premium wages in return for union acceptance of labor-saving devices. Thus, even when the railroads were allowed to improve efficiency, they did not enjoy the money-saving that improved efficiency ought to have brought. Union leaders in a number of other industries, including the automobile industry, obviously have not stood so firmly in the way of technological advances.

Featherbedding and similiar practices have afflicted freight trains much more than passenger trains, but when there is a strike, passenger as well as freight trains are affected—as they are by the general health of the railroad industry. Obviously, labor unions with antiquated work rules have helped to put railroads at a disadvantage competitively with other forms of transportation.

To cite one colorful example, under the terms of the Merger Protective Agreement won by rail unions in 1964, railroad workers whose jobs were eliminated in a merger would remain on the payroll for four years. But at the time of the merger of the Pennsy and the New York Central, the unions demanded, and got, as the price of their acceptance of the merger, an *open-ended* no-dismissal agreement. As a result, Penn Central found itself carrying about 10,000 more people on its payroll than it needed, at an annual cost of from $120 to $150 million, or $10 million plus every month. For 1972, the estimate was expected to rise to $165 million if the company continued carrying the nonworking workers.

Like passenger service, however, employment on the railroads has declined—from 1.4 million in 1950 to 625,000 in 1972. Penn Central, spurred by a court order to develop a plan to repay debts and taxes, was all set to eliminate 6,000 jobs after April 1, 1972, and 9,800 by 1976, by reducing freight-crew sizes to three men and in some cases to two—which, incidentally, is the standard in Great Britain. The company estimated that this crew-cut would save it about $98 million a year. (Penn Central planned to negotiate separately to eliminate those extra 3,500 firemen still being carried despite the repeal of state full-crew laws which had called for them.)

If other railroads followed Penn Central's example, some 25,000 jobs in the total industry would be eliminated, at a saving of some $400 million a year. Not surprisingly, the United Transportation Union threatened a nationwide strike to prevent the Penn Central move, arguing that four-man crews are vital for safety reasons. The railroads' position is that new electronic detection equipment could do the job better.

While that Penn Central dispute was receiving national attention, another rail strike was threatened by the Sheet Metal Workers Union over wages, benefits, and work rules. President Nixon signed an executive order postponing both strikes for sixty days, and at the same time established a three-man panel to investigate and make recommendations.

Of course, it is easy for an outsider to recognize that the rail unions, in an effort to protect jobs, are contributing to the economic rigidity of an industry nearly perishing for want of flexibility, and that in so doing they are hurting labor's long-range interests; but not so easy for a union whose members' jobs are at stake now.

Railroads also suffer from an economic phenomenon known as the Baumol-Bowen effect, which holds that productivity may vary from one industry or enterprise to another but wages, as a rule, rise uniformly everywhere. (William J. Baumol is a professor of economics at Princeton University, and William G. Bowen, formerly a professor of economics at Princeton, is now its President.) For this reason, any enterprise whose productivity is not increasing is at a competitive disadvantage in the labor market. Since the "product" of rail passenger service is passengers, and they have been declining dramatically in number since World War II, the service has had a big productivity problem that put it at a disadvantage in competing with other forms of transportation, as well as with other employers. The natural tendency was to raise fares to cover wage increases, and this drove "productivity" still lower.

It becomes increasingly clear that the historic struggle between rail labor and management is an impediment to the development of sound rail transportation and is never going to be resolved by the two parties themselves. Therefore, many who pale at the mention of "nationalization" are in favor of more federal legislation to stabilize the situation.

A plan that some observers feel can help wind down the conflict is President Nixon's 1970 proposal covering all forms of transportation. This calls for an 80-day injunction to head off a strike, after which there would be a 30-day cooling-off period; if no agreement could be reached, a three-man compulsory arbitration panel, composed of one union member, one management member, and one mutually acceptable member, would take over. This panel would ask for the last best offer from labor and from management and would then choose, as a binding settlement, whichever of the two offers it deemed the more reasonable. The idea is to encourage each side to submit a reasonable proposal in the hope that his will be the one chosen, whereas in other types of arbitration both sides may be tempted to make *un*reasonable offers in the hope of "splitting the difference."

Actually, rail management is apparently ready for compulsory bargaining out of sheer desperation—or exhaustion—but for the unions it evokes unpleasant memories. "We are absolutely opposed to compulsory arbitration," says the president of the United Transportation Union (representing firemen, brakemen, and other operating workers excluding engineers), Charles Luna. "We don't believe in letting somebody who doesn't know anything about the business come in and decide things like this." George Meany, president of the AFL-CIO, at a 1971 news conference urged amendment of the Railway Labor Act but said "we're not ready for compulsory arbitration."

The major obstacle to amendment of the Railway Labor Act or to enactment of Nixon's proposed legislation is that Congress is always reluctant to act on highly sensitive labor questions except to pass no-strike legislation *in extremis*.

Here is a sampling of editorial comment from the news media on Congress' inaction and on Nixon's proposal. *Business Week:* "The nation can expect nothing but endless crisis in transportation labor disputes until Congress acts." *New York Times:* "The Nixon plan died of total neglect in the last Congress. This Congress has an obligation to act on it or devise a better plan of its own." *Trenton Evening Times:* "The Nixon plan may not work, but we won't know until it's tried. So far Congress has not even deigned to hold committee hearings on the proposal." *Christian Science Monitor:* "For more than a year the House Interstate and Foreign Commerce Committee has sat on permanent legislation requested by President Nixon. His emergency public interest protection act may not be the best, but it is better than nothing." *Wall Street Journal:* "Even those legislators eventually are going to get tired of seeing that strike engine forever rolling out of the roundhouse."

So a solution to the railway labor problem is probably in sight. Optimists can point to a number of encouraging signs already mentioned, such as the allowance of runs of greater than 100 miles without crew changes, and the elimination of some featherbedding practices. Salaries of workers continue to rise, and this affects their attitudes, making them more cooperative, more willing to negotiate.

And some unions do seem to realize, finally, that their jobs depend upon the survival and revival of rail service. For example, the unions on the Central Railroad of New Jersey in July 1971 agreed to scrap old work rules to save their bankrupt line and with it approximately 2,700 jobs. Said the union spokesman, "We have to turn this railroad around, and look for more jobs down the line." The feeling expressed by many of the workers was that Jersey Central could pay higher wages and save money if it got a full day's work for a full day's pay. This would allow it to improve its service, and thereby attract the extra revenue it needed for solvency and future expansion.

But to the pessimist, the labor problem still seems insoluble

without federal government intervention. Meanwhile, labor problems reinforce the railroad's image as an archaic, inefficient
method of travel. Americans, who more than any other people
respect technology, view ancient work rules as a guarantee of
inefficiency on the railroads. And, of course, the traveling public
is sick of being threatened with strikes during holiday and vacation periods—the times unions choose to strike, since they want
to achieve maximum impact. A San Francisco commuter was
quoted in *The New York Times* as saying, "Most of us have
learned from previous experience to tune in the news before going
to the station."

Thousands of rail commuters and rail travelers between Long
Island and New York City were given new reason to hate the
railroads when on November 30, 1972, some 5,000 nonoperating
employes of the Long Island Rail Road (electrical and sheet-
metal workers, carmen, teamsters, clerks, etc.) in twelve unions
went on strike and shut the line down, forcing rail passengers to
fall back on other means of transport. Some commuters swore they
would not return to the railroad when the strike ended, but
clogged highways will probably cause them to eat those words.

---

*"They are going to put up the fares so high that no one will ride . . .
Then, like the guy who killed both his parents and pleaded for mercy
because he was an orphan, they are going to come in and ask to discontinue the service."*

> —REPRESENTATIVE ABNER MIKVA of Illinois, reacting to a
> fare increase by Illinois Central

CHAPTER Ⅴ

Enemies in High Places

A QUICK LOOK at the record reveals that Uncle Sam in recent years has been miserly with the railroads, preferring to lay his largesse upon the automobile and the airplane as means of carrying passengers. More interesting are the political reasons for this. But first a figure or two.

In 1970 and 1971, U.S. governmental entities—local, state, federal—spent $53 billion on highways and only $3 billion for public mass transportation; and a large proportion of that went for buses, suggesting what a relatively minuscule amount went to railroads. The Nixon Administration's budget for the fiscal year 1974 requested $4.9 billion for highways; $1.9 billion for airways and airports; only $494 million for mass transportation (buses and commuter rail service); and only $152 million for intercity rail passenger service. The Association of American Railroads estimates that out of nearly $25 *billion* dollars of public (tax) money spent on intercity travel in 1971, the railroads got only $6.5 *million*, or .026 percent. A news item in *The New York Times* in 1970 quoted a Department of Transportation (DOT) official as saying, "There are some people over at the Bureau [of the Budget] who just don't think that any money ought to be spent on rail service."

One should not forget, of course, that *in their day* the railroads were dealt with very generously by the federal government—to the point, actually, where it contributed to their present delinquency. The questions are, What has it done for the railroads *lately*? And, How do we make it clear that the railroads' day has come again?

Another statistical indication of whom the federal government loves is the 1972 personnel makeup of DOT: 5,350 persons assigned to the Federal Highway Administration; 700 to the National Highway Safety Bureau; 54,500 to the Federal Aviation Administration (a high figure because it includes personnel manning the air-traffic-control towers at airports across the country); but only 1,200 to the Federal Railroad Administration, and a mere 178 to the Urban Mass Transportation Administration.

It would be oversimplifying, and would serve no purpose, to make villains of the pro-automobile interests in America. All of us over 21 have had our love affair with the automobile, and plenty of those under 21 are having it now, and it is not surprising that an object so useful and so loved should have great economic and political influence. But now that our national survival requires that we get people off the highways and onto the rails again, we find ourselves up against powerful forces—which we ourselves have helped to create—whose momentum and short-range self-interest impel them to continue straight down the present road even though disaster clearly lies at the end of it. We need to understand those forces and the nature and extent of their power in order to achieve the essential turnaround.

———

The automobile gets a big break in Washington partly because it has back of it the most powerful combination of economic forces in the nation—in the world, actually: automobile manufacturers, highway builders, and the petroleum industry, much of whose product goes to fuel automobiles. Indeed, those three giants, sometime called the highway-auto-petroleum complex, have grown to the point where they now contribute far more to the Gross National Product than does the military-industrial complex. It would be a wonder if the automobile did not have good friends in Washington.

The awesome power of just one automobile corporation, General Motors, is suggested by this statistic from Ralph Nader, sometime torero to the auto industry's bull: GM, says Nader, in one year takes in "more money than any government in the western hemisphere with the fortunate exception of the United States." In 1970 it averaged $277,000 an hour right around the clock.

According to the Automobile Manufacturers Association, about 25 cents of every retail-sales dollar in the nation is related to the automobile, and 17 cents of every wholesale dollar. All told, over 800,000 businesses were dependent on the manufacturing, distribution, servicing, and use of motor vehicles in 1967, when the last census was taken. This figure includes 110,000 auto-repair shops, 14,700 highway-contracting firms, 62,000 auto dealers, 30,000 auto-accessory dealers, 235,000 motor-freight-transportation establishments, 3,100 automotive manufacturers (vehicles and parts), 438 petroleum-refining establishments, 66,000 automotive wholesale firms, 19,000 rental agencies, and 10,000 automotive-parking concerns. Also 216,000 service stations, 12,500 trailer parks, 3,400 drive-in theaters, and 42,000 motels.

As of 1967, there were 13.3 million people employed in businesses and industries related to highway transport. The total number of Americans employed then was 74.4 million. In other words, about one out of every six persons employed in this country at that time was economically dependent in some degree on the automobile. Some were employed in the businesses already mentioned, while others served as truck drivers (8.9 million); passenger-transportation employees (taxicab, intercity buses, school buses, and bus terminals—354,000); or public workers on state, county, and local roads (556,000). Furthermore, the 13.3-million figure would be even higher if it included the millions employed as construction workers for those 14,700 private highway contractors.

Still other groups qualify as friends of or dependents upon auto travel. Local chambers of commerce, real estate agencies, land developers, and other booster groups, for example, push for new highways and then understandably point out in brochures how close their communities, developments, and tourist attractions are to major highways or Interstates.

Naturally, the highway-auto-petroleum interests, like other interests, recognize the importance of lobbying in Washington, where the squeaky wheel is well known to get the oil, and while very little of their lobbying activity is directed specifically to taking money away from rail passenger service, much of it inevitably has that effect. And these interests have so many different groups lobbying for them, full or part time! To name a few:

Associated General Contractors, National Highway Users Conference, Asphalt Institute, Private Truck Council of America, Inc., American Trucking Associations, Inc. (64 organizations), National Parking Association, Highway Research Board, American Automobile Association, Keystone Auto Club, American Road Builders Association, Portland Cement Association, National Car and Truck Renting and Leasing Association, American Petroleum Institute, the American Right-of-Way Association and the American Association of State Highways. The list unrolls like I-95 going south.

In addition are the many lobbying groups representing industries involved in auto production. Most of their functions are clear from their titles, which include: Engine Manufacturers Association, Inc., Tire and Rim Association, Inc., National Tire Dealers and Retreaders Association, Inc., Automotive Electric Association, Independent Battery Manufacturers Association, Inc., Truck Body and Equipment Association, Inc., and the already mentioned Automobile Manufacturers Association, Inc. And so on.

We will turn later in this chapter to the lobbying activities of the petroleum industry.

Given the phalanxes of businessmen and workers dependent in some degree on keeping those automobiles rolling, it is not surprising that Charles E. Wilson, one-time head of GM and Secretary of Defense, once told a Congressional committee that what was good for our country was good for General Motors and vice versa!

Nor is it surprising that the automobile has important friends in high places. Among them has been former Secretary of Transportation John A. Volpe, who has also been Massachusetts Commissioner of Public Works, Federal Highway Administrator, President of the Associated General Contractors of America, and a highway contractor himself. In October 1970 Volpe, speaking at the Sixth World Highway Conference, said, "Highways are the backbone of our entire transportation network." The present Secretary, Claude S. Brinegar, was an oil-company president.

(President Johnson once tried to cut back on highway spending, but all fifty governors joined the chorus of protest, and California Governor Ronald Reagan not only protested but recommended "an accelerated program to beat inflation." Volpe, who was then Governor of Massachusetts, claimed that 41,000 additional miles of U.S. freeways were needed by 1985.)

There are always some Congressmen so close to the highway lobby that they seem a part of it, and when they have key committee posts they can be great friends indeed. Prior to 1972, Congressmen known as highway boosters included Representatives William Cramer (Florida), a member of the House Public Works Committee—and 1969 recipient of the American Road Builders Association annual award (defeated in the 1972 primaries); William A. Natcher (Kentucky), chairman of the Appropriations Subcommittee on the District of Columbia, who receives special attention in Chapter VI in his role as a proponent of Washington, D.C. freeways and an opponent of the Washington Metro subway; and John C. Kluczynski (Illinois), an ex-truck driver who rose to the chairmanship of the House road subcommittee and in that capacity has pushed for more highways, less highway beautification, heavier trucks.

Senator Jennings Randolph (West Virginia) is another big highway man. Formerly treasurer of the American Road Builders Association, he became chairman of the influential Senate Public Works Committee. (John P. Moss, president of the American Road Builders Association, once said that "Senator Jennings Randolph is not only our friend, he is one of us.") Anyone aware of this background should not have been surprised to hear the good Senator say in July 1970 that we needed to spend $320 billion dollars on national highways in the next fifteen years, or about $20 billion a year. A *Washington Post* editorial, in response, observed that this was "enough money for the government to buy all the railroads in the country, repair their roadbeds, fill all of their needs for equipment, operate their passenger and commuter trains without charge to the riders for the next 15 years and still have a big kitty left over."

Nevertheless, in January 1972 DOT confirmed that it favored the spending of that $320 billion, of which the federal share would be around $172 billion, with states and other governmental entities putting up the rest. Specifically, DOT's plan called for grading about 200,000 miles of rural and urban roads—five times the length of the Interstate system—during the 15-year period between 1976 and 1990. In a speech, Federal Highway Administrator Francis C. Turner talked about the plan:

"In show business there is a saying that might appropriately be applied to the highway program at this point, and that is, 'What do we do for an encore?'

"There are two main areas that we will need to focus our full attention on just as soon as possible. They are the urban areas and our primary highways.

"There must be no lag, no delay, no indecision. And, there must be no appreciable drop in the level of funding.

"At the present time, we are spending about $4 billion a year on the interstate system. We will need to have those kinds of funds available in the post interstate years in order to bring our urban and primary road system up to acceptable present-day standards."

He did not speak for meadowlarks on fence posts along "unimproved" country roads, or for air-breathers in general.

Even Presidents have been good friends to the automobile. Senator Francis S. Case (South Dakota) predicted that Dwight Eisenhower would go down in history as "Ike, the Builder" because he was one of the first to suggest a system of nationwide highways and became a big brother of the Interstate Highway System.

Standing as a formidable monument to the efforts of lobbyists for and friends of the highway-auto-petroleum complex in Washington is something called the Highway Trust Fund, which is finally getting the public attention it has long deserved. The HTF is made up of revenues from a special federal tax on automobile gasoline, oil, tires, and auto accessories, and until recently this gigantic fund could be used *solely to pay for highway construction.* Thus the highways—HTF is still almost totally theirs—have an almost bottomless source of funds and do not have to compete for their share of the tax dollar with educational, social, medical, environmental, and even defense needs.

The HTF was set up in the Eisenhower year of 1956 by the Interstate Highway Act to finance the building of a 41,000-mile "National System of Interstate and Defense Highways." Its author was former Representative George Fallon (Maryland), who at that time was House Public Works Committee chairman and whom environmentalists helped to defeat for reelection some fifteen years later. Under its terms, the federal government pays 90 percent of the cost of building an Interstate, and the states traversed by it pay the remainder. For primary and secondary roads—not part of the Interstate system—the federal government was empowered to fund 50 percent of the costs. After Interstate construction began, its total length was increased to 42,500 miles, and costs have almost trebled—from a 1956 estimate of $27 billion to $76 billion. This is several times what the federal government currently spends on education. *The New York Times's* Tom Wicker once wrote that the Interstate system has become "an $80 billion bonanza for a conglomerate of industrial, commercial, construction and political interests." But Senator Ran-

dolph has said we need *another complete Interstate system* after
the completion of this one—adding, to make it perfectly clear,
"This is a fact of life."

Though pressure for mass transit has now forced a tiny crack
in the Fund, it was until recently so airtight that the House Ways
and Means Committee did not even bother to hold public hearings when it came up for renewal in the Federal Aid Highway
Act of 1970. This act extended the Fund to 1977 and authorized
expenditure of $14.2 billion between 1970 and 1972. The 1970 Act
also increased the federal share of primary and secondary road
costs from 50 percent to 70 percent beginning in fiscal year 1974
(July '73). "I think we are very happy with this bill," said T.
Randolph Russell, director of public relations for the 6,000-
member American Road Builders Association.

The Trust Fund is sometimes defended on the ground that highway users pay the tax and should get highways in return. But its
opponents say that this is rather like arguing that the tax on
whiskey should finance only the building of more whiskey dis-
tilleries, or the tax on cigarettes the building of cigarette factories.
(Speaking of whiskey, the highway lobby's friend Senator Russell
B. Long, chairman of the Senate Finance Committee, proposed in
late 1971 that 7 percent of all federal alcohol taxes—amounting to
about $350 million a year—be diverted from general funds into
the Highway Trust Fund. His committee approved the motion, and
so did the Senate, but it was defeated in a joint House-Senate conference. The idea was not without precedent. Massachusetts diverts
a portion of its cigarette-tax revenues to its state highway fund.)

In his book *The Pavers and the Paved* (D. W. Brown, 1971),
Ben Kelley, former public affairs director for the Federal Highway Administration and presently in the Insurance Institute for
Highway Safety, attacks the HTF as a self-perpetuating system.
"Each time a new expressway is opened it produces an increase in
highway use, which in turn adds a new increment to gasoline and
tire sales, which . . . generates an increase in money available for
building yet more highways."

It was strong pressure from environmentalists that helped to force open a hairline crack in the HTF for mass-transit uses such as a new Metroliner station (see Chapter VII), and this pressure is now building up further as the social and environmental costs of automobile expansion are recognized. One way to open up the Fund and yet keep it related to highways was expressed in a letter to the editor of *Business Week* suggesting that the Fund, instead of being used solely for highway building, should help care for traffic-accident victims, help offset property-tax losses due to highway building, and help reduce automobile air- and noise-pollution levels.

Most opponents of the HTF, however, including conservation groups and many newspapers, say the fund should be expanded into a Transportation Trust Fund, to achieve a better-balanced system—aiding railroads and buses as well as the automobile.

Said *The Washington Post*:

You hear, over and over again, the argument that the government would break faith with highway-users if it spent any of the trust fund money on non-highway projects, that the taxes imposed on gasoline, tires, tubes and other highway related equipment are acceptable to the American public only because of the government's assurance that the money raised will be spent only on highways. One would think, from reading the speeches made on Capitol Hill and the propaganda spread by the highway lobby, that the trust fund is fed by taxes specifically created in order to finance it. If that were true, there might be some logic in the aura of inviolability that surrounds the trust fund. But it isn't true.

Of all the taxes that yield money for the trust fund, only two were created along with it in 1956—a tax on the rubber used in retreading tires and a use tax imposed on heavy vehicles. Most of the other taxes that feed the fund—including the one on gasoline that raises three-fourths of its income—had come into existence in 1932, although many of them were increased in 1956. Prior to the creation of the trust fund, the money from these taxes went into the general fund without being earmarked exclusively for highway purposes. As far as we can tell, nobody seriously contended between 1932 and 1956 that the government was breaking faith with highway users by spending part of the money from these taxes on non-highway projects. Yet today the highway lobby and some members of the Congress act as if something were morally wrong with the pre-1956 arrangement.

That's the background that has led us to describe the theory of the trust as a myth.

Senator Joseph Tydings (Maryland) introduced a bill in 1970 that would have allowed states to take some funds received from the HTF and use them instead for urban mass-transit needs, but it did not pass. Senator Edward Kennedy (Massachusetts) submitted a similar bill in 1971 for a Transportation Trust Fund, and in the House, Republican Edward I. Koch (New York) introduced such a bill in both 1970 and 1971. His would provide funds from the HTF for the combination of modes of transportation deemed best for given localities. Such legislation is certain to pass eventually as the public lets its Congressmen know how the wind is blowing. The wind had not been felt by Gilbert B. Phillips, president of the Automobile Club of New York, when he said not long ago of any mass-transportation fund:

"We recognize that there are those who advocate that motorist taxes be used for mass transit under the guise of balancing the priorities. However, so long as the Highway Trust Fund is derived from highway users, no portion of it should be diverted to non-highway purposes."

Some states, meanwhile, are setting a good example for the federal government by passing legislation permitting the diversion of some money from state highway funds to public transportation. And Maryland has set up a Transportation Trust Fund.

But in California, the country's biggest road builder (with 1.4 million road workers), a constitutional amendment that would have permitted the use of gasoline taxes to reduce air pollution and develop mass-transit facilities was defeated in the November 3, 1970, elections after an all-out attack by auto-highway interests.

California State Senator James R. Mills of San Diego referred to an "unlimited outpouring of funds by oil companies, road builders, and state auto clubs." He also called it "a classic instance of big spending to subvert the public will." He called it one of the greatest election abuses in the history of the state and estimated that the lobby spent between $700,000 and $1 million on billboard, radio, television, and newspaper advertising. "The highway lobby is prepared to spend as much as it takes to kill the development of mass transit," he said.

That lobby has also had its way in various U.S. cities including Los Angeles, Kansas City, and Seattle, where local transit bond issues have been defeated. Perhaps the voters agreed with Henry Ford II, who said: "The future of the Ford Motor Company and even transportation itself in the United States will be tied to automobiles for the indefinite future. Mass transportation is certainly a necessity, but if you think mass transportation is going to replace the automobile, I think you're whistling Dixie or taking pot. It just isn't going to be, not in my lifetime, anyhow." Even he, however, subsequently advocated spending a little HTF money on mass transit; that is, buses and trains.

In August 1970, a proposal that state governors should have some authority to divert federal highway money to other transportation needs was rejected by the National Governors' Conference. "There's no question in anybody's mind that there was significant pressure from some interest groups against this plan," said Washington's Governor Daniel J. Evans. Representatives from the Ford Motor Company, the AAA, the National Highway Users Conference, and other automobile and highway interests attended the Missouri conference urging that the HTF be kept inviolate. There had also been numerous telegrams from auto clubs and trucking interests. Meanwhile, most Americans, obviously, were unaware that such a proposal was up for consideration, and the antihighway forces were not as well organized as they now are (see Chapter VI).

"Under normal circumstances," commented Secretary Volpe, "when you offer governors more flexibility in utilizing funds, they jump at it."

But for environmentalists, this particular story had a happy switch ending: the governors had second thoughts, and forty-eight hours later reversed themselves and endorsed the idea.

Really opening up the Fund will require Congressional action, and the HTF still has strong support in Congress. One powerful pro-HTF group that will keep the pressure on Congress is the trucking interests, whose American Trucking Associations, Inc., ranks among the nation's top ten highway lobbies, spending $5 million a year for this purpose, according to John Burby in his book *The Great American Motion Sickness, or Why You Can't Get There from Here* (Little, Brown, 1971).

If more freight went by rail and less by truck, it would help clean up the environment, make motoring pleasanter and safer, and reduce highway-maintenance costs (many of our super-highways are cracking up under the weight of heavy trucks, and this sets the taxpayer back $1 billion a year in damages, estimates the Charles River Association). But no historical precedent suggests that if the railroads got more freight business they would voluntarily improve passenger service, and indeed the opposite might happen: passenger trains might be shunted aside even oftener to let the freight through. So while environmentalists favor more freight trains and fewer trucks, this cause is connected with the future of rail passenger service only indirectly—only because trucking interests are strongly prohighway, and the longer we keep building highways, the longer it will take the average citizen to discover that we already have too many automobiles.

(American Trucking Associations, Inc., ran a full-page ad in a June 1972 *U.S. News & World Report* in which it purported to answer questions "about the country's highway program" with "the facts." Here is one question with its "factual" answer: "Why isn't some of the Highway Trust Fund money used for mass transit? It already is. Excepting a few cities, buses are the only really practical mass transit system. And good highways make for better bus service. The real question concerns *rail* transit. As a matter of simple justice, we do not believe that car, bus and truck owners should have to pay for another transportation system out of special taxes they alone have paid . . . taxes dedicated in *trust* to a highway system.")

The move to treat sacred highway money like other tax revenues is opposed also by the Teamsters Union, whose political influence is of course legendary.

Anyone who still doubts the strength of what might be called the road bloc should try opposing the construction of a highway once its route has been approved. The prohighway Goliath is muscled by millions of dollars which can be spent for, among other things, the services of full-time professional publicists, and written off by the industries involved as business expenses. The antihighway David is usually a loose aggregation of conservation and other citizen groups operating on a shoestring, their publicity campaign manned by part-time volunteers. Moreover, as we write, most environmental groups are experiencing severe financial difficulties and are cutting their budgets drastically at a time when they are needed more than ever. Still, it *is* possible to stop a highway, as is made clear in Chapter VI.

The auto industry is fairly unselfconscious about its lobbying for highways. L. L. Colbert, as president of the American Chrysler Manufacturers Association, Inc., described his organization's contributions to the highway program: "Our recent published studies of highway economics helped to shape the legislation now moving through Congress and aimed at keeping the construction of the Interstate Highway on schedule and soundly financed."

Given the automobile industry and the highway-building industry as its competitors, American rail passenger service hardly needs another powerful enemy—but it has one. The petroleum industry has a stake in keeping more cars on more highways because: (1) much of the wealth of oil producers comes from the sale of gasoline and lubricants for automobiles (there is one gas station for every 380 automobiles), and (2) the oil industry supplies a major ingredient of the asphalt widely used in road building. (Even Interstates use about equal quantities of asphalt and concrete.) Many top officials in U.S. oil companies belong to both the American Petroleum Institute and the Asphalt Institute. Helen Leavitt in her excellent book *Superhighway—Superhoax* (Doubleday, 1970) quotes Joseph P. Walsh, general counsel for Sinclair Oil Corporation and a representative of the American Petroleum Institute, as saying at a Congressional committee hearing, "We all admit that good roads and sound highway policies are in the broad public interest, but they are also in the direct and immediate interest of our industry, which markets the bulk of its product for consumption by the side of the road."

Many diesel and gas-turbine locomotives, of course, also use petroleum products, but (good for the environment, bad for the oil business) in far smaller quantities per passenger-mile. So petroleum interests and highway interests tend to be friends.

If it is true that anybody with a great vested interest in the automobile is likely to be against a revival of the railroads, then the oil industry is worth a closer look. Is it an enemy to be reckoned with? Does it have much political clout?

Well, the oil companies are allowed a "depletion allowance" that relieves them of paying any income tax on the first 23 percent of their income from oil production. Does that suggest anything?

In fact, the oil industry's history has been characterized by attempts to control legislators, by the formation of great monopolies, by predacious infighting, by corruptive practices such as rebates, and by juicy scandals, including the great 1921 Teapot Dome scandal which involved public officials at the highest levels.

That leading oilmen take politics seriously is suggested by the fact that they contributed nearly $345,000 to Eisenhower's 1956 campaign and about $15,000 to that of his opponent, Adlai Stevenson. Other statistics compiled by Herbert E. Alexander, director of the Citizens Research Foundation, for his book *Financing the 1968 Election* (D. C. Heath, 1971), reveal that although corporations are forbidden by law from contributing to political parties, fifty-nine individuals who are members of the American Petroleum Institute gave $429,366 to the Republicans and only $30,606 to the Democrats in the 1968 Nixon-Humphrey presidential contest. By contrast, and indicative of how aggressive the railroads are, officials of the Association of American Railroads that year gave a modest $14,000 to the Republicans and nothing to the Democrats.

Not to suggest that everybody gets out of the federal government exactly what he puts in, but the oil people do get friendly treatment, specifically in the form of oil import quotas and the depletion allowance mentioned earlier. It was in 1959, during the Eisenhower administration, that oil import controls were established which in effect force Americans to buy the more expensive U.S. fuel—and to help use up the limited supply of it.

The oil (and mineral) depletion allowance gives oil producers (and mineowners) a big tax break ostensibly to provide them with an incentive to carry on costly high-risk explorations by compensating them for the decline in capital assets as the oil fields (or mines) gradually become depleted by production.

It started in 1913 when oil producers and mineowners were allowed to pay no tax on 5 percent of their gross income. The sponsor of this bill was the famous Pennsylvania political boss Senator Boies Penrose, a friend of oil magnate Andrew Mellon. In 1918 he increased the 5 percent tax advantage by pushing a proposal through his Finance Committee that depletion for oil wells (and mines) be based on "market value instead of cost." He succeeded, and Secretary of the Treasury Mellon was able to see his Gulf Oil obtain a depletion allowance 4½ times its net income.

In 1926 the depletion allowance was raised to 27½ percent, and the oil companies more than doubled their assets. The tax-reform bill of 1969 reduced it to 23 percent, but the principle of depletion allowance remained, and remains, sacred—and, according to conservationists, the consumer loses, because the depletion allowance encourages the exploiting of our earth's remaining resources at an accelerated rate.

Republicans are not the oilmen's only friends, by the way. Lyndon B. Johnson and House Speaker Sam Rayburn, from the oil state of Texas, were also friendly to oil and were in turn liked by the oilmen. The *Houston Post* once summed up this admiration: "The Democrats have Lyndon Johnson. Furthermore, there is speaker Sam Rayburn. These two men have stood like Horatio at the bridge for years defending depletion against all comers. Almost any oilman knows that without Lyndon and Mr. Sam, there might be no depletion provision today."

Indeed there would *not* be if another Democrat, President Harry S. Truman, had had his way. In his 1950 budget message, he said: "I know of no loophole in the tax laws so inequitable as the excessive depletion exemptions now enjoyed by oil and mining interests. A forward-looking resources program does not require that we give hundreds of millions of dollars annually in tax exemptions to a favored few at the expense of the many."

In 1967, Standard Oil of New Jersey paid taxes of only 7.9 percent, yet it earned $2 billion. Gulf's tax rate was 7.8 percent; Mobil's was 4.5 percent; Texaco's, 1.9 percent; Standard of California, 1.2 percent; and Atlantic-Richfield (formerly a member of the Standard Oil group) paid no taxes at all on its earnings of $145.2 million.

The reason all this is relevant to the railroads and balanced transportation is that it means the automobile-oriented oil companies have an enormous stake in federal politics, an enormous stake in helping their friends get elected to Congress. Once there, those friends of oil are not likely to be railroad buffs. This is simply a political reality that friends of balanced transportation—and of the environment—need to be aware of.

(Times are changing, though. Some oil companies—notably Mobil and Exxon and Gulf—have been running advertisements in favor of a balanced transportation system even if it means busting the Highway Trust Fund and banning automobiles from parts of cities. They are worried about their ability to keep up with the soaring demand for fuel—and perhaps about their reputation for responsibility.)

Another nonfriend of rail passenger service in Washington is the aviation lobby, which does what it can to get more money for the airlines. Insofar as it is successful, it takes the attention, and some of the funds, away from railroads. And it *is* successful. In 1972, the federal government inaugurated a spending plan through the Federal Aviation Administration of $530 million annually over a five-year period ($2.65 billion total) on aviation-improvement projects and air-navigation facilities.

The airplane benefits also from the Airport and Airway Development Act. Similar in nature to the act that spawned the Highway Trust Fund, this act supports air transportation through a "users pay" principle: an 8-percent tax on all airline tickets sold in this country. This revenue subsidizes 50 percent of the cost of new airports (which helps to explain why the number of U.S. airports has doubled in the last twenty years) and also airport and airway systems development.

In addition, local passenger airlines (such as Piedmont, Allegheny, Frontier, and Air West, to name a few) each year receive direct subsidies from the federal government. These subsidies, administered by the Civil Aeronautics Board, average about $50 million a year, and are intended to increase air service to small communities. At one time the major airlines also received direct subsidies.

The airplane interests guard their money sources as jealously as do the highway people, and to help them do so there are organizations such as the Air Transport Association, the National Pilots Association, and the National Aircraft Association.

Combine the airlines' friends with the automobile-highway-petroleum interests and the result is a formidable combination indeed, and one not likely to favor diversion of federal funds to rail passenger service. Many a Congressman is indebted to one component or another of that combination for campaign funds and other favors. When he must chose between doing something for his friends and doing something for rail passenger service, real pressure must be exerted to make him do the latter; and the railroads themselves—as was made clear in Chapter III—do not lobby for more passenger service.

These are facts of life that need to be understood by more of the friends of balanced transportation. To help them influence public and Congressional opinion in favor of rail service they can confidently anticipate some mammoth land and air traffic jams in the future, and some unprecedented environmental crises. And of course the gasoline shortage has already struck.

"We hear from the highway lobby, but we don't need to. We are all cousins."

> —REPRESENTATIVE JOHN C. KLUCZYNSKI of Illinois, Chairman, House Public Works Committee, quoted in *The Wall Street Journal* October 10, 1972

"It is difficult, if not impossible, to prove, but it's widely believed that oil invests more in American politics than any other industry. For example, a Western state's Governor involved in the 1968 and '72 Nixon campaigns told CBS News, quote: 'Oil interests contributed over 20 million dollars. Banking was a poor second, with 10 million.'"

> —DAN RATHER, *CBS Evening News,* January 26, 1973

PART THREE

SOME OF THE SIGNALS ARE GREEN

CHAPTER VI

Any Friend of Nature
Is a Friend of the Railroad

IF IN THE recent past American rail passenger service has had few friends in high places and zero political clout, that situation is now beginning to change. Increasing numbers of people, some of them in high places, are waking up to the urgent need for a rail alternative to the automobile, airplane, and bus.

True, the most significant battles for a rail revival are being fought by individuals and organizations who are not so much *for* railroads as *against* the pollution, congestion, and depletion of resources caused by unlimited increase of autos and planes, highways and airports. One cannot oppose those evils without being an advocate of the new railroad age. We will describe some of the battles that are indirectly benefiting the railroads, but first let us introduce a national association and some local organizations established specifically to improve rail service.

"Passengers of America unite! You have nothing to lose but your trains," quipped Peter Lyon in his book *To Hell in a Day Coach*, and that could be the motto of the National Association of Railroad Passengers, the outstanding organization of its kind in the United States.

Founded in June 1967, NARP was chartered in Illinois as a national nonprofit corporation "to represent consumers of rail passenger service together with all who believe that trains are an essential element of a truly balanced transportation system." It now has more than 6,000 members.

NARP is not a body of rail aficionados bound together by nostalgia but an aggressive political lobbying group with a full-time staff devoted to clearing the tracks for better passenger service *now*. Its Federal Period town-house office at 417 New Jersey Avenue, S.E., in Washington is within a train's length of the House office buildings and the Capitol—and has, appropriately, a view that includes the Penn Central tracks.

Although NARP does not attempt to tell Americans how to travel, it takes the position that rail travel must be a viable and attractive option; that this is essential to our national transportation system; that intercity train service must be made efficient and attractive once again, and that when it is, many Americans will voluntarily return to riding the rails and the open-ended destruction of land for highways and airports will cease.

Here is how NARP states its objectives:

The National Association of Railroad Passengers believes that railroad passenger service—long distance, high speed, and commuter— is an essential national asset which must be preserved, improved, and expanded. To achieve this goal, we are:
• urging Congress to pass constructive legislation, and maintaining contact with Government agencies whose decisions affect passenger service.
• participating in litigation before administrative agencies and courts which involves key railroad issues.
• acquainting the public with the benefits of good passenger service and with the economic and political issues at the base of the passenger service problem.
  Membership in the association is open to train riders and other concerned citizens who believe that modern passenger trains are a key element in a balanced transportation system.

The organization has been outspoken in its disapproval of basic railroad-industry attitudes. It acknowledges that many railroad companies cannot afford to maintain, much less modernize and improve, passenger service, but it does not accept the dropping of passenger service as the answer, as many freight-oriented railroad executives obviously do. NARP maintains that problems plaguing the railroad with respect to passenger service—antiquated work rules, worn-out equipment, the "grotesque" imbalance in governmental transportation policies—also hurt freight operations, and that any improvement in the industry's passenger service has to help its freight service. "To say that passenger trains have no future," said one editorial in NARP's monthly newsletter, replying to a railroad official, "is to suggest that railroading has no future."

NARP has no full-time lobbyist in Washington, but occasionally retains experts to work for the passage of legislation and provide Congressmen and their committees with background information. In appearances before the ICC and state regulatory agencies, NARP, with a Washington firm specializing in transportation law as its legal counsel, has acted as watchdog for the public by opposing most cases of train discontinuance. But in some cases it has worked with railroad operators for the elimination of underused trains in return for better service on remaining runs.

Like many other lobbying groups, it encourages members to write letters to newspaper and magazines, to speak up at public meetings, and to write their state and federal representatives. It issues press releases and advertises in newspapers and magazines. Its monthly newsletter and special mailings keep members informed of important rail hearings and the status of pending rail legislation. A brochure listing reasons why passenger service is needed in the 1970s has been widely distributed. And NARP members receive evaluation forms on which to report to Amtrak the conditions of that body's trains. The report ("A Rider's Report to Amtrak") is easy to fill out, involving little writing thanks to a checkoff grading system.

The guiding force behind NARP is its energetic founder and chairman, Anthony Haswell, whom many credit with being the person most responsible for saving the U.S. long-distance passenger train, insofar as it has been saved. As a dedicated crusader, he has been compared to Ralph Nader (both are lawyers, both bachelors) and to conservationist David Brower (who, like Haswell, has been a rail buff since childhood). Both Brower and Haswell have been called "preservationists" by their respective opponents—one for trying to preserve railroads; the other, wilderness. As a teen-ager Haswell worked as a signal helper on the B&O and later as a lawyer with Illinois Central. There, according to an interview by *Saturday Review*'s travel editor, David Butwin, Haswell learned firsthand how railroads were able to discontinue passenger trains by first overwhelming any opposition, usually weak, and then by winning ICC approval. He soon quit the Illinois Central for a private law practice in Chicago, and two years later became assistant public defender in Cook County courts. He remained deeply interested in the railroads and in trying to save intercity trains. Finally, urged on by friends, he decided that a consumers' lobby was the only effective tool for doing this, and he founded NARP, to which by September 1971 he had contributed over $362,064 of his own funds. He is heir to a Dayton, Ohio, department-store fortune.

NARP has a seven-man board of directors—one of whom is Otto Janssen, former NARP director of public relations, now the managing editor and promotional director of *Passenger Train Journal*, the only magazine devoted exclusively to passenger rail service—and an advisory board of thirty distinguished citizens including Roy Wilkins, Senator Claiborne Pell of Rhode Island, Pennsylvania Governor Milton J. Shapp, Professor Henry Steele Commager, actor Vincent Price, cartoonist Bill Mauldin, and writers Lewis Mumford and Peter Lyon, to name a few. John Chancellor of NBC News has said that NARP is "doing the work of the Lord."

In its few short years, NARP has won friends in high Congressional posts, and many are featured in a column in its monthly newsletter titled "Friends of the Railroad Passenger." Some of these are Senators Warren Magnuson of Washington, Vance Hartke of Indiana, Clifford P. Case and Harrison A. Williams of New Jersey (Williams is the Senate's chief transit supporter and sponsor of the 1970 Urban Transportation bill, and Case was considered by NARP to be the Senate's prime mover in upping Amtrak's appropriation for its crucial second year), and Lowell P. Weicker, Jr., of Connecticut. In the House there are such friends as New York Representatives Howard W. Robinson and Edward I. Koch.

Senator Pell is admired by NARP because he has been one of rail transportation's active supporters. In his first speech in the Senate, in 1960, Pell spoke out against the fast decline of passenger rail service. The partial arresting of that decline is credited to the Pell Plan, now called the Northeast Corridor Project. After the passage of the High Speed Ground Transportation Act of 1965, which he pushed in the Senate, Pell became known as "the father of high-speed ground transportation."

Although a David fighting a Goliath, NARP has won some significant victories. Prior to Amtrak, NARP's involvement before the ICC and in the courts managed to save from discontinuance such trains as the *Sunset* (New Orleans–Los Angeles) and the *James Whitcomb Riley* (Chicago–Cincinnati). NARP also made a major contribution in fighting Penn Central's March 1970 proposal before the ICC to discontinue thirty-four east–west trains. Included were such name trains as the *Broadway Limited* (New York–Chicago) and the *Spirit of St. Louis* (New York–St. Louis). When Amtrak took over fourteen months later, some of Penn Central's east–west trains were dropped anyway—although some were added, too; but largely because of NARP, the thirty-four continued fourteen months longer than they were scheduled to. (In a fight like this one, even small victories are celebrated.) No passenger trains could be discontinued until June 1973 under provisions of the law setting up Amtrak. A number of other NARP-initiated litigation proceedings are pending at this writing.

Its biggest victory, of course, was seeing the passage of the Rail Passenger Service Act of 1970, which created the National Rail Passenger Corporation, first nicknamed Railpax and now officially named Amtrak. Although conceived originally by DOT, the Amtrak idea might not have cleared Congress without the help of NARP. The original bill was redrafted (and improved from the standpoint of passenger service) by the Senate Commerce Committee with some help from NARP, and once the bill passed, NARP helped to bring about major revisions in the original Amtrak network to improve scheduling. For example, service had been omitted along the West Coast Corridor and through a number of large cities. West Coast service was reinstated between Seattle and San Diego, but a year later NARP still complained that Amtrak service was not being provided to such cities as Little Rock and Cleveland and to several entire states: Arkansas, Maine, South Dakota, New Hampshire, Vermont.

NARP, often impatient with Amtrak, now favors a proposal that the federal government acquire the nation's tracks, roadbeds, signal systems, and other field facilities and charge the private carriers for using them.

At this writing a bill is pending in Congress that instructs DOT to study federal acquisition, operation, and maintenance of all track and rights-of-way. That bill, the Interstate Railroad Act of 1972, was drafted by NARP. In addition to the study, to be completed within two years after the act becomes effective, the bill directs DOT to designate an initial network of some 82,000 miles (to be expanded later) that would meet new standards to permit speeds of 80 mph. Instead of government takeover of tracks, the bill calls for reimbursing the railroads for what they pay in state property taxes. It would also institute a rehabilitation fund for bankrupt or poor railroads and provide a $1-billion loan-guarantee program for emergency reconstruction, as well as some R&D funds.

Haswell told us that although this bill was "more modest" than

NARP's original proposal, it still was a step in the right direction; that it probably would not clear Congress easily but that he had hopes for its eventual passage. Senator Vance Hartke said deterioration of tracks and roadbeds had caused "widespread slowdown of passenger trains during the past ten years," and that "many Amtrak trains are running slower than 1941 runs over the same routes." He also cited an increase in derailments between 1963 and 1970. Senator Robert Taft, Jr., of Ohio in his remarks also mentioned the poorer train speeds and added that the bill was "consistent with the philosophy that railroads are in some respects equivalent to public highways" and as deserving of federal aid. He said "for over a century, this principle has been recognized by the Supreme Court of the United States."

While NARP looks out for rail passengers on a national basis, there are growing numbers of state associations of rail passengers: GARP in Georgia, CARP in California, VARP in Vermont, and so on, organizations of local commuters, mostly in the Northeast Corridor, set up to oppose fare increases and to fight for better service. In Westchester County, New York, for example, commuters organized the Committee for Commuter Service NOW, and in southern New Jersey, commuters formed the Delaware Valley Commuters Association. Another group is the Harlem Valley Transportation Association, which is able to call on the expertise of member Lewis Mumford, author and authority on urban and transportation problems.

The efficacy of this sort of organized action was demonstrated in a small but typical case involving an attempt by Penn Central in 1971 to increase fares and to drop commutation tickets on a 3-mile electrified spur running between the Penn Central main line at Princeton Junction, New Jersey, and the university town of Princeton.

This shuttle—to our knowledge the only one of its kind in the United States—had been in operation for over one hundred years and, as its station adjoins the Princeton campus, was used mainly by students and commuters to New York and Philadelphia. In fact, Frederic Fox, Recording Secretary of the University, remembering back to his undergraduate days at Princeton when students were not allowed to have automobiles, called it "our link to the outside world—our Burma Road."

Most riders refer to it as the "Dinky," because of its two-car size, or as "the PJ&B," for Princeton Junction and Back. Feelings toward it range from amused tolerance to strong affection. Its two conductors have served the PJ&B for twenty-five years each, are friendly to students and commuters, and have been known to drive a stranded passenger home late at night when taxis were not available.

So when Penn Central tried to up Dinky fares, six commuters— four lawyers, an operations-research expert with a New York bank, and a management consultant—organized to fight back, calling themselves the "Princeton Intervenors." Their number quickly grew to twenty-five, and they first took their case to the New Jersey Commuter Operating Agency, where Penn Central had filed the fare-increase petition, then to the ICC, whose approval was needed for the increase. Many hearings were held, including one in Princeton attended by two hundred protesting commuters. Penn Central viewed the PJ&B as an independent line, while the commuters saw it as a link to more distant destinations.

The ICC finally ruled in favor of the commuters, suspended the fare increase for a one-year period, and ordered an investigation into the Dinky's entire fare schedule. The Intervenors called their successful operation a "Children's Crusade." (A year later, in 1972, Penn Central again petitioned for a fare increase and the state set new hearings. Meanwhile, the Intervenors filed another brief with the ICC for further hearings should they be necessary.)

———————

But rail passenger service has probably benefited as much from the indirect help of pro-environment groups as from the direct help of specifically pro-railroad groups—from the growing success of organized efforts to slow down the auto-highway juggernaut, and in some cases actually to prevent highways from being built; airports, too. For, broadly speaking, any enemy of the unchecked proliferation of automobiles and highways and airports—and these enemies are becoming legion—is a friend of the railway.

Among these friends one would include the Sierra Club, National Audubon Society, Friends of the Earth (FOE), Environmental Action, the League of Conservation Voters, Zero Population Growth, Conservation Foundation, Wilderness Society, the Environmental Defense Fund. Together these organizations can be formidable, and despite the terrific odds against them, they have won a few notable victories against the auto-highway forces, reflecting a subtle but significant change in the public's attitude.

Worth examining in some detail is the seemingly endless battle to prevent the building of a freeway link and the so-called Three Sisters Bridge across the Potomac in Washington, D.C. (Legend has it that three lovelorn Indian princesses leaped into the Potomac, or fell out of their canoe on the way to join their lovers, and became three small islands at the proposed site.) The battle really began in the 1940s when a private study recommended that rail transit be made the backbone of the D.C.-area transportation system. The highway builders were not convinced, and they saw in the 1956 Highway Trust Fund and the projected new Interstate Highway System the means of making Washington as dependent on highways as, say, Los Angeles. In 1957 the D.C. Highway Department submitted a comprehensive plan to extend a downtown freeway loop over the Potomac via the projected Three Sisters Bridge to Virginia. Meanwhile, the long-talked-about District subway, the Metro, was officially proposed in 1959, but was soon eclipsed by the D.C. highway program.

Highway construction was started, but pressure from conservationists and influential homeowners forced abandonment of plans to bulldoze a section of the freeway through picturesque and historic Georgetown. By the mid-'60s, attention had shifted to another portion, the North Central Freeway, and the bridge itself. The former would have stabbed through the heart of D.C.'s predominantly black Northeast, and it was over this disruption of a community that matters finally came to a head.

In 1965, a conglomeration of neighborhood citizen groups recognized that their disjointed efforts to fight the freeway and bridge were inefficient, and they agreed to merge into the Emergency Committee on the Transportation Crisis (ECTC), whose membership thereupon included blacks, whites, rich, poor, suburbanites, the urban core, militants, and religious and political leaders—all with common interests and a shared goal: to stop the highwaymen.

A lawsuit filed in November 1966 bore fruit in February 1968 when the D.C. Court of Appeals ruled that the District's citizens had a right to public hearings on freeway decisions.

But Washington is run by Congress, which holds virtual life-and-death control over it through control of funds for the District. And those Congressmen are beholden not to Washingtonians but to their own "back home" constituents. So a handful of influential highway supporters in the House, among them Republican William H. Natcher of Kentucky, then head of the House Appropriations Subcommittee on the District, ignoring the 1968 court verdict, obtained passage of a bill in July 1968 ordering the building of the Three Sisters Bridge and some new freeway segments. The bill was introduced by prohighway Representative Kluczynski, mentioned in Chapter V.

Then in December 1968, the National Capital Planning Commission and the City Council responded to citizen pleas at hearings and agreed to oppose the freeway aspects of that plan, including the construction of the North Central Freeway.

Meanwhile, the D.C. Appropriations Subcommittee, under Natcher's chairmanship, had frozen all further District money for the Metro and threatened to cut off other federal funding that annually goes for the District until "irreversible" construction of both the complete freeway system and the Three Sisters Bridge had begun.

Nixon took office in January 1969, and the new administration and Congress pressured the City Council to accept the demands of Congress. The City Council at hearings in August 1969 approved plans to start construction on the freeway/bridge as the price of going ahead with the subway. Citizens attending the hearing at which this decision was made became enraged by the council's refusal to hear their testimony, as well as by the decision itself. They chanted, "No freeways, no freeways'"—but police, there in large numbers, arrested fourteen chanters, and "order" was restored. Two months later, DOT ordered that construction begin on the freeway/bridge.

The next episode centered around the bridge and received national attention when several weeks later—on October 15, 1969, Vietnam "Moratorium Day," the date set for bridge construction to start—thousands of citizens demonstrated against it at the site, and about 150 were arrested. The resultant publicity brought an offering of support from several national conservation organizations and the League of Women Voters. But construction did begin. (Metro subway construction began on December 9, 1969, the day Nixon signed the authorization and some ten years after it was first proposed.)

But then in August 1970, the District Court halted the bridge construction, leaving two sets of pilings standing in the Potomac. The decision was based on ECTC's contention that proper hearings had not been held by DOT. When DOT appealed, the case went to the U.S. Appeals Court for the District of Columbia. Finally in October 1971, a 2–1 ruling in favor of ECTC was handed down.

That decision too was based in part on ECTC's contention that proper hearings had not been held by DOT, and that DOT had not followed federal environmental guidelines. But there was more to it than that. "Even if the Secretary had taken every formal

step required by every applicable statutory provision," Chief
Judge David Bazelon declared, "reversal would be required, in
my opinion, because extraneous pressure intruded into the calcu-
lus of considerations on which [his] decision was based." The
judge also had an answer to any Congressional contention that the
bridge/freeway had to be built: " . . . nothing in the statute indi-
cates that Congress intended the bridge to be built contrary to its
own laws."

Still another indication of a change of attitude toward mass
transit, and yet another development in the bridge controversy,
came in late 1971 when the House of Representatives, under
pressure from the White House, overrode Natcher and voted 196
to 183 to release $72 million to the Metro. (Interestingly, Repre-
sentative Robert Giaimo of Connecticut, who led that House
fight, was the number two Democrat on Natcher's committee.)
The release actually amounted to twice the $72 million, because
other federal matching funds were involved. Up to that time,
Metro subway construction had been slowly proceeding with the
help of a $57-million DOT loan plus some funds from Maryland
and Virginia suburbs that will be served by the subway.

Time Magazine, in reporting the court decision, observed:
"Natcher has effective veto power over all appropriations for the
capital. If the bridge is not completed, he has said many times in
public, the city's unfinished 98-mile subway will remain mere
holes in the ground without further congressional funding."

At this writing it appears that Natcher may try to block a
pending bill authorizing a federal guarantee of $1.2 billion in
Metro bonds, but public pressure has built up to the point where
he would probably fail. Still, even if the Metro is no longer held
hostage, the future of the bridge/highway remains uncertain.

The then Attorney General, John Mitchell, at the request of
President Nixon, asked the Supreme Court to review the 1971
decision of the U.S. Court of Appeals, but his request was denied.
Chief Justice Burger, however, personally chided the Appeals

Court for frustrating "the will of Congress" and let it be known that he opposed a Supreme Court review of the case largely because it would take so long. Nevertheless, the Appeals Court decision was allowed to stand, and it is a landmark—though there was a precedent of sorts in the Memphis Overton Park case, on which the nation's highest court had already ruled favorably to antihighway forces. In that case, interesting in its own right, the Sierra Club, the Audubon Society, and a local group calling itself Citizens to Preserve Overton Park joined in suing the U.S. Bureau of Public Roads to prevent construction of a stretch of Interstate 40 that would slice 26 of the wildest and most picturesque acres out of the 342-acre park. The Bureau had approved the plan initially in 1956, and DOT's Federal Highway Administration had given final approval ten years later.

But in 1971 the Supreme Court ruled that federally financed highways may not be built through park areas except in the "most unusual situations." The Court declared that the Secretary of Transportation does not have the right to turn all or part of a park into an interstate highway simply because it would be cheaper or more convenient or would present fewer obstacles to the highway builders. The Court said construction of a highway through public parks was permissible only if all other routes had been fully explored and if there was absolutely no "feasible and prudent" alternative. So the case went back to the District Court for review. If it is found that the Secretary failed to investigate thoroughly all "feasible and prudent" alternatives, as is argued by the conservationists, I-40 will not go through the park, and Memphians will have saved some precious green space.

Two thousand miles away, another six-lane highway project was stopped as a result of a coalition of the Sierra Club and local civil rights groups. This was the proposed fourteen-mile, $100-million Foothill Freeway to run east of San Francisco Bay through three cities south of Oakland. The ruling by Federal Judge Robert F. Peckham was in response to a suit brought by the coalition which contended there was insufficient need for another Bay Area freeway and one that would displace five thousand low-income Mexican-Americans.

Judge Peckham ruled that the State of California had failed to establish a satisfactory relocation program for the many families that would be displaced, as required by the Uniform Relocation Assistance Act; failed to file an environmental-impact statement as per the Environmental Policy Act of 1969; and, as in Memphis, failed to seek "feasible and prudent" alternatives to the disruption of three public parks which the freeway would have traversed.

Despite the possibility of appeal, Anthony Kline, attorney for the coalition, called it a substantial victory. "The ruling challenges the validity of the planning process used by the federal government all over the country," said Kline. He also indicated that it was a victory for BART, the new transit system described in Chapter VII. "The purpose of the rapid-transit system is to cut down on traffic and smog. Why should we build another freeway to compete with it?"

Coast to coast, many other groups, like gnats buzzing around the head of a giant, are finally learning how to slow down, if not stop, the highway machine. In Seattle, a black community succeeded in obtaining a favorable Federal Appeals Court decision when threatened by a $250-million freeway; and New York's Governor Rockefeller in late 1971 conceded defeat in his arduous six-year battle against the Sierra Club and a number of citizens' groups to build a Hudson River Freeway. Declaring it a "dead issue" at last, Rockefeller said, "The people have spoken. In the midst of this turmoil it would be tragic if government, which quite literally is the creature of the people, is cast into the role of their enemy and not their instrument."

As of mid-August 1972, the Federal Highway Administration faced the task of processing some 950 environmental-impact statements before the year's end, and since 1966 there had been 84 lawsuits filed to halt construction of federally aided highways on social and economic grounds. Construction was halted in 16 of the suits, and prohighway decisions in nearly half of the remaining cases have been appealed.

A successful nationwide battle to arrest the spread of highways might simply force more people into traveling by air, with consequent damage to the environment from the spread of airports and plane pollution. But here again, conservationists and others who dislike airports because they take up so much land and are so noisy and dirty are indirectly promoting a rail revival by stopping or delaying construction of some big airports. To wit:

1) An attempt to put the fourth New York metropolitan jetport in either the Great Swamp or the Pine Barrens of New Jersey. (A suit has been filed by several New York towns to prevent its being built at the site of the former Stewart Air Base in Orange County, near Newburgh, New York, about 50 miles from New York City.)

2) An attempt to build a Miami supersonic jetport in the Florida Everglades.

3) An attempt to expand Kennedy International Airport through the Jamaica Bay Wildlife Refuge in Jamaica Bay, off Long Island.

Meanwhile, Palmdale International Airport near Los Angeles is being held up by a suit to prevent further funding by the federal government (see Chapter IX). Other jetport projects being opposed by citizen groups include the one proposed by the Metropolitan Airports Commission in Minneapolis on a site that would destroy a wildlife-management area, and the expansion of the Portland (Oregon) International Airport. Environmentalists are also fighting a plan to expand a small airport into a large jetport right in spectacular Grand Teton National Park. Congress has already appropriated $2.5 million for that one. This fight promises to be a classic, because not only is the future of this national park at stake, but such an airport could serve as a precedent for "urbanizing" other national parks as well. Opponents' arguments in this fight by now sound familiar: such an airport would foster jet air traffic that would shatter the park's serenity and defeat the very purpose of having a park, and the U.S. public would never wittingly subsidize the destruction of one of its parks.

Similar actions are delaying or blocking jetports in Cleveland, Boston, Chicago (for one on Lake Michigan), Atlanta, and St. Louis.

———————

The successful fight against the SST taught conservation groups that in unity lies strength. So, to coordinate their attack against unchecked highway building in general and against the Highway Trust Fund in particular, the Sierra Club and Environmental Action banded together in March 1971 to form the Washington-based Highway Action Coalition (HAC). Since its founding this group has allied itself with Americans for Indian Opportunity, Friends of the Earth, the Washington Metropolitan Coalition for Clean Air, the National Audubon Society, the Wilderness Society, and Zero Population Growth, and it has made contact with over 350 local antifreeway groups.

(NARP, recognizing railway friends in highway enemies, says it has established a number of "productive contacts" with the HAC —as well as with the Conservation Foundation and Ralph Nader's Center for Responsive Law. Furthermore, NARP tries, with growing success, to enlist members from the ranks of environmentalists.)

"We are out to bust the Trust," says HAC Board Chairman Theodore Kheel—speaking, of course, of the Highway Trust Fund. "We are Trust-busters." At a press conference during National Highway Week in September 1970, Kheel, best known as a New York City labor mediator, said of the Trust Fund, "The neglect of transportation for people is criminal . . . we are sick and tired of highway hearings occurring under the guise of transportation planning." He ended the press conference with the comment that "The highway lobby and the government are selling highways to the people. But this year, we're not buying."

HAC members acknowledge that dissolution of the Trust "simply is not in the cards through 1977," the date the present fund expires. In the meantime, the HAC is following a three-part plan: First, to try to open up the present Fund, make it a *Transportation Trust Fund*. Second, to "democratize the planning process" to allow the public an opportunity to decide whether a road will be built or not. Third, to require that all costs—environmental, social, and economic—be taken into account in all transportation planning. To help achieve these objectives, HAC needs funds, for it is taking on what Linda Katz, its coordinator, calls "most of the largest industries in the world."

But there have been encouraging, even startling, developments to spur the Trust-busters on. On the corporate side, the Mobil Oil Corporation has publicly advertised the need for a balanced transportation system; Gulf Oil Corporation and Jersey Standard executives have advocated publicly using state highway money for mass transit (trains and buses, to conserve fuel). The Ford Motor Company, in the person of Henry Ford II, had earlier become the first defector from the auto establishment when he recommended in early 1972 that some Highway Trust Fund money be shared with mass transit. General Motors, Chrysler, and American Motors subsequently took that position with respect to Michigan, at least.

But the most surprising breakthrough occurred on March 15, 1972, when Secretary Volpe released his DOT's 1972 Highway Needs report and proposed making some of the Trust Fund available for mass transit. Under his plan, nearly $1 billion (2 percent) would be spent in fiscal year 1974, $1.85 billion in fiscal 1975, and $2.25 billion in subsequent years. The money set aside would be designated as the Single Urban Fund. It would work this way: local governments in large urban areas would receive 40 percent of the annual amount, state governments another 40 percent, and the remainder would be used by the federal government for transit programs involving special projects.

The New York Times referred to Volpe's recommendation as "refreshing" and added, "Mr. Volpe deserves credit and support for rejecting the sacred canon that concrete is the answer to all of America's transportation problems." The paper did argue, however, that the "proposal falls short of the drastic shift" required.

Environmentalists generally agreed with the *Times* and maintained that highways still would receive 90 percent of the Fund, as they have in the past, while cities and states would have to put up 30 percent of the cost of transit systems. Furthermore, funds under the plan would be allocated to capital equipment and not to the operating costs that keep local transit systems in the red.

Some environmentalists expressed fear that Volpe's new plan might turn out to be only a replacement of the current urban-mass-transit program that expires in 1974. They worried that the actual funds available by 1974 might remain virtually unchanged or might even drop. Still another drawback: the Single Urban Fund does not *have* to be used for rail transit; it *can*, if local citizens so vote, be used for highways.

Still, Volpe's announcement was a symbolic victory and brought the Trust Fund issue into the open. And Volpe seemed to have the fervor of a convert as he charged highways with "destroying the quality of life in our urban areas," declaring, "This, very simply, is a self-perpetuating disaster."

Subsequently, in 1973, Senators Howard H. Baker, Jr., of Tennessee and Edmund S. Muskie of Maine introduced an amendment to a Federal Highway Bill which would open the Trust Fund to support urban bus and rail transit. At this writing, their modest proposal, watered down in House-Senate Committee and far less generous than Volpe's, seems likely to pass Congress.

Meanwhile, many states are considering the establishment of their own transportation trust funds to break up the auto-highway monopoly. Maryland has one. Although California failed by a whisker to pass Proposition 18, which would have diverted some state gasoline-tax revenues to pollution research and mass transit, the state does have a special gas tax that makes available $160 million per year to local communities for extra roads *or* mass transit, with the communities allowed to choose.

In Massachusetts, Governor Francis Sargent has restricted future highway building inside Boston's circular belt, famed Route 128, and observers predict that a proposal to allow gasoline-tax receipts to be used for transit will be placed before the electorate on the 1974 ballot and that chances for its passage are excellent. The legislature defeated such a proposal by just two votes in early 1972.

Missouri's Governor Warren Hernes came out for a transportation bond issue, and some eight months later approved tacking onto the bond issue an amendment creating a Transportation Trust Fund. Michigan is also leaning in that direction. Governor William G. Milliken failed to get through such a plan in 1971 but was expected to try again. New Jersey Governor Cahill moved to make road tolls available for mass transit, including rails.

In New York State, the motorist is already helping to support railroads. In the New York City area, tolls on nine bridges and tunnels of the Triborough Bridge and Tunnel Authority, totaling about $74 million a year (over one-fourth of the total national mass-transit budget), have been shifted to New York City for mass transit. "We have taken an important and historic step forward in having rubber help pay for rails," said Governor Rockefeller.

The HAC Trust-busters can point to still other favorable trends. A House-Senate subcommittee on economy in government recommended in 1970 that the Highway Trust Fund be abolished, and more and more Congressmen are coming to share that view. In fact, it is embodied in several bills already introduced. Also, both the National Governors' Conference, despite pressure from the highway lobby, and the U.S. Conference of Mayors have voted in favor of diverting some highway funds to mass transportation.

It was a heartening day for prorail and other environmental groups when, in the 1970 Democratic primary, Representative George H. Fallon of Maryland was defeated. He had been strongly opposed by the League of Conservation Voters, a group dedicated to defeating political candidates unfriendly to the conservation cause—and to supporting those who are friendly. As chairman of the House Public Works Committee, original sponsor of the Highway Trust Fund, Fallon stubbornly refused to support mass transit, which the league's organizer, Marion Edey, defines as the "only transportation system compatible with the environment." She said men like Fallon were indirectly responsible for East Coast smog. Since that primary, other Congressmen designated as "targets" by the League of Conservation Voters have also been defeated—a trend of more than passing interest to professional politicians.

The Environmental Defense Fund (EDF)—known for its legal expertise in court cases involving DDT and other pollutants as well as for its international efforts to save whales from extinction —announced in December 1971 that it intended to join the ranks of those challenging the Highway Trust Fund, and might join the HAC. Specifically, the EDF argues that when DOT requests the apportionment of Highway Trust money, the request be accompanied by an overall impact statement to conform with the Environmental Policy Act.

Whether or not HAC and its allies succeed in busting the Trust, there is no doubt that their efforts are making and will continue to make dents in its armor. And every blow struck at the auto-highway monolith is a blow struck for railroads, the natural—or at any rate, the nature-respecting—way to go.

Of course, the automobile itself has come under attack, mainly in cities, and many—including Baltimore, Boston, Philadelphia, St. Louis, and Denver—are actively studying "carrot and stick" methods of discouraging its uncontrolled use. Some are already in effect, such as raising parking prices, rationing parking spaces, encouraging bicycling, restricting truck deliveries to specified times, offering free transit tokens to employees, setting tolls in inverse proportion to the number of riders per car (a California study showed that 95 percent of the commuting vehicles checked carried only a driver), and free parking for car pools. The Boston branch of the Prudential Life Insurance Company of America for years has offered free parking to car pools; parking priority is based not on rank but on number of passengers. San Francisco has experimented with allowing cars with three or more occupants to cross the San Francisco–Oakland Bay Bridge free during rush hours. In its first test, car-poolers sped across the bridge while other cars clotted up at toll gates for the usual ten to fifteen minutes. The early results were termed "promising," as car pools doubled to about 2,200 daily. (Some single drivers zipped through toll-free with mannequins seated beside them.) On the nearby Golden Gate, toll collectors are now handing out free bus tickets and urging commuters to leave their cars home the next time.

Taxation as a means of reducing auto use, and auto pollution, is also being studied. Progressive taxes on auto horsepower, on weight, and on the amount of space an auto occupies on the road have all been suggested, along with a special tax on new autos to help pay for disposal of roadside junk heaps. Obviously, as automobile use is restricted, and as automobiles grow more costly, the advantages of going by train will become more apparent. So it is interesting how many localities are becoming inhospitable to automobiles.

New Jersey's Clean Air Council has recommended some deterrents to auto use, including higher taxes on some parking facilities; priority (special lanes) on expressways for buses (this is now being tried in Washington, D.C., in the Metropolitan New York area, and in a number of other cities); increasing the state gasoline tax; limiting the number of vehicle registrations per household. The council also emphasized "the pressing need for mass transit."

Restricting automobile parking because of sheer glut is being tried in some cities. San Francisco in 1971 imposed a 25-percent tax on downtown parking lots. The financial district of Manhattan became so congested, even with staggered work schedules, that parking meters were removed and parking was banned in a fifty-block area. Washington, D.C., is plagued with commuters' cars, and it has been proposed that on-street parking by Maryland and Virginia cars be prohibited between 7 A.M. and 5 P.M. Monday through Friday. NARP's Vranich, testifying before a D.C. Bureau of Air Pollution Control hearing, said an auto quota plan would jolt Maryland and Virginia "into the realization that their lop-sided transportation policies hurt the District and are no longer welcome."

Several cities contemplate the banning of autos from downtown areas, a step that is becoming increasingly acceptable to the public according to a recent poll taken for DOT by the Opinion Research Corporation of Princeton, New Jersey. The poll revealed that 60 percent of urban residents would be willing to curb downtown auto trips and 57 percent of the public at large would like to see traffic limited in downtown areas.

New York City has banned autos from some downtown areas when air pollution reached emergency levels, and a Detroit suburb has already partially said No to the auto by closing two major through streets to traffic. (Although automobiles have not yet been banned in their old hometown itself, Detroit did temporarily ban new filling stations during 1971 because they were proliferating beyond reason.)

Two demonstrations against the auto received attention in the news media. The first was in early April 1970 when Citizens for Clean Air, Inc., the Sierra Club, FOE, and many other conservation and environmental groups, totaling some five thousand people, gathered in front of the General Motors Building in New York City to protest against—in their words—"the insult of the automobile." They then marched to the Coliseum, where the New York International Automobile Show was being held. Included among those who took part in the six-hour demonstration were such public figures as Representative Edward Koch of New York; New York City's then consumer protector, Bess Meyerson Grant; and Jerome Kretchmer, then head of the city's Environmental Protection Administration.

One year later another demonstration was held outside the Automobile Show, and this time the city's Environmental Protection Administration exhibited an anti-automobile display at the show; Kretchmer and Robert N. Rickles, commissioner of the Department of Air Resources, also participated in discussions. Rickles, in a letter written to Mayor Lindsay a few days before the show, described the auto as "this most insidious of urban insults."

A demonstration of a slightly different order occurred when a handful of "Nader's Raiders" picketed the American Automobile Association's 1971 annual meeting. One of the demonstrators charged the AAA with being "incredibly subservient" to the auto industry. It was another chapter in Nader's dispute with the AAA, which has been under study by a team of his student investigators. "The auto clubs are ripe for a take-over by the consumer movement," says Nader. The president of the 14-million-member organization, William B. Bachman, has accused Nader of being not a consumer spokesman but a "dictator."

But many AAA members have criticized the organization. An article on the AAA in *The Wall Street Journal*, by staff reporter James F. Carberry, featured San Francisco businessman Bert Schwarzschild, who is trying to put a dissident on the club's board of directors. Schwarzschild was furious that the CSAA, an affiliate of the AAA, spent money from dues in California to defeat Proposition 18. "The AAA should expand its horizons to consider all transportation needs, not just those of the freeway lobby."

Los Angeles City Councilman Marvin Braude went one step further and sued another California affiliate of the AAA, the Automobile Club of Southern California, charging that it keeps dissidents off its board.

Stressing the point that autos must be controlled in order to make motoring a pleasant possibility, Professor Donald H. Gray of the University of Michigan wrote the Automobile Club of Michigan, "Sitting in monstrous traffic jams amid the miasma of exhaust fumes may be your idea of mobility, but it's not mine." Other members have simply resigned in protest over AAA's link with the auto-highway lobby.

A different method of attacking the automobile was initiated by FOE when it wrote to WNBC-TV requesting that the station balance its commercials for automobiles and gasoline with messages proclaiming the harmful effects of autos. Gary A. Soucie, FOE's executive director, argued that the fairness doctrine that affected cigarette commercials, before they were dropped, applied equally to "high performance" cars and high-test gasoline since they too were hazardous to health, particularly in the city.

The station turned FOE down, contending that the auto was a necessary form of transportation and, besides, that it had shown many programs on air pollution caused by automobiles. FOE appealed to the Federal Communications Commission, which ruled in favor of the station. FOE then took the case to court. In August 1971 the U.S. Court of Appeals for the District of Columbia, in a 2-to-1 vote, overturned the FCC decision, and Judge McGowan, speaking for himself and Judge Robb, wrote: "Commercials which continue to insinuate that the human personality finds greater fulfillment in the large car with the quick getaway do, it seems to us, ventilate a point of view which not only has become controversial but involves an issue of public importance. When there is undisputed evidence, as there is here, that the hazards to health implicit in air pollution are enlarged and aggravated by such products, then the parallel with cigarette advertising is exact."

When we asked Soucie what he thought the significance of the judge's decision would be for the future, he told us, "Advocates of mass transportation should be happy about this decision . . . and not just because it's a blow against their archenemy the private automobile. With all that auto and gasoline advertising, the networks can hardly afford to put the knock on the car all the time, so the easiest way for them to discharge part of their fairness-doctrine obligation is to promote mass transportation."

The decision, as it turns out, affected only past performances of the station, but it did lead to an agreement between FOE and NBC that the station would show messages on the need to replace city driving with good mass transit. FOE also hopes to reach agreements with ABC and CBS.

The published book as an instrument of social change has gained respect since Rachel Carson zapped the careless use of DDT and other chemicals with her *Silent Spring* (Houghton, Mifflin, 1962) and Ralph Nader gave the auto makers the shakes with *Unsafe at Any Speed* (Grossman, 1965). Now we are getting books about the highway builders and auto makers that may help to bring about better rail service.

Widespread publicity was given to Helen Leavitt's *Superhighway–Superhoax* (mentioned in Chapter V), which deals with—in the author's words—"the men and institutions who promote highways and how they destroy our churches, schools, homes and parks." The book takes a hard look at the Highway Trust Fund, the power of the highway-auto-petroleum complex with its friends in the right places, and the efficiency of the highway boosters in pushing highways through locales by using a "divide and conquer" technique. Like many citizens who become conservation activists when a highway threatens their own backyards, Mrs. Leavitt was aroused by the bulldozers bearing down on her home in Washington, D.C., and went on to become the Rachel Carson of the antihighway forces. Her book plants seeds that will be growing for a long time.

Although *The Road to Ruin* (J. B. Lippincott Company, 1968) by A. Q. Mowbray was written earlier than Mrs. Leavitt's book and covered some of the same ground, it came at a time when the public was a little less ready for it, and received less attention. Too bad, because it might have triggered opposition to the highwaymen two years earlier. Mowbray calls his chapter on the decline of railroads "A Nation Derailed."

A more recent book and one that received wide coverage and good reviews was Ben Kelley's *The Pavers and the Paved* (D. W. Brown, 1971). This one gained impact from the author's being former director of the Federal Highway Administration's office of public affairs. As an insider he could—and did—tell how "The Pavers" operate, and what "The Paved"—embattled citizens —can do to defend themselves. He recommended litigation in federal courts on grounds of planning deficiencies as the best way "To Halt a Highway" (the title of that chapter). He revealed past, costly-to-the-taxpayer mistakes by interstate highway planners, discussed neglected highway safety, and, like the other authors, came down hard on the sacred Trust Fund.

Autokind vs. Mankind (Norton, 1971), by a sociologist, city planner and conservationist, Kenneth R. Schneider, dealt with the same general themes but brought fascinating new facts and insights to them. Samuel Mines in *The Last Days of Mankind* (Simon and Schuster, 1971) dealt more broadly with man's assault on his environment, but his chapter "The Road Builders" offered further ammunition for use against the highway lobby.

What's Good for GM by Edward Ayres (Aurora, 1971) was another in the series of books attacking America's auto orientation. It zeroed in on General Motors but dealt generally with the car as an enemy of society, and questioned the desirability of our viewing national prosperity and success in terms of the number of vehicles that come off the assembly lines. Ayres told how industry had failed to search aggressively for alternatives to the internal-combustion engine and had opposed safety devices.

The Death of the Automobile by John Jerome (Norton, 1972) accuses the American automobile of causing or compounding a horrifying range of problems, and it comes down particularly hard on the Interstate Highway System. As *The New York Times* noted, Mr. Jerome "writes with clarity, concision and enough humor to make the book palatable without lessening its punch."

The leading environmental organizations have published ecology and conservation paperbacks that are in effect field manuals and handbooks for activists, and many of these deal with the automobile and the highway as hazards to mankind. FOE's *The Environmental Handbook* (Ballantine Books, 1970) was one of the first, and it came out in time to be used before Earth Day 1970. Close behind it in publishing date, also before Earth Day, was the Sierra Club's *Ecotactics* (Pocket Books, 1970). Environmental Action, the organization that coordinated Earth Day 1970 activities, did not get its *Earth Tool Kit* (Pocket Books, 1971) out until 1971, but it is just as hard-hitting as the others and also offers a strategy for combating the "freeway establishment."

Since publication of its first handbook, FOE has published two other paperbacks of value to anticar activists. *The Voter's Guide to Environmental Politics* (Ballantine Books, 1970) reported the environmental voting records of current Congressmen and showed how the individual can bring about change "before, during, and after the election." It explained the workings of our legislative process and how to counteract power interests, including the highway-auto-petroleum lobby. The chapter titled "Transportation and America's Environment" was written by Robert C. Fellmeth, a "Nader's Raider," and dealt with the need for better passenger rail service.

The other, *User's Guide to the Protection of the Environment* (Ballantine, 1970), described how one's purchasing habits affect the environment and how to be a civilized buyer. Like all of these books, it helps to consolidate public opinion in favor of better rail passenger service as a civilized alternative to the nature-destroying highway.

And so goes the battle for a rational, balanced transportation system. The odds still seem almost insurmountable, but pressures continue to mount as some groups rally to demand good rail service while others attack the present auto-intoxicated national transportation policy. *Business Week* has predicted that "The militancy of the critics and the broadening base of public involvement in mass transit issues will force the government to make a substantially better effort." The reference is only to mass transit, and not to coast-to-coast or intercity trains, but, as we have said elsewhere, what helps rail travel of one kind is likely to help rail travel of all kinds.

". . . there has recently been considerable public discussion concerning nationalization of the entire railroad system. Our Nation must have a modern and responsive rail passenger system. Amtrak can and should meet that need. If Amtrak fails, public demand for passenger service will doubtless not disappear and may be redirected back toward the railroad corporations. Since the railroads generally have been unwilling or unable to meet this demand, total nationalization will inevitably be advocated as the only alternative which promises a positive passenger train solution. But, if Amtrak achieves the objectives for which it has been established, there should be no rational ground for proposing nationalization on account of passenger service deficiencies."

—Report of the Senate Committee on Commerce, April 20, 1972

CHAPTER VII

Good New Trains at Home

THOUGH THE United States trails all other developed nations in rail passenger service, there are some innovations in equipment and service now being tried in this country which are well worth reporting.

The most nearly modern train in U.S. long-distance railroading is the *Metroliner*, which runs the 226 miles between New York and Washington, D.C., in two hours and fifty-nine minutes. Operated by Amtrak, the quasipublic corporation that has taken over most of the nation's rail passenger service, this electrified six-car train, built by the Budd Company and using General Electric motors and control equipment, ranks with the world's fastest. If it had, like the Japanese Tokaido Line trains, a new roadbed and no grade crossings (one advantage of Interstate highways is that they have no grade crossings; the *Metroliner* crosses nineteen public roads and three private ones), it could maintain a much higher average speed than its present 80 mph. It is actually capable of more than 160 mph. On one short stretch along its route it hits 110 mph, and along a 68-mile stretch between Baltimore and Wilmington, Delaware, it holds—for forty-three minutes—a respectable 95.4 mph. It cuts one hour from the travel time of conventional trains and, of course, beats the car by even more. (There are, at this writing, no speed indicators in each car to tell passengers how fast the train is going, as there are on the bullet trains and many in Europe.)

While it is like the Japanese bullet trains in that 65 percent of its track is now continuous-welded, it still uses old-fashioned (and cheaper) wooden ties instead of the more stable prestressed-concrete ones now supporting the tracks of most of the world's other fast trains. Though unlike the Tokaido Line it has no rubber pads or springs between tracks and ties to absorb lateral thrust, its ride is still fairly smooth. Its rapid acceleration is surprisingly gentle and its braking quick without being jerky. One is conscious of some vibration and noise, and cannot help wondering how exhilarating the same trip could be if the *Metroliner* had a Japanese-style roadbed and could zip along at maximum speed all the way.

For the American railroad passenger long accustomed to slow, dirty, uncomfortable, and unprompt trains and rude and surly service, the *Metroliner* is a happy surprise. Its silvered exterior is eye-catching and displays the familiar Amtrak symbol. (For those readers not familiar with it, the symbol suggests both the feathered end of an arrow and, at the same time, a track. "Amtrak" appears in print over the arrow.)

Through a public-address system the conductor welcomes his passengers aboard and, when they leave at the end of the run, invites them back. In between there are clearly audible station announcements and (not everybody's dish, but still . . .) soft background music. The train makes a fetish of punctuality, it is of course air-conditioned, and the scenery—except for liberal portions of urban blight—isn't bad. No Fujiyama, but some good American woods and fields, and the freedom to look at them.

There is not the gracious dining-car service that older patrons remember—the opportunity to dawdle over a deluxe meal amid snowy linens, heavy silverware, and finger bowls during about half the New York–Washington run. Instead, hot sandwiches and beverages may be consumed standing up at one of two snack bars or taken back to one's seat in cardboard containers. Or, in the extra-fare Metroclub Car (luxury parlor), meals may be ordered and will be served at seatside. Here, seats are reclining wing chairs which are able to revolve full circle. It is still possible to tip, whether at the stand-up bar or in the Metroclub, though not everyone does.

Much attention has been directed to safety, and a number of safety-related features have been incorporated—some new to railroading, others representing improvements over conventional standards. Examples: advancement in braking equipment, a number of emergency push-out windows in a more rugged car body, safety glass in all windows. Cab signals provide continuous monitoring of traffic conditions ahead. There is also an "alerter" device requiring that the engineer respond to warnings. Should he fail to respond, "deadman" controls would take over and automatically stop the train. Similarly, if he fails to observe speed limits, automatic braking reduces the speed.

Passenger-pampering features include high-level, nonskid platforms at every *Metroliner* station, eliminating that awkward stepdown. There are noise-damping carpets and wall coverings, insulated ceilings with good lighting, comfortable reclining seats with plenty of leg room, airline-style reading lamps, and spotless interiors with clean windows tinted against the sun's glare. Onboard telephones, in booths, enable passengers to make long-distance calls to anywhere in the world en route, a convenience offered by no other train in the world. Incoming calls are also possible, if disruptive of the railroad passenger's traditional privacy. The Japanese bullet trains, if you recall, have telephone connections only with Tokyo or Osaka.

Except in the club car, individual seats are not assigned, but seating is on a reserve basis, arranged through a telephone call to the nearest Amtrak reservation office—though patrons often wait a long time before Amtrak picks up the phone. The computerized ticket can then be picked up at the boarding station—airport style —or at one's local station even though the *Metroliner* does not stop there. The computerized system will in time allow refinements to be made streamlining ticketing procedures even more, and it is hoped that there will soon be ticket offices in the downtown areas of all cities served by the *Metroliner*.

(Another aid to the Metroliner traveler, and one that affects all Amtrak passengers, is the acceptance of American Express, Master Charge, and Rail Travel cards. As we write, additional ones expected to be authorized are BankAmericard, Diners Club, and Carte Blanche. So far there is no indication that gasoline credit cards will ever be accepted, but who knows?)

The change in attitude of railroad personnel is striking. Cheerfulness is standard, possibly inculcated by a special training program for *Metroliner* assignees. Or it may be simply that employees are happy to be there, since *Metroliner* duty brings with it prestige (many of the emplcyees are ones with the most seniority) as well as better hours and working conditions than on other trains. This is true particularly for engineers who have graduated from freight trains. (Crews, by the way, call the *Metroliners* the "rockets" or "six-packs.") The term "engineer" is a misnomer; "motorman" would be more appropriate, since electrical equipment has replaced the engine. As if to support this new title, he wears slacks, sports coat, and tie while driving the *Metroliner.*

Metroliner conductors at this writing still wear the familiar black suit with brass buttons, but more fashionable new uniforms are beginning to appear. Red berets, paratrooper boots, and Eisenhower jackets will be worn by baggage handlers, while ticket agents will sport white eyeshades and double-breasted red vests. (Passengers presumably will wear raised eyebrows.) *Metroliner*s may eventually carry hostesses, as some Amtrak trains now do, and one would suppose that their attire might be spectacular.

Statistics attest to the *Metroliner's* growing popularity. The number of riders—or at least, the number of tickets sold—more than trebled from its first year, 1969, to 1972. In the latter year more than 160,000 tickets were being bought each month, or 1.9 million a year. Incredibly, the *Metroliner* has actually been showing a profit, all earned on passenger tickets—proving that under the right circumstances Americans can be got back on the rails.

The Lindenwold Line (KEITH S. JORGENSEN, LOUIS T. KLAUDER AND ASSOCIATES)

The steel-wheeled, steel-rail linear-induction-motor vehicle for research (LIMVR) undergoing tests at the Federal High Speed Ground Test Center near Pueblo, Colorado (DEPARTMENT OF TRANSPORTATION)

Passenger dome cars of the Auto Train (DAVID W. HAMILTON)

The Auto Train's temporary auto loading and unloading ramp (STAN JENNINGS)

The Metroliner
(DEPARTMENT OF
TRANSPORTATION)

BART (BAY AREA RAPID TRANSIT DISTRICT PHOTOGRAPH)

Tracked Air Cushion Research Vehicle (TACRV) undergoing tests at the Federal High Speed Ground Test Center near Pueblo, Colorado (DEPARTMENT OF TRANSPORTATION)

Five-car United Aircraft turbotrain on Amtrak route between New York and Boston (SIKORSKY AIRCRAFT DIVISION OF UNITED AIRCRAFT)

CN's Supercontinental *passes through the mountains of western Canada.* (CANADIAN NATIONAL RAILWAYS)

CP Rail—The Canadian *crossing Stoney Creek Bridge, B. C.* (CANADIAN PACIFIC)

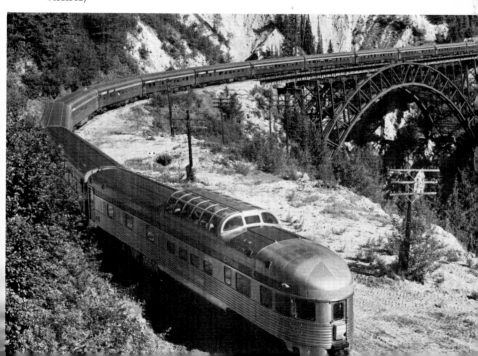

Canadian TurboTrain (seven cars) (CANADIAN NATIONAL RAILWAYS)

Light, rapid, comfortable—(and beautiful). . . . *On display outside the builder's shops in Montreal, where it has been undergoing tests, this prototype diesel-electric locomotive boasts 2900 hp, is of lightweight aluminum construction with a low center of gravity, and is capable of 120 mph. It is specially designed for operation on existing main-line track. With Britain's APT and France's turbos, the LRC is a lively contender for service on Amtrak routes. It was developed by Alcan Canada Products, Ltd., Dominion Foundries and Steel, Ltd., and the MLW Industries division of MLW-Worthington, Ltd.* (GRAETZ BROTHERS, LTD.)

The French turbotrain TGV-001 (Très Grande Vitesse, or very high speed) is colored orange and white and has a speed of more than 190 mph. It is being considered for use in the future by Amtrak. (RAILWAY AGE)

Le Mistral (FRENCH NATIONAL RAILROADS)

Fast and reliable turbotrains such as the ones shown are now a regular part of French rail passenger service. The speedsters can hit 150 mph, and plans are being drawn for 188-mph units. Amtrak has purchased two of these trains for service in the Midwest. (FRENCH NATIONAL RAILROADS, *above;* RAILWAY AGE, *below*)

The 250-mph French tracked-air-cushion vehicle (TACV) known as "Aero-train," now in service from Paris to Cergy-Pontoise. (UMTA, DEPARTMENT OF TRANSPORTATION)

Le Mistral—*the "Boutique"* (FRENCH NATIONAL RAILROADS)

Le Mistral—*the bar* (FRENCH NATIONAL RAILROADS)

British Rail's APT (Advanced Passenger Train) project's objectives are to exploit fully the potential of existing track and signaling equipment and provide superlative comfort at a 155-mph top speed. (BRITISH RAILWAYS BOARD)

Japan's famed New Tokaido Line—the "bullet train"—streaks by Mount Fujiyama. (JAPANESE NATIONAL RAILWAYS)

Japanese "bullet trains" on the New Tokaido Line (JAPANESE NATIONAL RAILWAYS)

Japanese "bullet train" (JAPANESE NATIONAL RAILWAYS)

The Trans-Europe Express (TEE Train) takes a mere four hours from Zurich to Milan. Here the TEE train is passing Baar. In the background is the Zuger See, to the left the Rigi, and to the right the Pilatus in central Switzerland. (SWISS NATIONAL TOURIST OFFICE)

Mexico City Collective Transportation System (Sistema de Transporte Colectivo Ciudad de Mexico), *March 9, 1972. This section of line uses former rapid-tramway right-of-way. Trains have rubber tires with conventional flanged wheels for guiding through switches.* (JOHN J. BOWMAN, JR.)

German manufacturer Krauss-Maffei's magnetic-levitation system (magnetic attraction). This is an experimental vehicle. (R. A. MOPE, RAILWAY GAZETTE INTERNATIONAL)

The *Metroliner,* because of its reliability (better than 90-percent on-time performance) and its speed, offers the airlines serious competition on a door-to-door basis. Eastern Airlines in 1970 moved to eliminate its Newark–Washington shuttle because of a drop in passengers which is attributed mostly to the *Metroliner.* Obviously, few would consider flying between intermediate *Metroliner* stops—Trenton, Philadelphia, Wilmington, Baltimore —but how about between its end points? There, time gained by the traveler by flying is lost in getting from town to airport and from airport to town. Rail terminals are in readily accessible downtown areas. Rail travel is also cheaper and, except to the most fervent flying fan, more comfortable.

There are planes faster than those now flying between New York and Washington, but they would not shorten the flying time much, if any, because faster planes have to go higher, thus lengthening the trip, and they take more space—and time—to make their turns, as when they orbit airports because of traffic or bad weather.

Metroliner service started as a cooperative effort between Penn Central and DOT when the High Speed Ground Transportation Act of 1965 was passed. At that time it had become obvious that transportation needs within the urbanized intercity corridors had outstripped capability, particularly in the Northeast, where 20 percent of our population lives. Under the provisions of the act a DOT "demonstration project" was established to develop alternative modes of transportation in the densely populated Northeast Corridor.

DOT drew up a two-part contract (a one-year base period and a two-year test period) with Penn Central in order to test improved passenger rail service between New York and Washington. The contract totaled $12 million. This particular contract included conventional trains as well as *Metroliner* service, though most of the time, effort, and funding has gone to the *Metroliner.* Since the contract was initiated, a dozen amendments—mainly covering equipment modifications—have been added. One provided a suburban station at the Capital Beltway, Maryland, exactly ten *"Metro"* minutes outside Washington; another, a similar station, Metropark, at Woodbridge, New Jersey, on the Garden State Parkway. At this new station, free parking space is provided for 820 cars, with room to expand to 1,200 cars. Metropark, costing $2.6 million, was built with funds provided by the State of New Jersey, the Federal Railroad Administration, and, of more significance, the Highway Trust Fund. This was the first time the sacrosanct HTF—described in Chapter V—had been used for other than highway-building purposes, and it was made possible by an amendment tacked onto the 1970 Federal Highway Act. Whether it will be an important precedent remains to be seen.

The *Metroliner* started running in 1969 with six daily round trips, and in January 1971 another one was added. Because the seven trains consistently ran so close to capacity, Amtrak, as soon as it took over (May 1971), added two more. One year later the number of daily round trips had been upped to fourteen, approaching the frequency of the sixteen daily Eastern Airline shuttle flights operating between New York and Washington, and more cars are on order. At the same time schedules were simplified, so that the liners began departing from Washington every hour on the hour and from New York every hour on the half-hour, from early morning to midevening with a few brief exceptions. In November 1971 *Metroliner* service was extended northward to New Haven, Sunday through Friday.

The new additions may have resulted from criticisms such as that of Senator Charles McC. Mathias, Jr., of Maryland who said in 1971 that the *Metroliner*'s big shortcoming was its dependence on too little rolling stock. The number of daily runs was ample, he said, but the trains were so overused that there would soon be a rash of equipment breakdowns. There were just not enough cars so that some could be pulled off service at intervals for replacement of worn parts and for other servicing. He told us at the time that "You cannot operate equipment continuously, as is being done on the *Metroliner*, and not experience trouble at some point." He also pointed out that when equipment trouble did develop, it might come all at once, since most of the equipment was about the same age.

DOT studies show that, comparing *Metroliner* passengers with New York Washington airline passengers, a greater proportion of *Metroliner* travelers are females. Surveys showed that 96 percent of *Metroliner* passengers rated the train's cleanliness and attractiveness "good to excellent"; 95 percent gave the same rating to comfort, lighting, and courtesy of the conductor.

Amtrak is considering introducing free meals, a special *Metroliner* lounge in stations (already opened in New York's Penn Station, serving free coffee and tea), more frequent inspections in maintenance pits, experimentation with schedule variations, fare reductions on weekends and during off-peak hours, an entertainment car (movies, or even live music), rentable space for office work, rentable dictation machines or stenographers. One experiment, a 50-cent bus ride from the station to all hotels and the business districts in Washington, will be introduced in New York if it works well.

If the *Metroliner* is our number one intercity train, then number two would be the Boston–New York *TurboTrain*, so named because it is propelled by six 400-hp gas-turbine engines, each weighing 300 pounds. No space is wasted, since three are located in the forward car and three in the rear car—both domed observation cars, in which passengers ride above the engines. Only five are used for traction, the sixth providing on-board auxiliary power. An additional bay makes it possible to add still another turbine to the train. Like the *Metroliner*, the three-car *Turbo* is a product of the DOT–Penn Central "Northeast Corridor demonstration project," and it has been running regularly since April 8, 1969. In the *Turbo*'s case, however, the mission was to demonstrate a propulsion system new to American railroads which might result in faster and more economical operation.

At present there are only two *TurboTrains* (DOT-1 and DOT-2). Originally each consisted of only three cars, but in August 1972 two cars were added to each, increasing the seating capacity from 144 to 240.

Although the *Metroliner* has received more publicity, the *Turbo* may have greater significance for the future of U.S. railroading. The *Metroliner's* dependence on electrical power limits it to its present route, the country's only major intercity electrified rail line. Although many favor electrifying the New York–Boston line, the significance of the *Turbo* now is that its engines can take it wherever there are tracks, making it a possible replacement for the diesel engine, workhorse of American railroads since the end of steam. It is the first new nonelectrical intercity train to operate on a regular basis in the last fifteen years. Newer, faster propulsion systems now under study (see Chapter IX) will not soon be competitive with the *Turbo* because of the great time interval needed for development—unless we purchase some of Britain's new APT trains described in Chapter II.

The basic gas-turbine engine is not new. It has a long history of aviation, marine, and industrial usage, and the Indianapolis 500 recently brought fame to the gas-turbine automobile. As we mentioned in Chapter II, French National Railways has operated high-speed gas-turbine trains for a number of years and is in the process of expanding the service. Our *Turbo* is basically the same engine used by Canadian National Railways on its Toronto–Montreal run (the Canadian train is longer: seven cars), and both were built by the United Aircraft Corporation. Jet-engine expertise by the Sikorsky Aircraft Division of United Aircraft, builder of Pratt-Whitney aircraft engines, went into the design of the *Turbo's* ST6B gas-turbines, providing a major link between the aircraft and rail industries.

Its kinship with aircraft is evident in the train's streamlined shape, the lack of visible protrusions along the sides, the rounded nose, the smooth and curved underbelly, its overall sleek look—not too unlike an elongated aircraft fuselage. The train not only looks lower than other trains, it is 2½ feet lower. Even the dome in dome cars is below the top of conventional cars. An "overland plane" might be a better description of the *Turbo*. Basically white, it wears a shiny bright red band with black stripes (the red band widens near the extremities). The stripe effect bears a resemblance to auto racing stripes. There are also flush, aircraft-type mechanical-access doors, windows, and passenger doors. Observation domes are not new to passenger trains, but the two on the *Turbo* look more like giant cockpits than like domes.

The train's plush beige interior also reflects its aircraft heredity. (There is no distinction between first class and tourist on the *Turbo*.) There are luggage-storage areas beneath the seats and in overhead racks. The comfortable reclining seats with headrests have individually controlled reading lights and airline-type pull-down trays for eating. The floors are carpeted, windows tinted, with attractive draperies. The cars have soft indirect lighting and wood-paneled end walls. There is a PA system, but passengers are spared piped-in music on it—though in DOT-1, music can be heard at one's seat through headphones. The lavatories are chemical units, airline style, located in the center of each car.

Fast food service is available at a compact galley at mid-train, and there is also a beverage bar in one of the pale green dome cars. The *Turbo* has followed the airlines' example of having hot dinners—though not free ones—served at the passengers' seats by a Penn Central hostess, in maroon and yellow. An Amtrak hostess is available to assist the conductor and passengers when needed.

Another cue from the airline industry is the maintenance of a slight pressure in the air-conditioned cars (electric heat with ample ventilation in the winter) to keep out dust and to dampen noise. Access doors are electrically powered, and all can be operated by the conductor by remote control from any one of them.

Outside folding steps adjust to different platform heights. One of the most untrainlike features of the *Turbo* is the absence of doors between cars, giving it the open-tube appearance of a very long airplane.

But as modern, high-speed ground transportation the *Turbo* doesn't measure up, its speed being restricted by the following factors: a poor, unimproved roadbed (inferior to the *Metroliner's*), unfavorable track conditions characterized by too many curves, a large number of grade crossings, poor right-of-way conditions, and inadequate signaling at various points. Like the *Metroliner*, the *Turbo*, if opened up, could exceed 160 mph (it exceeded 170 mph in tests on welded track between New Brunswick and Trenton, New Jersey). Instead, its average speed is a poky 63 mph, although it does top 100 mph for one short interval south of Providence, Rhode Island, where there is a section of welded track. Its run of 229 miles is only 3 miles greater than the *Metroliner's*, but it takes about forty-five minutes longer to complete it: that is, three hours and forty-five minutes from New York to Boston.

It's a nice ride, though. There is a gentle sway similar to the *Metroliner's*, but acceleration is fast and smooth. The ride, when one is seated in the regular compartments, is relatively quiet; the only noise heard is the clickety-clack of the nonwelded track. In the dome cars, however, one hears a combination whistle, whine, and hum because of their location over the engines. The noise is not excessive, but United Aircraft is working to reduce it.

A special "pendulous banking suspension" system enables the *Turbo* to take curves by banking at speeds much higher than conventional trains. The welded aluminum skin, the aerodynamic design, and the aluminum underframe contribute to the train's lightness and also reduce wind resistance. *Turbo* also saves weight by having only two wheels at the ends of cars, instead of the four-wheel truck at the ends of conventional train cars. A four-wheel swivel truck is employed, however, at the beginning and end of the train.

Like the Japanese bullet trains and the *Metroliner*, the *Turbo* does not have to turn around when it reaches its destination. The rear dome car simply becomes the forward dome car, since both are power sources and have the necessary controls.

The *Turbo*'s on-time efficiency is also high (87 percent), and its passenger space is normally about 70 percent occupied, which is over twice the national average. But there are still complaints, including the old familiar ones: poor ticketing procedures, mediocre food, and an interior not kept in sparkling condition. One unwelcome carry-over from the airplane is the train's narrow aisles. Seats in the dome cars are slightly cramped, and some always face backward regardless of the train's direction. When we rode the train, the outside striping paint had begun to peel, and the dome's double-thick windows were dirty, as was the carpeting. The one conductor wore that same old-fashioned uniform. Housekeeping on the Canadian National's *Turbo* is said to be much tidier.

Still, a good train, and aboard it we noted an air of informality lacking on the *Metroliner*. The crew was friendly, and most willing to answer passengers' questions.

———————

In mid-1971, one of the *TurboTrains* (DOT-1) was pulled from its New York–Boston run to make a 12,000-mile, one-month tour, sponsored jointly by Amtrak, United Aircraft, and DOT, through thirty-one states. It was a festive affair—the handsome red-white-and-black train with "*Turbo*" on each side in white letters, along with DOT's emblem, a red ball with a white pinwheel inside it, and the Amtrak logo—and was a big success. Unexpectedly large crowds turned out all along the way. Said one DOT official, "The interest in this train was just fantastic. The crowds went wild." During the tour over 100,000 people traipsed through the train, and another 6,000 were given demonstration runs. "Yes, people can be lured back to the trains," editorialized the *Arizona Daily Star* after the *Turbo*'s visit to Tucson. It got equally fine notices in other cities, but Southern Pacific president B. F. Biaggini (see Chapter III) remained bearish when *Turbo* visited the San Francisco Bay Area. "Southern Pacific once had trains as comfortable," he said, "but they didn't attract riders. It would be pretty silly to put a lot of [these] trains in service if nobody would ride them."

True. Even a shiny new train won't succeed just anywhere, under just any conditions. Four months after the *Turbo* tour was completed, DOT-1 was refurbished, and, amid much controversy, it began service on February 7, 1972, between Washington, D.C., and Parkersburg, West Virginia, a mountainous route of 351 miles.

The controversy involved Representative Harley O. Staggers of West Virginia, a former brakeman on the B&O, who, as chairman of the House Interstate and Foreign Commerce Committee, was a key figure in Amtrak and DOT funding authorizations and an early, outspoken critic of Amtrak. Some who disapproved of the move charged DOT and Amtrak officials with putting the *Turbo* on that run to appease Congressman Staggers, who denied he had exerted any pressure. He was quoted in the press as saying he only wanted to see Washington "opened to the West." He said, "I'm hoping for Parkersburg to be the gate west to Cincinnati. If the *Turbo* is proved practical across the mountains, I think we should get more all across the country." Also upsetting to many was the estimated $40,000 spent advertising the scenic beauty of the route when the westward trip was run at night and half of the eight-hour return trip took place in the wee morning hours, starting at 4:00 A.M.

Meanwhile, Amtrak and DOT said it was just an experiment for six months or so, and they had some pretty convincing arguments in favor of it. Amtrak's president, Roger Lewis, said the idea was "to gauge very quickly public reaction to better equipment, improved schedules and reduced travel time on what has been a lightly patronized line." But DOT officials were particularly interested in the route because of its extraordinarily rugged terrain. So rugged, in fact, that one DOT official told us he didn't know of

"any main line in the country equal to the challenge of this one."
But despite long uphill climbs, many a tight curve, and a vener-
able roadbed, *Turbo* made the run in eight hours, or one and a
half hours less than conventional trains, though still nowhere near
Turbo's potential speed.

As might have been expected, the train was still lightly patronized, and the run ended after three and a half months. But traffic
was picking up considerably toward the end of the trial.

Getting back to *Turbo* as a link between New York and Boston,
that run was established originally to test equipment, and friends
of rail passenger service were pleasantly surprised when President
Nixon announced that the *Turbo* demonstration would be extended two years beyond its original two-year period, which
ended in October 1970. He said the extension had been recommended by Secretary Volpe "because of our resolve to apply
space-age technology and expertise to earthbound problems." He
added that the project had proved the public will use such trains.
At the end of the second period Amtrak bought the TurboTrains
and continued operating them.

An indication that *Turbo* would be around longer than its extension period was provided by its linkup with the *Metroliner* in
early 1971. Then the *Turbo*'s New York terminal was moved from
Grand Central to Pennsylvania Station, enabling *Metroliner* passengers arriving in New York to make across-the-platform connections with the *Turbo*. Before that time, *Metroliner* passengers
arriving in New York had to cross the city to get to Grand Central.
The linkup now allows one to go from Washington to Boston in
close to seven hours—a reputable time, but nothing to what the
two trains could do if allowed to travel at top speeds. Unfortunately, at this writing, there is only one *Turbo* round trip a day,
none on Saturdays and Sundays.

What is still needed is a greater resolve to sell passengers on
rail travel and to keep them sold. Better scheduling would help,
but freight still takes precedence over intercity passenger trains

when it comes to scheduling. The *Metroliner* and *Turbo* schedules are no exception. They are not shunted aside to let freight trains through, but their schedules have been rearranged so as not to interfere with freight.

When we asked a DOT Federal Railroad Administration official about the chances for more funds to rebuild the roadbeds for the *Metroliner* and the *Turbo*, he said Amtrak did not have the funds. "Would DOT push for this, since the improvement would be so advantageous?" His reply seemed to suggest the government's present attitude toward any all-out effort to achieve high-speed ground transportation: "We don't even talk about it anymore."

To show how fast things are changing, though, DOT announced in September 1971 that high-speed trains not only make sense but are necessary to solve the traffic problems of our crowded urban corridors. This amounted to a major DOT policy shift from a "highways only" approach and was backed up with a plan to upgrade the *Metro* and *Turbo* roadbeds in order to achieve the objective of a two-hour run between New York and Washington and a three-hour run between New York and Boston. In October 1972 DOT said it would spend $30 million on eliminating grade crossings between Washington and Boston.

A remarkable little railroad with the singable name "the Lindenwold Line," and another with the more down-to-earth name "BART" (for Bay Area Rapid Transit)—in the Philadelphia and San Francisco areas, respectively—are to commuter travel what the *Metroliner* and *TurboTrain* are to intercity travel. They are pacesetters that may revolutionize American commuter habits and in time have far-reaching social consequences.

The 14.4-mile Lindenwold Line, serving commuters between the suburban town of Lindenwold, New Jersey, and Philadelphia, with nine stops enroute, was the first of the two lines, and to a large degree was copied by San Francisco for BART. Lindenwold was discussed in 1950, construction began in 1966, and it started operating on February 15, 1969. By the time it was three years old, in early 1972, it had racked up 25 million fares. It opened carrying 17,000 passengers daily, surged to a peak of over 37,000 in late 1970, and now averages over 41,000 daily. It is expected to carry even more in the future—which will require more equipment, because it now operates at close to passenger capacity.

But perhaps the greatest indication of its success is that a whopping 40 percent of its riders (about 16,400) formerly drove to work. Were there no Lindenwold Line, an estimated 10,900 more autos would be on the road, since statistical studies show that each automobile carries 1.5 persons. Giant parking lots totaling close to 9,000 cars enable the non–wife-chauffeured commuter to leave his car behind. Philadelphia city officials and environmentalists love that Lindenwold Line because fewer cars entering the city means less congestion and less pollution.

The commuter likes the train because it is fast, reliable, convenient, comfortable, and economical. The train flows along over new or renovated roadbeds on continuous welded track. It accelerates rapidly on leaving the station and reaches speeds as high as 75 mph, driven by high-powered GE traction motors, one per axle. Electrical supply is received by a covered third rail. The train's speed so impresses riders that locally it is known as the "Hi-Speed Line."

To drive a car into Philadelphia from Lindenwold before the line was in business took anywhere from 45 minutes to an hour. The train trip takes 22 minutes, despite those nine intermediate stops and a number of speed restrictions. Two such restrictions occur when it passes through portions of the original Camden and Philadelphia subways, another when it crosses the Delaware River into Pennsylvania via the Benjamin Franklin bridge (speed limit 40 mph). But top acceleration rates and quick braking enable the train to change speed requirements rapidly. On express runs, with fewer stops, it makes the trip in 19 minutes. "I don't think I'd ever want to drive again," said Lindenwold commuter Irvin Shoemaker in a *New York Times* interview. "With the parking problem at Camden, it was getting impossible to take your car. I really didn't realize how good public transportation could be."

Not only has the railroad commuter benefited, but those who still drive to work in that area now enjoy a drop in highway and bridge traffic. In fact, they can now drive at a steady speed across the Ben Franklin during the peak rush hours, instead of in the stop-and-go pattern characteristic of a few years earlier.

During the rush hours, trains depart every 5 minutes and at other times (from 6:00 in the morning to 11:30 at night) every 10 minutes. After midnight, trains run every hour. On Sundays, trains are run at 15-minute intervals. Overall, the Lindenwold Line's on-time performance efficiency is about 99 percent. Most of the trains consist of only two cars, but during peak periods six cars are often used. Passengers sit two on either side of an aisle. Seating capacity in regular cars is 72; "married-pair" cars—i.e., inseparable cars that share control booths—seat 80 each.

Philadelphia commercial interests have benefited because the convenient scheduling has made the train attractive to suburban housewives who want to shop in the city, and to sports fans who can come in for major sports events. Extra trains are also available for special excursion and charter groups. For those attending the theater or the Academy of Music there is the added advantage of having a station located only a couple of blocks from the theater district.

Local stations along the line are clean and air-conditioned, and passengers on the platform are sheltered from the weather.

The cars, built by the Budd Company, are comfortable, with climate-controlled heat and air conditioning, tinted windows, up-holstered high-back transverse luxury bucket seats, and thermal insulation that also helps to screen out noise. From inside there is a faint, faraway, high-speed, whistlelike sound, but nothing more. Fortunately for residents who live near the tracks, it is relatively quiet even on the outside, and quieter by far than the roar from a highway. And cleaner. Not only do roadbed and track contribute to a smooth trip, but the cars ride on four-wheel air-suspension trucks with both dynamic and electropneumatic braking. A suspension system providing automatic leveling and load weighing helps maintain smooth acceleration rates.

The train's exterior is not particularly sleek or racy, but it is neat and eye-catching with its stainless steel rectangular sides contrasting with dark, almost black, tinted windows and a thin horizontal painted red stripe running the length of the train. In automatic-car-wash fashion, train cars are washed in thirty seconds (every three days), cleaned inside daily, and repaired on computerized schedules. Each car's two doors per side tell the viewer at first sight that this is no ordinary train, as the doors are not located at the end of each car, but rather a quarter of the way from the ends. This location of the doors makes for less congestion and greater accessibility.

But perhaps the most science-fictional aspect of the line is its automation, not duplicated on any other transit system. No featherbedding (see Chapter IV) here. The engineer—or, more precisely, motorman—is its only crew, and it takes only about 210 employes to run the entire line. (This is a major factor in the line's economy. Fares on the Long Island line, by comparison, are twice as much per mile.) More than 80 percent of the transit costs of the other East Coast lines is wages, and all suffer a deficit. Because the Lindenwold Line started from scratch, the original labor contract was free of the complexities so characteristic of other rail lines, and employees are represented not by railroad labor unions but by the Teamsters Union.

The motorman sits at a control panel up front, operates the doors, and presses a "start" button after the train comes to its automated halt. The rest of the time he serves merely as a monitor, but he *can* take over and run the train manually in emergencies, such as when heavy rain or snow causes poor traction on the tracks.

To operate the train automatically obviously requires sophisticated equipment, much of it electronic. There are two systems: automatic train control (ATC) and automatic train operation (ATO), both capable of meeting demanding requirements. Braking has to be, and is, so accurate that the train can stop within a few feet of the center of station platforms, and acceleration and deceleration rates must be very precise to maintain the train's rigid schedule. When the train is operated manually, it loses time.

Automation also extends to the stations, where attendants are conspicuously absent. Passengers enter the stations through automatic turnstiles, receive exact change from bill-changing machines, and purchase their magnetically coded plastic tickets from vending machines which operate much faster than the quickest cigarette machine. The passenger, proceeding to the station platform, inserts his ticket in an entry turnstile that in less than a second reads his magnetic ticket and returns it to him. After he reaches his destination, an outgoing turnstile rereads his ticket and, if it is correct for that station, retains it and lets him pass.

What about the bewildered newcomer who has a question to ask and no railroad personnel in the station to ask it of? He simply picks up a highly visible red telephone connected directly to the railroad's control center in Camden—called Center Town—where someone with the title of TV monitor fields his question while observing him on a television screen (in case he makes meaningful gestures?).

The Lindenwold's control center looks more like a smaller version of Mission Control at Houston than like something to do with railroads. There are elaborate-looking control panels, an assortment of computer-type equipment, circuit diagrams, telephones, and a bank of twenty television screens, each showing a section of one of the commuter stations. A train dispatcher observers all train operations on a control panel, is in communication with each motorman, and can even take over the operation of the automatic switches and signals. The TV monitor, in addition to answering passengers' questions, operates the PA system heard inside the stations. Another key person in the center is the power director, who can control substations, line breakers, or high-voltage feed.

Lindenwold's security is well under control. The tracks are patrolled by its own police force and a squad of K-9 dogs. Robbery in the stations is minimal, because with automation there are no cashiers, no cash out in the open, and all activity is under constant twenty-four-hour TV surveillance. As an added precaution, there are phones tied to the line's own police radio system plus a "hot line" to Philadelphia police headquarters.

If all this seems a bit Orwellian, the commuters seem to like it. They get more attention than do commuters on other transit lines, and take pride in "their" line. Officials apparently share in this feeling of pride.

The Lindenwold Line is operated by the Port Authority Transit Corporation (PATCO), a subsidiary created by the Delaware River Port Authority (DRPA) for this purpose. The line cost PATCO $94 million to build, and during its first year a deficit occurred. In 1970 it just about broke even, and it is anticipated that the line will now start showing a profit. Still another distinctive feature of this line, and one that may in time be a common one for other transit systems, is the practice of having the motorist help subsidize it through bridge tolls. Proponents claim it makes sense to do this because lighter bridge traffic benefits motorists.

There is no lucrative freight service to distract the LL offices from their role of serving—or to make them independent of—the passenger. One result is that compared with other lines, PATCO is conspicuously aggressive in promotional activities. Signs are in evidence everywhere in the region, and LL is advertised on TV and radio and in newspapers. Besides offering the special excursion trips already mentioned, PATCO provides free parking after 10 A.M. in certain areas to encourage trips by the shopper during off-peak hours. About a third of the 8,000 commuter parking spaces are free, the balance accessible through coin-operated gates.

As a result of the line's booming business, many other communities in southern New Jersey are calling for similar rail service. If PATCO's parent organization, DRPA, has its way, these communities may soon get their wish, and DOT's Urban Mass Transportation Administration (UMTA) has already awarded $750,000 for an eighteen-month study by the Port Authority to refine plans for expanding and extending the line.

(UMTA also made a $1.5-million grant for the establishment of a Dial-a-Ride minibus service, to take Haddonfield, New Jersey, citizens to the Lindenwold Line's station. The service when developed will offer personalized door-to-door service for rail commuters.)

To carry out its Lindenwold-improving plans, the Port Authority needs federal assistance, and has applied in a preliminary way for $106 million, or about two-thirds of the estimated cost.

Not only do U.S. city officials, planners, and engineers flock to Camden to study the Lindenwold success story; official visitors have come from Europe and even the Soviet Union. A *Fortune* Magazine article (July 1971) devoted to Lindenwold ended with a quote by a Detroit mass-transportation planner who said, "Don't confuse me with a lot of engineering studies—just show me how to build a carbon copy of PATCO." It is no coincidence that the BART system bears strong resemblance to the Lindenwold.

San Francisco, which ranks high on anyone's list of American cities worth seeing, appealing as it does to both traditionalists and the avant-garde because of its blend of eastern sophistication and western openness, can now add BART to its cable cars as something for tourists to ogle and local residents to make good, practical use of.

Threading a 75-mile route through neighboring towns and suburbs in the Bay Area, this snazzy-looking train is in some ways a carbon copy of Lindenwold, but there are some interesting differences. Like Lindenwold it receives its electric power from a covered third rail, and it has similar computerized automatic train control (ATC) to monitor and adjust train speeds, to govern stops and starts, to open and close doors, to maintain safe traffic control, and to govern the spacing between trains. And its labor problems should be few, with automatic electronic fare collections. But unlike Lindenwold, it has one human attendant per station to back up the automatic equipment. It has a Lindenwold-type nerve center located in Oakland, geometric center of the line.

It will be cheap to ride BART. At this writing the longest trip one can make is 45 miles, at a cost of only $2.60 round-trip. A *Christian Scientist Monitor* writer has estimated that driving this same distance by car would cost a minimum of $4.50, and this seems conservative, since automobile costs are usually put at 10 cents a mile, and the AAA puts them at 13 cents a mile. In addition are parking fees and tolls.

Credit cards will enable passengers to charge up to $20 worth of rides, using their cards in the automatic fare devices.

Service is convenient and fast. Cars reach a top speed of 80 mph and an average speed of 50 mph, including station stops. Trains depart during rush hours every 90 seconds, every 3 to 4 minutes normally, every 5 to 15 minutes on weekends. Late at night, train frequency is slowed to half-hour intervals. Station stops are brief —20 seconds. Rush-hour trips that now take more than one hour by auto can be made in about half the time on BART.

Electronic indicators tell the passenger all he needs to know about schedules and travel times. BART's estimated initial patronage is 200,000 persons daily, probably a conservative estimate. Moreover, BART officials predict that passenger usage will increase once the new train becomes known—up to 1975, when they expect usage to level off. The hourly capacity of seated passengers on BART is 30,000 one way, or 60,000 both ways. The number of cars now is less than half the 1975 goal of 250.

BART stops at 34 stations, one of which is a junction to receive passengers from one San Francisco trolley line. All 34 stations at this writing are completed or nearly so, and since 21 architectural firms worked on their designs, they vary greatly in appearance. They use a variety of materials such as stained glass, marble, mosaic, steel, concrete, and bronze, and each was designed to reflect the nature of its community. BART officials plan to display works of art at some of the clean, well-lighted stations, and a local touch will be community bulletin boards.

Stations have been attractively landscaped, as have some areas between stations. Large parking lots at suburban stations hold from 500 to 1,400 commuters' cars each. There are feeder bus stops nearby for the commuter who wants to leave his automobile at home. For the ecology-minded, there are even bicycle parking areas. The one-car family begins to be a possibility once more.

"Train convenience" is a consideration largely determined by route location; that is, whether a train goes through where the customers are. On this score, BART rates high. Not only does it pass through areas surrounded by vast suburban housing tracts whose residents commute to the commercial centers of Oakland, San Francisco, and Berkeley, but it passes through the black ghetto areas in these cities, serving large numbers of *no*-car families. Other well-known ghetto areas it serves include San Francisco's Chinatown and the Spanish-speaking neighborhoods of San Francisco's Mission area and southern Alameda County. In fact, 16 of the stations are located in neighborhoods classified as low-income, where no-car families abound. Youth too is served: BART passes near 30 colleges and universities.

For Californians who now have to go great distances in their automobiles just to exist—to get to work or school or do the shopping, not to mention attending films, theaters, and the like— BART can be a great time and money saver. And according to an estimate made by a California air-pollution official, BART, by replacing automobiles, will reduce air pollutants in the Bay Area by fifteen tons a day. Then too, San Francisco is noted for its fog, a handicap to motorists but not to the train.

The highway builder's bulldozer has had little fresh earth to turn in behalf of BART, whose track goes alongside freeway lanes and over existing railroad rights-of-way. The fatigued motorist who sees BART zip by him may have second thoughts about the way to go.

For greater stability, BART has wide tracks—5½-foot gauge: wider by almost a foot than standard track. (Lindenwold track width is the standard 4 feet 8½ inches.) The right-of-way is almost equally divided among underground, surface, and elevated stretches. (BART public relations people refer to the elevated section as the "aerial transit line.") A portion of the subway section passes under San Francisco Bay through twin underwater steel-and-concrete tubes 4 miles long. The Transbay Tube, as it is called, rests on the bottom of the bay at a maximum depth of 130 feet.

The 450-square-mile San Francisco Bay is the geographical center of the area served by BART, so it is natural that Oakland, located right on the bay, should serve as BART's center. From Oakland the double-track line extends in two directions: (1) north to Richmond and northwesterly to fast-growing Concord, whose population has zoomed from 15,000 to more than 900,000 in twenty years; and (2) south to Fremont, almost 30 miles away. On the San Francisco side the line, after surfacing from under the bay, extends through the historic Mission District south to Daly City, a distance of about 10 miles.

The unpainted BART aluminum train is very modern-, not to say futuristic-, looking with its wide, square windows, subway-type sliding double doors, lack of protrusions, and jutting, stream-lined nose, dominated by an off-side large front window. "We had to design a car which would be a trend setter, yet an enduring design," said Detroit industrial designer Carl Sundburg of Sund-burg-Ferar. "We realized that the BART car would have to look just as new twenty-five years from now. After all, transit cars do not have yearly model changes."

Trains consist of two to ten cars, each seventy feet long and capable of seating 72 passengers. As with Lindenwold, an air suspension system combined with new roadbeds should guarantee a smooth ride. The braking system is like Lindenwold's, and as on Lindenwold, each car is propelled by four traction motors, though on BART each car totals 600 horsepower, or 100 hp more than on Lindenwold.

Each car is well insulated against outside noises, and each has wool carpeting, air conditioning, wide aisles, recessed lighting, large tinted windows, reading lights, and an on-board public-address system. The seats are extremely comfortable—contoured, upholstered, and four inches wider than those of any other transit system. They are also cantilevered from the wall to make floor cleaning easier. BART has the distinction of being the world's first transit system to offer service to passengers in wheelchairs. Another distinction claimed by BART is a ventilation system so effective that smokers can smoke without damaging anyone but themselves—a questionable improvement over the old no-smoking car.

To anyone interested in how things get done in America, or anyone thinking of starting a new transit system, the background of BART is worth looking into. It was born in a joint Army-Navy study in 1947 that recommended an underwater transit tube beneath the bay. Thereupon both San Francisco and the state, over the next few years, gave lip service to the need for rapid transit to achieve full utilization of the harbor, but their hearts were in freeways and automobiles. By 1951, though, it had become evident that the region's major arteries were already hardening and that certain sections within San Francisco were starting to decay because of suburban sprawl. It was then that things began to happen. The San Francisco Bay Area Rapid Transit Commission, composed of members from nine Bay Area counties, was created by the California Legislature to study transportation requirements for the area.

The commission reported back to the legislature a few years

later, saying unified rapid mass transit in the region was an absolute necessity. Their report also recognized the need for detailed studies of the best way to achieve mass transit. The State Senate agreed and provided some of the finances for a master plan. The remainder came from the nine Bay Area counties.

The engineers' study, completed in January 1956, offered alternative plans: one, the more expensive and elaborate ($717 million), required the building of an underwater tube across the bay; the other ($586 million) called for using the existing San Francisco–Oakland Bay Bridge. (It also called for a second-phase construction plan that would raise the cost to $892 million.)

In effect seconding the report, the Stanford Research Institute two months later recommended the creation of a public transit district, which was accomplished in June 1957 when the legislature passed the bill drafted by the BART commission.

By the time the commission was actually given the authority to create a Bay Area Rapid Transit District as its own successor, only five of the original nine counties remained in the project: San Francisco, San Mateo, Alameda, Contra Costa and Marin. But their merchants, manufacturers, and civic leaders were enthusiastic. Particularly was this true in the large cities of San Francisco and Oakland. Environmentalists were for it because they knew the population of the area was expected to double sometime between 1987 and 2000; and, then as now, they favored mass transit to reduce the ecological damage caused by the automobile. Businessmen and the Chamber of Commerce saw transit as a way to lure people back to the city to shop in their stores and even to live. Property owners could visualize the profits to be made from the sale of land, and developers could see a resultant need for new construction.

That was the background of public attitudes when a $792-million BART bond issue came before the voters in July 1962. The amount of the bond would have been greater had not the state legislature accepted the then novel proposal of authorizing $133 million from Bay Bridge automobile tolls to help finance the construction of the Transbay Tube used by BART. By this time only three counties were involved. Marin County (the county connected by the Golden Gate Bridge with San Francisco) and San Mateo County (south of San Francisco) having voted to withdraw. In San Mateo, according to *Science* Magazine writer Robert J. Bazell, several large property holders, fearing BART would retard suburban growth and development, pressured the county's board of supervisors to withdraw. Marin County, located across water, would be too expensive to reach without San Mateo's help, so it was asked to withdraw by BART officials. A major, well-financed public relations campaign supported by the likes of the Bank of America (the commission's chairman, Alan K. Brown, was an executive officer of the bank and former president of San Francisco's Chamber of Commerce) was launched to persuade the voters in the three remaining counties that BART would provide great direct and indirect benefits to offset increased taxes. "Save Money—Save Time—Save Lives" was one of the campaign slogans.

The state sternly required that the three counties vote as a single entity and, further, that the bond measure had to be approved by 60 percent of those voting. The campaign was successful, but barely. BART got 61.2 percent of the vote. San Francisco County gave BART its widest margin, 68 percent—high enough to offset the lowest, 55 percent, in Contra Costa. According to the San Francisco Chamber of Commerce, the mandate to build BART was "the largest public works project ever undertaken in an American metropolitan area."

BART's troubles were just beginning. First, a taxpayer's suit challenged the legality and validity of the vote; the suit was lost after six months of litigation. Then came cost overruns due to inflation. Surprisingly, the overruns by mid-1971 were only about 3 percent of the original contracts, but more funds were needed, and officials and voters wondered where they would come from.

Fortunately, the state passed a ½-percent tax measure in the three BART counties, and this meant BART was home free financially. Then came engineering problems.

Obviously, any highly complex engineering project of this magnitude is subject to delays, particularly when much of the technology is new. Possibly contributing to BART's delays was the fact that the winning bidder for BART cars was the Rohr Corporation of Southern California, a concern inexperienced in railroad-car building. Debugging and testing proceeded slowly.

One two-month delay was caused partly by an "act of God"—the Southern California earthquake in the spring of 1971, which destroyed the facility of Hurst Airheart, a subcontractor responsible for the car's disk brakes. It was located at the epicenter of the quake. BART then ran afoul of conservationists and environmentalists unhappy about potential land overdevelopment and land blight as a result of BART's plans. At Berkeley, famous for university protests, a large segment of the community opposed running the tracks on unsightly elevated structures, and claimed besides that the tracks would physically split the community, as highways so often do. A "Committee to Bury the Tracks" spearheaded that attack so successfully that BART officials finally agreed to run the tracks subway-fashion under Berkeley if the city would foot most of the bill. A special city election was held, and the project won. The subway portion was built.

Conservationists have long opposed the chamber-of-commerce–type civic boosterism that pushes a mayor into trying to bring more people and more industry into an area regardless of the expansion's possible aftermath, and BART was seen by some as a promoter's dream.

And though California may be the home of the automobile, California's Bay Area is conservationist country, headquarters of the fast-growing, aggressive Sierra Club and containing a major office of the equally aggressive Friends of the Earth. Other active conservation groups abound in nearby college towns as well as in

San Francisco. In that city an anti-BART group was formed expressly to fight what it called the "Manhattanization of San Francisco": that is, the building of high-rise, canyon-forming office and apartment buildings along BART's path. They were soon joined by many other conservationists who had become alarmed at the building boom brought on by BART. There was delay, but the developers had their way. San Francisco in particular has seen over a billion dollars' worth of office buildings, hotels, stores, and apartment complexes go up, much to the delight of the local Chamber of Commerce. Oakland has also done well in new construction, and all along the route property values have skyrocketed.

So even railroads aren't all good; but at least BART will get some autos off the highways and clean up the air. Or will it? Not according to some critics. Bazell, mentioned earlier, again writing in *Science*, summed up such criticism: "The Bay Area could end up with both high-density development encouraged by BART and sprawling suburbs fed by new highways. That would mean more people, costs, suburbs and buildings." In other words, more development—even when inspired by mass transit—may mean more cars. In the state that defeated a statewide mass-transit trust bill in the November 1971 election, a state known for its layers of freeways, there is obviously a certain built-in momentum for highway-building. As Bazell said, "In California it might be easier to eclipse the sun."

Another discouraging post-BART development is the projected building of the Southern Crossing, a bridge paralleling the Bay Bridge. It is bitterly opposed by the Sierra Club, which more than once has come to the aid of oil-splattered, dirt-filled San Francisco Bay. The organization charges that the bridge will help steal business from BART by encouraging more driving into San Francisco, and says it must be headed off if transportation problems are to be solved by mass transit.

On a more encouraging note, UMTA is now financing a study of the desirability of running BART from its present terminal in

San Francisco to the San Francisco International Airport. A proposal is also under consideration to do the same thing for a connection to Oakland's National Airport and another to the airport in San Jose. In addition, the Department of Transportation has provided $150 million for the construction of BART cars, and a number of substantial grants have been made toward BART station construction. (The city of Berkeley was awarded $4.7 million for its subway construction.)

The future for BART will be a rosy one indeed if it is as successful as its promoters predict. Once the neighboring counties see BART's advantages, it is felt that they too will want to get on the bandwagon.. Chances are that the six counties that dropped out along the way will be first in line.

Joe Asher, transit critic-at-large for *Railway Age,* said of a test ride on BART in the summer of 1972:

This system represents a dividing for the transit industry: everything built prior will be dated B.B. (before BART); everything built after will be A.B. (after BART).

I went on a test run with a bunch of *San Francisco Chronicle* people. You remember all the years they badmouthed BART editorially? Their tune is very different now. All I heard was oohs and aahs, and one cry, "It's Disneyland!" Frankly, Disneyland and its monorail are flashy plastic bonbons by comparison.

The cars ride like a dream—and this run was done on manual, not automatic control (the automatic goes in later). We seemed to be coasting at about 35 mph when one *Chronicle* type called out, "Hey, take it up to 80." I had my head half in the cab and looked at the speedometer. We were doing 82 at the time.

All I can say is—nobody can stay jaded about transit after seeing BART. A few hard-line scoffers, maybe. My advice to them: Eat your hearts out. It works.

As the nation's longest all-new transit system, BART could have a profound influence on other cities and urban regions. Said *Business Week:*

A lot more will be riding on BART than its passengers. The entire world of transportation—Washington bureaucrats, city officials all over the country, highway promoters and anti-highway promoters, professionals and amateurs—will be scrutinzing BART's progress with anxious eyes.

Not unexpectedly, once BART began its period of shakedown operation it drew criticism, some detractors saying it was over-automated and hence unsafe. One BART train did overshoot a station at the end of the line and leave the track, injuring five passengers. But massive pileups occur on California freeways frequently enough to remind rational citizens that railroads are still far safer.

"Tragically, the efficiency of America's railroads has been jeopardized by deteriorated track and roadbeds. Such deterioration presents a serious safety problem for the American people. Between 1963 and 1970 train derailments caused by defects in track and improper maintenance of track increased by almost 250 percent. Freight loss and damage claims paid out in 1970 are almost double the amount ten years earlier."

—SENATOR ROBERT A. TAFT, JR., of Ohio.

CHAPTER VIII

Rail Travel for Pure Pleasure

SINCE WORLD War II it has seemed that nearly everyone—including the railroad companies themselves—has wanted to stamp out rail passenger service in America, or at least to let it die a dignified natural death. So conspicuously lacking was any effort to lure passengers back to the rails that Amtrak, when it began running showy full-page ads in *The New York Times* for its New York–Washington *Metroliner*, seemed almost to be violating good taste —as if brain surgeons were suddenly to start advertising. Surely the least overworked of all Americans in recent years have been those engaged in the marketing of rail travel.

But now, almost imperceptibly, that is beginning to change. Not only does Amtrak's *Metroliner* advertising take a few genteel pokes at automobiles and airlines, but some originality and inventiveness are finally being shown in what might be called the packaging of rail service. We will describe some of the American "cruise" trains in a moment, but first a word about a train that carries both passengers and their automobiles—a fairly new wrinkle here, though something Europeans have been doing for some time.

The Auto-Train Corporation (ATC) carries passengers and their automobiles nonstop between Alexandria, Virginia, and Sanford, Florida, once daily in each direction. The train originates in Virginia (just south of Washington, D.C.) instead of New York, where most of its passengers come from, because obstructions such as tunnels and overpasses north of Virginia prevent the passage of the tall dome and bilevel cars.

ATC started operations on December 6, 1971, with its two trains, each powered by two diesel locomotives. The size of the trains has since been increased, and each, at this writing, consists of twelve to fourteen enclosed, bilevel auto carriers, three or four sleepers, two buffet cars, a so-called nightclub car, and five bilevel coach lounge cars, which are domed and seat 70 passengers each. There is also a steam-generator car. Compartments sleeping two are available for an extra $40, but the coaches have deep reclining seats with leg rests for fairly comfortable sit-up sleeping. On the other hand, the compartment passengers can have breakfast in bed and their own television sets. A children's car is planned, with soft-drink dispensers, free hot dogs, pinball machines, jukeboxes, a section permitting dancing, and, for the youngest, romper rooms furnished with toys.

The spectacular if fluctuating success of the venture is revealed in its financial history. When ATC went public in the summer of 1971, it sold 700,000 shares of common stock at $10 per share. The price rose steadily to about $60—but eleven months later had dropped to about $23. Market experts attributed the drop to Amtrak's new "Free Wheels" plan under which a passenger is provided with one free rent-a-car, for a limited period, with every three adult round-trip fares from Chicago or New York to any one of seven key Florida cities. Amtrak subsequently initiated special car-rental rates at major terminals in eleven western, midwestern, and southern states. Nevertheless, the ATC stock was still holding at nearly twice its original price, and its plan has some advantages, though we applaud Amtrak for its enterprise in providing another attractive option for the I-love-Florida-but-hate-to-drive-there set.

ATC's operation was made possible by a fifteen-year agreement with Seaboard Coast Line and the Richmond, Fredericksburg &

Potomac for the use of their tracks. The locomotives (with one spare) were purchased from General Electric, the auto carriers from Canadian National, and the dome passenger cars from the Santa Fe. Interiors were completely rearranged and attractively redecorated, with emphasis on bright colors and much attention devoted to the well-being of the passengers: comfortable seats, color TV, movies, stereo, and a player piano for sing-alongs. Specially trained stewardesses perform helpful services including the serving of impressive complimentary meals (beef Wellington and lobster, for example) in their seats to those who do not wish to go down to the lounge areas on the lower levels. *Time* called it the "*Queen Elizabeth* on wheels."

Auto-Train, which obviously appeals to families with young or adolescent children, chose Sanford as its Florida terminus because it was only 37 miles from the then newly built Walt Disney World. It is also 20 miles from Orlando, about an hour's driving time from Cape Kennedy, an hour and a half from the Tampa area and three and a half hours from Miami. Both terminals are located near Interstates (I-95 in Virginia and I-4 in Florida) for easy accessibility. One-way fare is $190 for one car and up to two occupants. Additional occupants are $20 each. The cost is much less than that of flying a family of four or five to Florida and then renting a car. And it is, of course, much more relaxing, safer, and quicker (fourteen hours nonstop) than driving down, and the costs are comparable, on the basis of auto cost of 10 or 13 cents per mile plus motel and meal costs en route—and wear and tear on parents' nerves. Months before its first run, ATC took out full-page ads in East Coast newspapers ("Ride the Auto-Train. You'll never drive to Florida again") and was booked solid for two months in advance. It has continued to run at full capacity and nearly broke even in its first full year in operation, carrying 51,834 autos and 157,329 passengers. People who have taken the trip report an agreeable experience and express amazement at the speed and ease of loading and unloading their cars.

Says Kenneth L. Howes, operations vice-president, in discussing ATC's future plans: "Tomorrow, as a going concern, we can anticipate being a key factor in bringing the public back to long-distance rail passenger service . . . We anticipate expanding our service to other routes and developing more sophisticated equipment than is presently available and economically feasible for our service. This equipment will incorporate loading and unloading advances and the ability to make intermediate stops along our routes."

Expansion of the Auto-Train scheme across the country would allow a family from the East to travel with its car by rail to such potential jumping-off cities as St. Louis, Chicago, or Minneapolis–St. Paul or even farther west, out to where the driving is easy and the scenery exciting, without all that truck-passing and boredom on the way.

It has been suggested that the car carriers be designed with extra-large windows and with an aisle along the side so that one could actually remain in his car, except to stretch and to visit a lounge car, and watch the landscape go by. This would be advantageous to smaller families who could easily sleep in their cars, and would be perfect for those owning campers.

Much has been written of the plague of automobiles in our national parks. A study is under way of the feasibility of using rails in the parks to reduce automobile traffic. The researcher is a California concern and the park, Yellowstone National. "Park experience is getting too much like the rush hour in Washington, D.C.," said Interior Secretary Rogers C. B. Morton. "We ought to develop transportation systems that will limit the use of roads."

––––––––

Besides trains that take people to and around vacation spots, some train trips are now being billed as vacations in themselves. One, the *Transcontinental Rail Cruise*, is a New York–Los Angeles luxury train which provides an overnight stay in New Orleans (until noon the next day), makes stops at a number of south-western cities, and is the longest-distance sleeper on the North American continent (3,400 miles). The train is Amtrak from New York to Washington. From Washington to New Orleans it runs on Southern Railway tracks, on the route of the *Southern Crescent* (Southern is one of the rail companies that did not join Amtrak); and from New Orleans to Los Angeles it takes Southern Pacific tracks, the route of SP's *Sunset Limited.* (SP *did* join.) The complete trip is listed in Amtrak's timetable as "Southern Crescent/ Sunset Route." It originated in the fall of 1971 as a trade-off agreement with the ICC so that SR and SP could reduce the number of runs of the *Southern Crescent* and the *Sunset Limited* through still unspoiled scenic areas—though, strangely, at this writing a panoramic dome car is available only on the Atlanta–New Orleans portion of the cruise. The trip is not cheap: a roomette is about $228 one way, or about $45 a day, not including meals.

Vacation trains that involve extended trips to scenic places, departing from several U.S. cities, are now being offered by Four Winds Travel, Inc., the country's largest rail-tour organization, the only such organization located in New York City and the only one offering transcontinental-rail-tour departures from New York, Newark, Philadelphia, and Washington. Some tours can also be picked up in New Orleans or Chicago.

During 1971, Four Winds reportedly spent over $100,000 to advertise its more than fifty transcontinental rail cruises; whether thanks to advertisements or not, business was considered good, and no wonder, considering the exotic nature of the trips.

A typical example is the "Grand Circle Americana," a 23-day tour of spectacular American and Canadian scenery, including famous national parks of two nations, from Arizona to Alberta. The contrast is memorable. Consider having an itinerary that takes in Flagstaff, Arizona, and a breathtaking view of the world's most extraordinary geological phenomenon, the Grand Canyon— followed by Yosemite with its giant sequoias, cascading falls, towering granite rocks, and emerald green meadows. Then on to the scenic splendors of Glacier National Park; to Banff and its mirrorlike Lake Louise; to Canadian national parks with their rugged snow-capped peaks, unspoiled lakes, and shimmering glaciers, all framed by giant evergreens. The scenery-intoxicated passengers are sobered by stops at Los Angeles, San Francisco, Seattle, Victoria, and Vancouver.

Many of the nights are spent on board, but fifteen nights are spent at luxury hotels, such as the Beverly Hilton in Los Angeles, the Washington Plaza in Seattle, the Empress in Victoria, and the Banff Springs. Although the passenger naturally has to change trains from time to time, he is always assured of comfortable sleepers aboard "name" trains.

The passenger is pampered by a tour escort who takes care of all details, including baggage moves, makes informative briefings about stops, and arranges for sight-seeing tours. Though expensive —$70 a day (and higher)—the cruise is about as worry-free as travel can be, and the cost includes tips, hearty meals (except those on a few private excursions), and the overnight stays at fine hotels.

The most popular trip is the Canadian Rockies/Pacific Northwest tour, called the "Timberline Tour." It costs about the same per day but is five days shorter than the "Americana," which it resembles, and includes Yellowstone and Grand Teton National Parks.

There is also a 24-day "Alaska/Americana" tour (starting at about $83 a day) that includes Yellowstone en route and Glacier on the return and is highlighted by a trip through lovely fiords along the unforgettable inside passage of Alaska's Panhandle. Passengers on this one get two train rides generally regarded as unsurpassed in North America for spectacular scenery. One is on the Alaska Railroad from Anchorage to Fairbanks, along broad valleys and rugged, snow- and cloud-covered mountain peaks of the Alaskan Range. This one also takes in North America's highest peak, Mount McKinley (20,320 feet), in Mount McKinley National Park; great stretches of flower-covered tundra; remaining stands of America's disappearing wildlife; and massive glaciers.

The Alaska Railroad is not an Amtrak line, but is owned by the federal government and is doing a booming business. In the past six years, passenger fares have jumped from 50,000 to 94,000, a gain of 88 percent—enough to encourage the railroad to add to its passenger fleet a number of surplus cars, originally valued at $3.5 million, including dome cars, reclining-seat coaches, diners, and bar cars.

The other unusual train trip is the historical Skagway–Whitehorse on Canada's famed White Pass and Yukon narrow-gauge railway. There, too, the scenery combines delicate beauty with savage wilderness. (As the train has to stop occasionally to urge a moose off the tracks, it is referred to by local wags as the "moose-gooser." That it does not always *stop* for this purpose is suggested by a regrettably high moose mortality rate.) That line was completed in 1900 despite great engineering difficulties, and it remains today an active conventional carrier as well as a scenic railroad. The White Pass railway follows what the travel brochures call "the trail of the sourdoughs" and runs alongside the original gold-rush Klondike Trail of '98. The train passes near cataracts tumbling between giant Sitka spruces, along roaring rivers (some boiling white) and clear, blue-green lakes. Along the way are Dead Horse Gulch, where three thousand pack animals died during the '98 gold rush, and the White Pass tunnel, which emerges a thousand feet above the floor of a gulch and offers a magnificent view of the surroundings. This tour is made in summer months when the days are very long, giving the passenger more daylight for sight-seeing.

Dropping south for one more tour: "The Fiesta Americana" is a 19-day rail cruise into Mexico. A little cheaper than the others, it averages something over $52 a day. (Incidentally, all of these prices are as of this writing, subject to change. We include them only to give the reader a rough idea.) It affords sights of wild Mexican country and makes stops in a number of colorful cities, including New Orleans, Corpus Christi, Mexico City, and Acapulco. Accommodations include luxurious hotels such as the internationally known Continental Hilton in Mexico City. This is the only tour with year-round departures; all the others leave from May through September. (It is possible to start out on one tour and switch to another, by the way.)

Four Winds also sponsors a number of separate western tours ("Western Wonderlands") that last two weeks and are cheaper per day (about $45). These tours are not exclusively rail tours, but most feature some trips by rail. They all involve flying to and from the embarkation points of the tour, and this is included in the tour price.

When we asked a Four Winds official what role he thought Amtrak would play in the rail-cruise business' future, he was optimistic. "Amtrak is good for us. It will help revive passenger rail service, and the more people who are pleased with improved rail service, the more there will be who want to go on rail tours."

The Midwest Travel Service, of Midwest City, Oklahoma, also offers popular three-week rail cruises: to Mexico in the winter, a midsummer tour of our most spectacular national parks, and an early-fall trip to eastern Canada.

An idea taken up and dropped was "Polis '76," which would have had 200-mph trains running from Boston to Miami, linking major cities in between (with a side trip to Atlanta) in time for the 1976 celebration of the Republic's two-hundredth birthday. Not only would this have been a lasting boon to U.S. transportation, but it would have allowed celebrations to be held in many historic locations. Also, it would have been a symbolic and literal linking together of twelve of the thirteen original colonies.

The plan needed approval by Congress, since it would have involved an appropriation (for rebuilding existing rail roadbeds, eliminating grade crossing, and straightening curves) of between

$1.5 and $2 billion. It had originated with a citizens' group in Boston, and at one point the American Revolution Bicentennial Commission said it was seriously interested. Melvin Spector, director of the commission, told *The New York Times* it was an "exciting and stimulating idea."

It stimulated the railroad industry a bit more when somebody suggested that not only passenger but container freight trains should be allowed to use the new route. (Trains of container freight cars were chosen over conventional freight cars because the latter are heavier and would damage the roadbeds.)

The whole idea seems dead at this writing, but that it was ever seriously considered is somewhat encouraging.

Amtrak not only cooperates with the planners and promoters of rail cruises; it plans and promotes some itself. With the cooperation of the Las Vegas Chamber of Commerce, it initiated in early 1972 the *Las Vegas Party* train between Los Angeles and Las Vegas, a distance of 250 miles. Round-trip cost: $60. Known also as the "Las Vegas Fun Train" and the "Gambling Special," it ran every weekend through the end of May. It sought no speed records, took six hours; the Chamber of Commerce furnished bands, folk singers, balloons, and paper streamers to make each trip like New Year's Eve. Business in the two bar cars was booming. For those who, once into Nevada, couldn't wait to get to Las Vegas, there were poker and other card games. The trains were clean, were air-conditioned against the Mojave Desert heat, had hostesses aboard, and offered roast-beef dinners for $3.25.

The Las Vegas train had counterparts in the *Reno Special* operating between San Francisco and Reno. This train started a couple of months earlier than the "Gambling Special" and, according to officials, carried 35,000 passengers in just its first two months of operation. Another specialized train introduced by Amtrak was the week-long ski train from Los Angeles to Sun

Valley, Idaho. Called the *Snow Ball Express,* it ran once in January 1972 and again in March 1972. It carried stewards instead of hostesses, and two music groups flown in from Sun Valley.

So unaccustomed are most Americans to long-distance rail travel that any long intercity train trip is in the nature of a cruise. Since Amtrak operates most intercity trains now, Amtrak can be said to be in the travel-for-pleasure business more deeply and in ways more significant than the specials just mentioned would indicate. And in many ways Amtrak is showing more enterprise than some of its critics expected—particularly since its first official act was to cut the number of passenger trains in service to fewer than 180, an all-time low. But the critics were heartened when in September 1971 Amtrak announced it would spend $16.8 million to buy 1,200 passenger cars which had been in service on twenty-four lines prior to the May 1, 1971, Amtrak take-over. Amtrak had its pick of 3,000 cars, many of them from western railroads. The ones it bought were fairly new and of stainless steel, which has saved Amtrak some maintenance costs. In June 1971 Amtrak restored the southern Montana service it had earlier cut out.

Two weeks later it announced a plan to introduce still newer trains, to reinstate some other trains, and to offer many additional improvements in service. One follow-up move was the initiation of the first direct rail service in history between Milwaukee and St. Louis. Another was the restoration of long-abandoned through service between Boston and Miami, Boston and New Orleans, and Boston and Chicago.

Amtrak's decision not to abandon the wintertime *Florida Special* —reversing an earlier decision—was welcome but not very surprising, since it was a popular train and had even made money for the Seaboard Coast Line: popular in spite of so-so speeds, which Amtrak improved by eliminating stops from Richmond to Florida. Its respectable speed still would not qualify it as a crack train by European standards, but it is clean, the service good, and the choice of food in the dining room varies from light snacks to four-course dinners with prime ribs of beef or charcoal-broiled steak. Stewards wear tuxedos (remember?) and serve free champagne, or were doing so the last time we checked.

Recreational activities have long been and still are a major feature of the train. One can bet on filmed horse races, play bingo, view color television or movies, participate in songfests, or watch hostesses model the latest fashions—including, naturally, bathing suits.

One might suppose that most *Florida Special* riders were leery of flying, but that seems not to be the case, according to a *New York Times* piece by Robert Lindsey, which quoted a 33-year-old Washington insurance executive as saying, "I just think it's a relaxing way to travel. You have time to read and unwind." Another rider thought it was "more like a cruise ship than a train." A Seaboard Coast Line executive said, "We feel that if you give the public good equipment, good service, and good schedules, you can get passengers on trains, regardless of what some people say."

(At this writing the on-again, off-again *Florida Special* is off again, but Amtrak's *Silver Meteor* has been upgraded to include many of the *Special's* passenger-pleasing features, and New York–Florida service was doubled in 1972 over '71.)

Amtrak has retained its one Chicago–Florida train—now called the *Floridian*—and has changed Chicago departure time from morning to evening, a popular move.

Doubling the number of trains on the Boston–Washington route made some friends for Amtrak, as did restoring overnight sleeping-car service between those cities. And Amtrak then moved to establish transcontinental schedules that would avoid overnight stops in Chicago by resuming through sleeping-car service between New York and California. At the time of that move, the *Hotel on Wheels* train via New Orleans was the only through coast-to-coast sleeper. In June 1972 Amtrak added another New York–Los Angeles train that bypasses Chicago, going via Indianapolis, St. Louis, and Kansas City on what is called the "National Limited Chief Super Chief Route."

Amtrak put the United States back into international rail service in July 1972 with the *Pacific International* from Seattle to Vancouver, providing connections with the Los Angeles–Seattle *Coast Starlight* and the Chicago–Seattle *Empire Builder* and *North Coast Hiawatha*. Moreover, it announced resumption of abandoned New York–Montreal service via the *Montrealer*, and a train into Mexico via Nuevo Laredo, just across the border from Laredo, Texas.

Amtrak also gets points for its effort to convenience the passenger through a linkup with the U.S. Travel Service. The idea is to woo foreign visitors to ride U.S. trains by offering them a 25-percent discount. Not much when you consider what the Eurailpass does for Americans in Europe, but still helpful.

The Southern Railway, America's largest passenger road independent of Amtrak, in an attempt to be accommodating, shifted its Washington–Atlanta *Piedmont* run from overnight to daytime, then added food and bar service. Also, the Southern during the summer of 1971 added a dome car for the 139-mile leg between Salisbury and Asheville, North Carolina, to give passengers a better look at those Southern Appalachians.

Presumably the revival of comfortable seasonal East Coast trains offering access to Maine is under consideration. After all, for years people flocked to ride the comfortable *Bar Harbor Express* before it was discontinued. They might again, given the crowded state of our highways, not to mention the casualty statistics. And what about seasonal trains to the vacation areas of Michigan for vacationers from Chicago and Detroit and other neighboring cities?

No doubt these and many better ideas are being run up the pole at Amtrak.

Though it is reassuring to know that at long last someone on the inside is trying to revive rail passenger service in America, no friend of rails can feel complacent on the strength of what Amtrak has been able to do so far to erase the railroads' "Legacy of Ill Will" dealt with in Chapter III.

From time to time there is a rash of letters-to-the-editor in magazines and metropolitan newspapers protesting that Amtrak service is terrible, and no doubt in some instances it is—though often there will be another rash of letters defending Amtrak. Some ardent rail advocates claim that Amtrak itself is a kind of Trojan iron horse designed to bring about the total abandonment of intercity rail service. The fact to bear in mind is that a good passenger train, efficiently run and conveniently scheduled and courteously serviced, is an excellent way to travel from city to city. That in America we have not yet learned, or relearned, to run trains properly should not be allowed to reflect on passenger trains as a way to go.

"The public demand for a decent environment grows stronger each year, and this awareness is translated into expectations of governmental actions to clean the air and water and protect the land."

> —NEW JERSEY GOVERNOR WILLIAM T. CAHILL. *The New York Times,* February 18, 1973

CHAPTER IX

Far-out Trains in Our Future

IN RECENT years, most research-and-development efforts on behalf of travel in the United States have been conducted by automobile companies to improve cars and by aerospace companies to improve planes. But at long last both the government and the railroad industry have begun to show serious interest in R&D work on new concepts that will revitalize and eventually revolutionize rail travel in America.

The emphasis so far has been mainly on bringing rail cars, operating systems, and tracks up to some of the standards long ago set in Europe and Japan. As a result, higher speeds are now feasible. Car bodies are lighter, thanks to new metallurgical adaptations of stainless steel, LAHT (low-alloy high-tensile) steel, aluminum, and fiber glass. Transistorized cab signaling has led to automatic train control, and solid-state chopper (modulated) controls have led to more precise signaling. Laser beams are used for track alignment, and old-fashioned track in some places is being replaced with welded rails; acceleration is now faster, and braking is both faster and more reliable. Finally, automatic fare collection makes possible more efficient processing of passengers. At this writing several of these advances are now in use, though so far only Lindenwold and BART have incorporated all of them into their systems.

General Steel Industries' president W. Ashley Gray, Jr., summed up what has been happening: "It's true there hasn't been enough R&D. But the scope of innovation was limited anyway by the reluctance of the operators to try something new. They needed compatibility on the older systems. Now, with new systems, there's a whole new ball game."

If we continue our investment in railroad R&D, as we surely will, by the end of the '80s we should see many exciting new developments ranging from the fairly superficial to the out-and-out science-fictional: trains that can go faster than today's fastest jet planes; trains powered by jet engines, or pneumatic pressure, or linear-induction motors, or gravity; trains that travel in tubes; trains that ride on cushions of compressed air or on magnetic fields; and trains suspended from an overhead rail which they do not touch, being separated from it by atmospheric pressure rather than by an air cushion underneath. All of these possibilities and more are now on the drawing board, or being investigated, or, in some cases, actually being tested in the United States.

DOT's recent report "Recommendations for Northeast Corridor Transportation" predicted that rail transportation in the northeast urban corridor for the 1980s will revolve around three rail systems:

1) A continuation and expansion of DOT's demonstration projects (the *Metroliner* and *Turbo*) under a program labeled Improved High Speed Rail (IHSR). Given upgraded rights-of-way, these trains could travel at around 150 mph. To place this system in full swing would cost approximately $460 million over a three-year period. New York–Boston trips, nonstop, would take two hours; New York–Washington, one hour and a half.

2) The advanced High Speed Rail Concept (HSRC) goes one step further and involves building new rights-of-way with less track curvature, plus minor improvements in certain items affecting train performance. Cruising speed would be brought up to 200 mph, allowing the New York–Boston run to be covered in roughly one hour and a half and the New York–Washington in one hour and a quarter.

3) Fastest, least conventional, and certainly most exciting of the three systems involves the use of the earlier-mentioned tracked air-cushion vehicle, or TACV. This type of train could be so fast (300 mph) that it would surely reduce plane travel and thus alleviate intolerable air congestion in our urban corridors. One could go from New York to Washington in just under one hour.

As might be guessed from its name, the TACV is designed to skim, wheelless, along a U-shaped concrete guideway or trough —which it does not touch while in full-speed motion. A one-inch cushion of air, generated by on-board compressors, separates the vehicle from its track so that it literally rides on air. "Flies" might be a more appropriate verb. As a consequence, there is no wheel friction or wear caused by wheel–rail interaction.

The TACV is the offspring of the development of the peripheral jet air cushion by Christopher Cockerall in England in the early 1950s. Applied originally to water vehicles, or "Hovercraft," the air-cushion principle is adaptable to transportation over the ground, and studies performed on both sides of the Atlantic have led to the combining of an air-cushion vehicle with a guideway.

The British refer to their TACV as the "Hovertrain," and by now they are well into their test program. But it was the French who in 1965 became the first to start the operational testing of a full-sized TACV, the "Aerotrain." It rode on an inverted-T rail of prestressed concrete, and was driven then by an aircraft turbo-prop engine. It now has an aircraft jet engine. The Aerotrain remains today the TACV closest to being ready for regular service.

In this country, TACV research and development—like R&D in any transportation system—must concern itself not only with science but with economics, engineering, and the environment. Some studies, with limited funds, have been made so far of the guideway and of the vehicle.

Since there is pretty surely some form of TACV in the American traveler's future, an attempt to describe this system in layman's terms may be in order.

First, about the guideway, which is the equivalent of, and by the cognoscenti is called, a track, but bears no resemblance to the conventional railroad track. We said earlier that the TACV skims along a U-shaped trough, but there are at least three possible designs for the guideway: the inverted T (French), the box beam (British), or—the one so far favored by this country—the U-shaped channel. The French and British guideways are very similar, and in both cases the train straddles the guideway and rides over it. The only difference is that the cross section in one case is an inverted T, in the other a square box. The U.S. version has the train riding inside the U-shaped guideway, a trough some twelve feet four inches across. The diagrams below may make all of this more intelligible.

BRITISH   **FRENCH**   **AMERICAN**

The British appears to be the cheapest of the three possibilities. Guideways can be set in a tunnel, on an elevated platform, or at grade level, at respectively decreasing cost. Regardless of its type and elevation, the guideway must be relatively straight, must allow for switching, should not be unsightly, and should not have the effect of a wall or barrier within a community.

A variety of designs is possible for the vehicle itself. For example, the propulsion can be provided by a shrouded fan (in effect, a propeller encased in a cylinder), a turboprop, a jet engine, or—the one favored by DOT—the linear-induction motor (LIM).

The cost of an air-cushioned system is high, but the returns in speed are enormous. DOT estimates at $2.7 billion the price of providing such service between Boston and Washington. Included in this figure are routeway preparation, guideway construction, system electrification, terminal construction, yards and shops, purchase of land, communications, testing, and purchasing the number of vehicles estimated to be needed during the first year of operation. Because right-of-way preparation and guideway construction are the most expensive items, decisions affecting them will be the crucial ones. So the choice of guideway type is extremely important. In its report, DOT recommended that TACV research and development efforts "be expanded and accelerated and should include heavy emphasis on the environmental impact of the system (including electric power sources)." It further recommended that the R&D be completed and a decision made by 1976.

That R&D is now under way. The Grumman Aerospace Corporation in March 1970 received a $3.5-million DOT contract for construction of a tracked air-cushion research vehicle (TACRV). At the same time, Rohr Corporation and Vought received contracts totaling $2.9 million to produce various TACV designs and mockups powered by LIM. The TACRV will be used to study vehicle, guideway, and system-related problems. It will feature a wayside power-collection system to receive and dispense electrical power, a fan-jet air compressor, and a secondary mechanical suspension system.

(The Federal Railroad Administration in November 1972 announced a technological breakthrough resulting from tests of an experimental wayside power-collection system for high-speed trains. The tests proved that power could be distributed to trains traveling 300 mph or faster. Electrified trains receiving power via a standard third rail can go no faster than about 130 mph because of a spring-loaded connector that bounces too much. Electric trains using overhead pantographs are restricted to about 200 mph because of cable vibrations.)

The TACV line (also mentioned in Chapter X) was to serve the Los Angeles International Airport and would have complemented the TACRV effort, but plans for it have been temporarily shelved if not abandoned—partly, according to DOT, because of second thoughts evoked by the February 9, 1971, Los Angeles earthquake, but mainly because of the controversy surrounding the building of the Palmdale Intercontinental Airport near Los Angeles.

This new airport was to be connected with Los Angeles and its International Airport via another TACV line, after the first line was built, but because airports, like highways, hurt parks, wildlife, and human eardrums, they are often bitterly opposed by conservationists and nearby residents. In this case, the Sierra Club has filed suit to prevent further funding of Palmdale by the federal government until environmental studies can be made. Besides complaints of the anticipated trapping of air pollutants—the projected airport's location is a valley—it is also within 20 miles of seven wildlife sanctuaries, seven regional parks, thirteen county parks, and one state park.

The initial TACV line to the Los Angeles airport would have traveled on troughlike guideways elevated from 20 to 60 feet along the San Diego Freeway on its 16.3-mile route at speeds of 150 to 200 mph. It was to be funded equally by the UMTA and the Los Angeles Department of Airports and would have cost an estimated $50 million. It was originally expected to begin revenue operations in mid-1973 (with initial operations scheduled for late 1972). By mid-1972 Los Angeles had not even submitted a request for funds because of the legal tie-up of the new airport. Should that problem be resolved in time for initiation of service late in the '70s, engineers would still be able to make an early evaluation of a TACV system operating on a daily basis. Volpe in 1970 described the airport project as "perhaps the most exciting new development in the field of transportation and environmental control."

To understand why a TACV can go so fast, aside from its aerodynamic design characteristics, one needs to consider the linear-induction motor which propels it. The LIM, whose speed is theoretically unlimited, is impossible to describe clearly to the layman in a few words. It has been called a "simple rearrangement of the classic asynchronous motor, but with its rotary motor cut along a radius, unrolled and laid out flat." See what we mean? "A small airgap remains between the primary and the secondary windings so that relative linear motion is permitted between the two." For those who understand such things, the (AC) currents in the primary induce currents in the secondary by induction, and these secondary currents in turn interact with the primary's electromagnetic field to produce a force that pulls the primary (the vehicle) along the lengthened secondary (the rail).

In the United States, engineers so far have favored a double-sided LIM, on the ground that "this design features no attractive forces between the vertical rail and the vehicle, whereas gravity attracts the vehicle to the horizontal-rail-type the British propose. The British single-sided LIM design requires extra power to provide the necessary air gap, but it has the advantage of focusing the thrust down the vehicle's centerline." Another LIM design consideration has to do with the source of electric power for the motor. It can be produced by on-board gas-turbine generators (also called turbo alternators) or picked up by the vehicle from wayside collection rails—like a subway's third rail. The latter, although technologically more difficult, features lower air- and noise-pollution levels.

Most of the LIM work now being done in the United States centers around the linear-induction-motor vehicle for research (LIMVR). Built by the Garrett Corporation (another aerospace company and a subsidiary of Signal Industries of Los Angeles), it is rated at 2500 hp, can reach speeds of 250 to 300 mph, weighs a whopping 24 tons, is 56½ feet long—and, at this stage, carries two people.

It is the kind of snappy-looking craft that Buck Rogers would approve of—red and white, highly polished, with a large, eye-catching DOT emblem just aft of the cockpit. Its missile-type nose suggests speed, as do the two red racing stripes that run the length of its sides.

The LIMVR rides on special high-speed trucks, or sets of wheels, over regular rails that include, running down the center, an aluminum reaction fin necessary to receive the LIM's electromagnetic field. (See sketch.) An on-board aircraft-type gas turbine

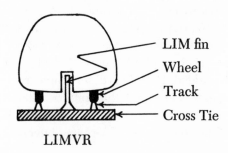

LIMVR

drives an AC generator to provide its only source of electric current. The LIM is its own braking system. That is, currents in the LIM can be reversed, producing almost two tons of braking thrust—which is a lot of braking thrust, they tell us.

As Under Secretary of Transportation, James M. Beggs was enthusiastic about LIM and likened it to U.S. achievements in space. "A great part of its significance lies in the future—in the door it has opened for surface transportation development. As the development of rocket propulsion enabled man to break loose from earth's gravity, so the LIM promises to enable us, on the ground, to be freed from dependence on the wheel."

Crucial to the development of LIMVR and the TACVR is the testing that goes on at the Federal High Speed Ground Test Center, a 45-square-mile grassy plain area 20 miles northeast of Pueblo, Colorado, where not only far-out experimental vehicles but conventional railroad equipment and safety devices as well are checked out. Colorado was chosen because of its varied climate. Still under development, the test center eventually will have a 20-mile oval with three tracks (one for conventional rail, one for the LIMVR, and one for the TACVR), a 20-mile straight-away for a tube test system, a 9-mile UMTA track, a 16-mile Federal Railroad Administration (FRA) track, and a giant building housing the Wheel/Rail Dynamics Laboratory: all told, a $100-million facility.

If the initials are confusing, FRA and UMTA are major sub-divisions within DOT. Under FRA is the Office of High-Speed Ground Transportation (OHSGT), and it is this office that has performed much of the work and provided most of the technical advice for the TACRV's development.

"We added 'High Speed' for glamour; it helps to win votes in Congress," said one of the drafters of the legislation establishing the test center. But Myles B. Mitchell, director of OHSGT, is more down-to-earth: "We are interested in real workaday problems."

Those workaday problems include some having to do with railroad freight rather than passenger service. DOT contends that research into freight—the railroads' traditional first love—may lead to discoveries of value to passenger service.

That may indeed be one result of research being performed there by the Santa Fe on its coaxial-freight-train project—some-times referred to as the flextrain. SF has already built, for testing purposes, a model (one-eighth size) flextrain and plans to build three more. Though freight-inspired, this innovation may in the end help to improve passenger service, so we pause for a quick look at the flextrain.

To begin with, it rides on conventional tracks, but not on con-ventional wheels with fixed or rigid axles. Instead it has many smaller wheels, in pairs, individually powered, fastened at four-foot intervals to a flexible "spine," or center sill (a jointed steel beam several inches wide and about a foot high), running the entire length of the train. The wheels are fastened to the sill by transverse beams. Roller-bearing plates enable these beams to "float" under the forty-foot cargo-carrying containers. This arrangement permits a long, rigid car to—in effect—"bend" around curves while carrying heavy loads.

The advantages of the flextrain are that its cars need no conventional coupling, and that at high speeds it would provide a smoother, more stable ride by preventing "wheelset-hunting," a lateral oscillation common to conventional carriers which greatly increases wheel and rail wear and keeps train speeds low.

The flextrain has a very low center of gravity, since the approximately 16-inch wheel diameters are roughly one-half those of a standard wheel. It works out that the deck of the container is only 24 inches above the rail, compared with 42 to 46 inches for a conventional flatcar. This reduced height means less wind resistance and less turbulence beneath the train. It is estimated that even with heavy loads, it could reach speeds of between 100 and 200 mph.

When we asked a Santa Fe official whether the train could be used for passenger service, he said it was possible, but that the railroad was concentrating on freight because "let's face it, that's where the money is."

Back to the Pueblo test center: The impressive research and testing programs now going on or planned for the future there include analyzing ride qualities of existing trains, making safety studies, performing prototype shakedowns, designing and using "lab cars" to record track profiles of lines and systems, developing new control systems, and exploring new rail advancements. If these programs receive adequate funding in the future, enough information could be produced from them to bring American passenger rail service up to modern times and even to give the United States some international prestige in this field—but only, of course, if we as a nation are *committed* to good rail service.

The steel-wheeled, steel-rail LIMVR has already undergone a number of tests there. Until the summer of 1971 the highest speeds obtained were a low 35 to 40 mph. Then, with Transportation Secretary John A. Volpe aboard (and wearing a ten-gallon hat), it reached a new high, 95 mph. Past performances had been limited not by propulsion problems, but by the length of the LIM track then in existence—about 3 miles. The trackage has now been extended to 6.2 miles, and the LIMVR is expected to whoosh along at speeds up to 180 mph. The goal of achieving speeds of 250 mph may not be realized until the necessary funding makes possible the completion of the 20-mile track.

Grumman's 300-mph TACRV was completed in mid-1972 and, like the LIMVR, is powered by a Garrett-built LIM. (Garrett was also selected to build the wayside power-collection system, or electric pickup system, that furnishes power to the motor, since, unlike the LIMVR, the TACRV has no gas-turbine generator aboard.) The Grumman vehicle has a souped-up LIM of 12,000 hp, exceeding the one in the LIMVR by 9,500 hp and providing exactly four times as much thrust, or 15,000 pounds compared with 3,750. The TACRV will undergo tests on its own special 20-mile U-shaped concrete guideway at Pueblo through the end of 1974. (See sketch.)

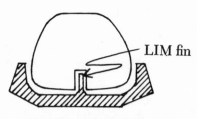

TACRV and TACV

The testing will be thorough and should do much to further the development of tracked air-cushion vehicles and to ensure their use in the future. Technological areas to be investigated include the performance of the vehicle guideway system, switching techniques for the guideways, characteristics of the new LIM, power requirements, and vehicle aerodynamic performance and stability. (In any high-speed vehicle, the aerodynamic drag effects must be considered, especially the effects on vehicle control in a crosswind.) Passenger-oriented problems, with special emphasis on comfort, are also being studied and evaluated; and finally, detailed cost studies are being made, with a view to selling TACVs to future operators whether they be Amtrak, independent railroads, or—who knows?—the federal government itself.

Pending completion of studies, rough cost estimates have been completed and were included in DOT's Northeast Corridor report. Although the initial investment obviously would be high, the report states that unit cost per passenger-mile for TACVs would be low in the Northeast Corridor because of the high volume of travelers—a fact consistent with past cost comparisons between rail and other modes of transportation.

While the advantages of TACVs—high speed, low unit cost, and large capacity—are widely acknowledged, it had been feared that, in the words of *Railway Gazette International*, "they could be noisy and create problems in tunnels." This rather Thurber-esque statement may have been inspired by the fact that the French Aerotrain is propelled by jet engines, hardly ideal companions in a tunnel. But there is no reason to suppose that an economically feasible engine cannot be designed that will conform to acceptable noise levels. True, these vehicles have a racket problem because of their air-compressor fans, but recent studies by DOT's Office of Noise Abatement indicate that noise levels can be reduced to acceptable levels by the time TACVs are in full operation.

The TACV emits few air contaminants, particularly when its power is received from wayside collection rails. Obviously, some air pollution occurs at the power stations that create the power in the first place—the amount depending upon the type of fuel consumed. But air pollution would be virtually eliminated from power stations if energy from nuclear fusion, as opposed to the present nuclear fission, became a reality, which many predict may occur in the next twenty years. (Fusion energy would not eliminate all pollution; its fantastic heat would generate thermal pollution as a by-product of its energy-conversion process: that is, such heat introduced into waterways intensifies the effect of pollutants already there, lowers the oxygen content, and kills aquatic life. But producing fusion energy would not by-produce the tons of highly radioactive ash that comes from fission energy, with its residue of plutonium so dangerous it has to be buried.)

One environmental consideration would remain: the aesthetic. If the TACV's concrete guideways were elevated, they would resemble the unsightly old "el" trains. But the guideways *can* be placed at ground level, along existing rights-of-way, with adequate crossing barriers. Elsewhere, they could go into tunnels if the cost of tunneling could be greatly reduced, which is not impossible.

Actually, speaking of tunnels, if one looks beyond the TACV, one sees that the next big rail innovation will probably be the train running in a tube that has been wholly or partly vacuumized. Such trains would be free of the frictional forces that limit the speeds of other kinds of trains, even the relatively friction-free TACV. Conventional trains, of course, never move fast enough so that aerodynamic drag (air resistance, the frictional force experienced by airplanes) is a problem. Their problem is old-fashioned wheel–rail friction. By eliminating that frictional factor, the TACV should be able to achieve speeds up to 300 mph; but its speed would then be limited by aerodynamic drag, which is greater at ground level than in the air and, whether acting on an airplane or on a surface vehicle, increases with speed. A train traveling in a vacuumized tube would be free to achieve speeds up to 500 mph, maybe more.

The tube concept can be hybridized. The vehicle could ride on conventional rails or on one of the air-cushioned guideways. It could be powered by a LIM, jet, propeller, pneumatic pressure, or gravity. The tube's cross section could be square, semicircular or circular, although the last might be the easiest to construct.

The tube could be in complete vacuum, partially evacuated, or at atmospheric pressure. It could be tunneled all the way or emerge at certain points and travel at ground level.

Drag force in a tube decreases as the amount of air in it decreases, until drag is nonexistent in a completely airless, or evacuated, tube. So the fastest combination would be an air-cushioned vehicle, powered by the LIM, in an evacuated tube. Then gravity could complement propulsion by accelerating the vehicle in the downhill portions of the tube and braking it in the uphill sections. (Estimates of the depth of a New York–Washington, D.C. tunnel vary from 50 feet for a non–gravity type tube to 50 miles for a gravity one—assuming this latter depth could actually be achieved.)

The tube-train system offers advantages other than speed. It permits passage through the hearts of cities and would be more dependable, since the adverse effects caused by weather would be eliminated, as would the danger of vandalism from outside and the polluting noise of surface trains. The disadvantage would be that the traveler would see no scenery as he sped along.

Constantinos A. Doxiadis, an internationally known Greek architect and city planner, is one who strongly favors underground transportation systems:

We ought to learn from biology and go underground. In biology, the circulation systems are always on the inside. The idea in our cities is to take all things that have to do with machines and put them underground. This would leave the area above the ground to the walking people. Eventually, all urban transit will have to go underground, no matter what the cost.

Should the tube in certain areas have to be aboveground, it could run along existing rights-of-way. Some means would need to be devised for preventing its being an eyesore. Landscaping, probably.

In general, the fast tube trains, particularly the gravity–vacuum-tube ones, will require extensive research, extending present rail technology to new frontiers. Under a $500,000 UMTA grant, the Johns Hopkins Applied Physics Laboratory is evaluating several Fast Transit Link (FTL) systems, including tube trains. An initial report by the laboratory assessed some of the problems of various tube-train concepts, and they seem formidable but not insoluble.

A tricky problem for both the tube vehicle and the TACV is how best to switch tracks, particularly at high speeds. This, incidentally, has been one of the drawbacks of the monorail, which once seemed the rail system of the future and enjoys some use abroad, but which in the United States has been largely confined to Disneylands and the Seattle World's Fair. Seattle still has the monorail fair trains. LIM vehicles, to get back to that switching problem, would have it in spades because of their higher speeds and dependence on wayside power-collection systems.

Tube Transit, Inc., of Palo Alto, California, is working on a tracked tube vehicle powered by a combination of gravity and pneumatic pressure. The company admits that the "track smoothness would have to be 10 times greater than on Japan's famed Tokaido rail line, built from the ground up and carefully maintained to be the smoothest railroad in the world."

A vacuum tube costs two or three times as much as the same tube built to sustain ordinary atmospheric pressure. If the tube is then placed underground, the costs become extraordinary, and for this reason DOT's Northeast Corridor report eliminated the tube as a possibility for the 1980s, but saw some value in continuing tube-train R&D: "If . . . a major breakthrough is made in reducing the cost of tunneling, underground high speed (tube) systems could prove a practical alternative in some spinal intercity as well as urban applications. . . . Therefore, a major effort should be undertaken in tunneling technology to achieve significant improvement in cost."

One new way of tunneling that promises to reduce costs significantly is through the use of powerful laser beams to penetrate rock and bore through the ground. Further research is needed, but since tunneling with lasers would benefit the mining industry, the research seems assured.

Another tunneling devise DOT is showing an interest in is the "subterrene," now built in prototype. According to its developers at the Los Alamos Scientific Laboratory in New Mexico, the subterrene—with its tungsten tip, molybdenum shell, and graphite heating element—within fifteen years will be able to penetrate the side of a mountain and produce a round, glass-lined tunnel 35 feet in diameter at 300 feet per day. Also referred to as the "hot-hole digger," it is capable of melting rock (and forcing the molten rock into voids in the tunnel wall)—an impressive feat considering that most rock melts at 1,200 degrees Centigrade. But it would use a fantastic amount of power, obviously, which may doom it unless thermonuclear fusion resolves the coming energy crisis.

Circulating water or gas is required to cool the walls of a sub-terrene-made tunnel and help "freeze" the molten rock in place, but it does eliminate one major problem, debris removal. Scientists on the project predict that it will also eliminate cave-ins.

A small prototype digger has been tested successfully, and the testing of a somewhat larger one is planned. Interest in tunneling and excavating techniques is being demonstrated by the Advanced Technology Applications Division of the National Science Foundation, whose budget request for fiscal year 1973 was $6 million—a skyrocketing jump from the $700,000 requested the previous fiscal year.

DOT plans to construct an experimental ground-level tube test system at the Pueblo Test Center to experiment with evacuated and atmospheric-pressure systems and with various types of vehicles—though, according to DOT's Mitchell, "Our tube vehicle won't be ready for 20 to 30 years."

While some scientists work on tube problems, others are experimenting with the magnetic-suspension, or magnetic-levitation, system described in Chapter II in connection with Germany's dream trains. If the Germans are correct in their claim that such a system can carry heavier loads, while using less power, than the TACV, then magnetic suspension *could* be the next evolutionary stage for the TACV in this country. (The Germans point out that a magnet's heat losses are much less than the air losses of a TACV, a fact that would make the magnetic-suspension system more efficient.) It also, according to DOT, is potentially usable in evacuated tubes to obtain still higher speeds.

Stanford Research Institute scientists, on the strength of theoretical designs completed several years ago, received an initial $121,000 grant in 1971 from DOT to determine the feasibility of adapting the magnetic-levitation system to accommodate a passenger train capable of traveling up to 1,000 mph through a tube and propelled by electrical magnets chilled to 450 degrees below zero Fahrenheit. (In an evacuated tube there would be no sonic boom, and in a partially evacuated tube the boom would be considerably weakened.) Advances in the field of superconducting materials have made it possible to use immense currents without melting the rail, and scientists say liquid helium is a strong possibility to be used as the supercoolant needed for the superconducting magnets.

What about that old darling of the Sunday supplements, the "dual mode" system, whereby a private automobile or bus can be attached to an automated guidance and power system to combine the best features of the auto and the train on a long trip? That is, with each vehicle becoming in effect an element in a trackless train.

Well, research goes on, and the idea interests environmentalists because—since power would be transmitted from a "third rail" or guideway to an electric motor on the vehicle—poisonous emission gases (except at the point where the power originated) would be reduced to zero. If the guideways could be built on the road's surface, instead of elevated as most present studies seem to favor, the aesthetic effect on the landscape would not be disastrous.

There is much interest in dual mode on the part of industries and individual transportation experts. In Wisconsin, Ford, American Motors, Allis-Chalmers, and Dwight Baumann Associates have joined with Milwaukee County in submitting a multimillion-dollar proposal to DOT aimed at demonstrating the feasibility of dual mode. The Bendix Corporation is also conducting research into dual-mode operation and plans to install an elevated guideway test section at Columbia, Maryland. UMTA has shown interest in dual mode but at this writing has not put its money on the line.

Obviously, much research remains to be done into such questions as how to reduce accidents and malfunctions in a system where cars would move at high speeds virtually bumper to bumper, and how to handle great volumes of traffic on these "automated turnpikes" at rush hours and on holiday weekends. But probably the most important thing to be researched is the public's attitude toward dual mode. Would they buy it?

Getting back to railroads, those who favor a return to rail consciousness in America can take some heart from the work now being done at many American universities: research into new kinds of trains and new systems and, perhaps of greater importance, the establishment of new training programs to turn out persons qualified to carry on such research.

In the past, the transportation field has had the reputation of not being able to attract top engineers and scientists, and the few who were so attracted too often became bogged down in transportation problems and approaches that were extremely narrow in scope—the study of traffic flow patterns, for example. As a consequence, transportation people have been constantly criticized for taking an "engineer's" approach to problems without considering the "human" element.

The new attitude of universities has been brought about in part by a growing environmental awareness and in part by the growing public disenchantment with the automobile. UMTA is now sponsoring a University Research and Training Program in urban transportation that will benefit travel by train, since it will broaden approaches to the study of transportation. Funds for this program have just about doubled every year since its inception in 1969. (The amount authorized for 1972–73 was $3 million.) Guidelines are explicit, and universities submitting proposals must have transportation programs in existence that include both research and training. Multidisciplinary approaches are encouraged, and preference is given to applicants proposing continuing programs of research.

To take a quick look at one university's activities in this field, the multidisciplinary transportation program at Princeton University, under the direction of Professor Paul M. Lion, involves faculty and students from the School of Architecture and Urban Planning, the School of Engineering and Applied Science, the Woodrow Wilson School of Public and International Affairs, and the departments of Statistics and Economics. The program combines research, training, and practical experience and includes both undergraduate and graduate students. The core of the program is a joint curriculum leading to the Master's degree. According to Lion, there is a greater need for Master's-degree holders than for Ph.D.s, at this point, because the latter often become too specialized. In his words, "the person with the Master's degree becomes the practitioner, the Ph.D. the researcher." And Lion feels that transportation research should follow "real problems," instead of the other way around—that is, where the researcher comes up with a solution and then begins searching for a problem to apply it to. He cites the SST as an example of something the scientists came up with before solving the problem of how to get to and from the airports.

UMTA is not the only governmental agency supporting university research that may have an effect on future rail travel. The National Science Foundation in 1971 funded an urban-transportation laboratory at MIT to train students in seeking solutions to urban transportation problems. The laboratory will try to determine the social, economic, and political implications of various transportation systems and weigh their advantages and disadvantages. DOT in 1972 announced it would spend another $4 million to fund university studies of transportation.

There are those who, despite the fact that federal R&D funds have climbed steadily during the last few years, are still dissatisfied with current research efforts and feel that what is being spent is minuscule compared with the size of the problem. For example, an editorial in the December 1971 issue of the magazine *Industrial Research* had this to say:

One area, urban transportation, where most current and complex needs exist now is funded to the tune of only $50-to-$60 million a year for R&D. This is a paltry sum considering the fact that urban transportation costs, based on the automobile, are estimated to approach $100-billion annually!

The magazine offered some practical advice:

We suggest the Transportation people retire to their offices, listen again to Secretary Volpe's earlier stirring rhetoric concerning the solution of this country's transportation problems, and draft a solid statement with a real commitment to technology.

William F. Hamilton II of General Research Corporation is one who feels that research efforts are still too restricted to conventional systems, as opposed to the development of new concepts: "This research focuses on incremental and relatively minor improvements to conventional mass transportation, and makes no mention whatever of the major conceptual innovations which are now within reach."

Train safety is one area of badly needed research singled out by the National Transportation Board: "There has been no research whatever involving the interaction of train, track and passenger during and after initiation of a derailment or crash. By contrast, most other modes of public transportation are actively engaged in crash testing of safety during system failure."

Those words were given new meaning in the fall of 1972 when one Chicago commuter train rammed into another, killing forty-four passengers. It was the worst U.S. rail disaster in fourteen years. While no one should minimize its significance, the loss of life was not spectacular in comparison with lives lost in plane and automobile crashes.

Balance is, of course, the key to a sound research program. It is exciting to look far ahead, but we need to keep one eye on the present and immediate future. To quote Joseph Vranich, executive director of the National Association of Railroad Passengers (see Chapter VI):

"Our political leaders and technocrats must offer immediate relief from traffic congestion. In other words, we should not allow consideration of esoteric systems—such as tracked air cushion vehicles—to be an excuse for not taking action to improve conventional rail and bus transit. The exotic system may not be ready for another 10 years. The frustrated commuter doesn't want an improved system when he's old and retired. He wants one tomorrow morning when he has to face his steering wheel again."

"We have a recognition of the fact that you just can't continue to lay down asphalt all over the State."

> —JOHN P. GALLAGHER, executive director of The New Jersey Highway Authority, commenting on Governor Cahill's State Mass-Transit Program through revenues from superhighways (January 20, 1973)

CHAPTER X

Getting Commuters Back on the Rails

THERE ARE other developments in U.S. local rail service less spectacular than Lindenwold and BART—evolutionary rather than revolutionary; improvements in existing services rather than "from scratch" innovations—but still of great significance as indicators of things to come.

The early '70s saw a flurry of studies undertaken and plans drawn up as cities and states finally began to face their traffic-congestion problems and to realize that rails had to be a major part of the solution. And they knew this approach would be hard to sell, because 82 percent of all American commuters were using automobiles to get to work, and although the trend had to be away from cars and highways and toward rails, commuters are a stubborn breed and would not change their habits overnight—particularly since many had endured the poor scheduling, outmoded equipment, and high fares characteristic of postwar commuter rail service.

Developments in mass rail transit are coming so thick and fast that some of what we now report will inevitably be out of date by the time this book appears. But to show how the wind blows, we will review rail-transit developments in several major U.S. cities, starting with Chicago and ending with New York, all of which promise to have their equivalents of Lindenwold and BART by the mid-1980s.

To Chicagoans, the sight of a tall, double-deck suburban rail car (about three feet higher than conventional ones) evokes no comment, because commuters have been riding bilevel cars on the Burlington Northern (BN), Rock Island (RI), Chicago & North Western (C&NW), and Milwaukee Road (MR) for several years. (The first double-deck streetcar had a trial run on July 4, 1892, in San Diego; the first double-deck railroad coach was built in August 1830 and used on the Baltimore & Ohio.) But today on the Illinois Central Gulf (ICG), commuters are riding new, modern ones. The IC—before its 1972 merger with Gulf, Mobile & Ohio— purchased 130 of these "Highliners," as they are called, and started introducing them in mid-1971, with a peak rate of introduction of eight per month.

The great advantage of the double-decker, obviously, is that it can seat nearly twice as many passengers as a conventional car of the same length, thus reducing costs and moving more people faster.

Even though the Highliners run on ICG tracks, ICG actually does not own them outright but leases them from the Chicago South Suburban Mass Transit District. (The district is one of four public transit agencies in addition to the Chicago Transit Authority serving the Chicago area. This one serves eleven communities south of the city.) A $26.6-million UMTA grant funded two-thirds of the equipment cost, and although it would not own the cars, IC, in the interest of modernizing its line, was willing to put up the other one-third (13.3 million). The St. Louis Car Division of General Steel Industries is the manufacturer. (Other Chicago double-deckers are made by either Pullman-Standard or the Budd Company.)

The Highliners are different from other bilevel cars in the Chicago area in several ways. Each car is self-propelled electrically by four GE motors (640 hp per car), whereas more conventional two-deckers must be moved by diesel "push-pull" locomotives which push the cars going in one direction and pull them going in the other, to avoid turnarounds. Highliner cars, because electrically powered, have a rather unconventional silhouette. The roof is stepped down (one foot ten inches) about five feet from the front of the car to allow room for the pantograph. Owing to the train's height and minimum-maximum pantograph-clearance factors, the overhead wire had to be raised or lowered at 175 locations, and at one point the wire could not be raised so the tracks, instead, were lowered six inches.

These have wheels 36 inches in diameter instead of the 33 inches of more conventional double-deckers, and attractive paint jobs combining light silver-white with orange and black. Each has electronically controlled pneumatic sliding doors on both sides: one double door just aft of the center, and one single door at the extreme forward section—all equipped with ice-defying door-track heaters for those Chicago winters. Other Chicago double-deckers have only the one center sliding double door per side. Interestingly, IC introduced sliding doors to American railroads in order to handle the crowds at the Chicago World's Fair in 1893.

Inside, the Highliners are all climate-controlled and have some 156 contoured seats in a 2–2 arrangement (two seats on either side of the center aisle), tinted safety-glass windows, overhead steel luggage racks, a good lighting system—and a No Smoking rule throughout: not out of sympathy for nonsmokers, but to save the very substantial costs of cleaning up after smokers and replacing or repairing burned seats. The motorman sitting up front is in two-way radio communication with nearby trains and base and tower stations, as well as—through a PA system—the riders and conductors on his train. Unlike those of BART and Lindenwold, Highliner ticket sales are automated only at fare-collection gates at main stations, but complete ticket automation, using vending machines, is now in the testing stage. The major stations are now undergoing a renovation and modernization program.

Passenger Train Journal has described the new Highliners as "modernistic looking with sleek silver pantographs. The cars are smooth—although the track needs more work—the seats are

medium soft, the lighting superb, and the ride is amazingly quiet."
The cars are built to ride in pairs, and two to six cars make up
a Highliner train. Top train speed is 75 mph, but the average
is only 40 mph because of stops—even though ICG has fewer
grade crossings than other Chicago lines, 75 percent of its trackage being free of such crossings.

(Most of the forty-four persons killed in the Chicago train wreck
mentioned in the preceding chapter were passengers on a Highliner rammed by an older, more conventional commuter train.
At first there was some suspicion that the Highliner's design and
light-metals construction might have been partly to blame for the
fatalities, but analysis did not bear this out significantly. The real
cause was human error, compounded by signal-system error. A
nonautomated Highliner had overshot a station and was backing
up when struck.)

How successful will ICG's new trains be? If C&NW's new bi-
levels are any indication, quite. When C&NW first added these
cars in 1968, the line began experiencing a 5-percent increase in
business per year. But C&NW is an unusual railroad. It is one of
the very few American rail commuter lines to show a profit in
recent years, and this has been due largely to aggressive efforts,
including a willingness to innovate. The railroad let commuters
buy monthly commutation tickets rather than tickets based on
distance, an idea new to Chicago. Not only that, it billed its commuters and gave them ten days to pay. More important, trains are
prompt, rides comfortable. Effective advertising has exploited the
auto commuter's plight in foul weather and traffic jams. Of course,
the line has had a hard time staying out of the red, and though
many cite C&NW as proof that commuter railroads can make a go
of it if they try, this line would be hard pressed to fight a subsidized rival.

Chicago is already considered by many to have the best mass
rail-transportation system in the country, and a major $277-mil-
lion, five-year transit-system capital-improvement program is
planned by the municipally owned Chicago Transit Authority

(CTA). Not all of that sum will be spent on rails; some will go to purchase 1,000 air-conditioned buses. In accordance with the Urban Mass Transit Act, CTA requested and has already received some $53.1 million from UMTA. Included in CTA's plans to bring about a "completely modern system in 1990" are the purchase of 100 new air-conditioned rapid-transit cars plus a large investment in track renewal, cab signals, maintenance facilities and station modernization. Also included are major outlays for improving passenger comfort, safety, and convenience.

Chicago is improving its transportation with the aid of a $900-million bond issue authorized by the legislature—which, in a pattern familiar throughout the country, earmarked most of the funds ($600 million) for highways. Airport development got $100 million, and though the remaining $200 million was for mass transportation, the CTA received a modest $19 million for rail-travel improvements.

The six privately owned railroads in the Chicago area have been urging the Illinois legislature to create a new local public-transportation super-agency which would operate and supervise passenger transportation, both bus and rail, in the six counties in and around Chicago. They argue that the single agency (they would call it the Chicago Metropolitan Area Transportation System) would be better able to coordinate transportation planning and operating within the area. Motivating these private railroads, they warn, is the fact that if CTA receives subsidies for the bus and rail lines it operates and the privately owned roads are not subsidized, the latter would be placed "in the intolerable position of facing publicly subsidized competition" where they compete directly with the services operated by the CTA—which would inevitably lead to a deterioration in their rail services.

In Baltimore, too, help for commuters is coming down the track. There a 28-mile rapid-transit rail network is projected, the first phase of an eventual 65-mile system. Baltimore looks to UMTA for two-thirds of the estimated cost of $656 million for the 28-mile phase. Its one-third share will be funded at the state level, since Baltimore's local transit authority was absorbed by the State Department of Transportation. (Maryland is one of a few states with their own Transportation Trust Funds.)

Atlanta, too, has improved commuter rail service coming, after a wrangle over ways and means. Voters in two of the four Georgia counties that make up the Atlanta area approved in 1971—by a narrow margin—a mass transit plan to finance a 1977 rapid-electric-rail and busway system by increasing local sales taxes 1 percent. The two smaller neighboring counties that rejected the plan will be without rail service at the start, but could join up later. (A 1968 transit plan that called for financing of such a program through a property tax had been rejected.)

The narrowness of the 1971 margin may be attributed partly to an emotional campaign in which the opponents of mass transit argued that it would give the downtown degenerates and other undesirables (Atlanta was having its share of urban crime at the time) a way to fan out cheaply and quickly to all suburban neighborhoods and do their thing—apparently forgetting that most enterprising degenerates nowadays have automobiles and motorcycles. Former Governor Lester G. Maddox saw something else in the woodpile: "This rapid-transit idea is a scheme to accelerate the residential integration of our fine suburbs," he said. Still others objected to any increase in taxes for any purpose.

Proponents countered that bus fares would drop from 40 cents to 15 cents as promised, and that the federal government had already pledged two-thirds support of the proposed system. What probably spoke loudest in its favor, though, was the recurring mammoth traffic jams Atlanta had been experiencing, plus parking problems, increased air pollution, and traffic accidents. City officials also were able to promise an economic boom if Atlanta could have rapid transit. Richard Rick of Rick's, Inc., a big department-store chain, was quoted in *The Wall Street Journal* as saying that Atlanta "will be a first-rate city or a second-rate city depending on how well she moves people. That is the key to her future."

Atlanta's new system will include some 50 miles of rail rapid-transit lines with forty stations and a coordinated busway system with 490 new air-conditioned buses, all under the Metropolitan Atlanta Rapid Transit Authority. As the system fans outward from the city, two-thirds of the rail lines will use existing rights-of-way. Nine miles will be subway; almost half will be elevated. Trains will run every ninety seconds during rush hours and will be able to run as high as 65 mph and average 40 mph. Cars will be air-conditioned, of course—an important plus in Georgia summers.

Here are brief notes, city by city, on other rail transit developments, before we zero in on New York.

St. Louis has long-range, detailed plans for a rail transit system. Originally Missouri Governor Warren E. Hernes said the state could not financially back such a plan, but in August 1971 he changed his mind and supported a $730-million transportation bond issue which called for the diversion of some gasoline-tax money to finance rail transit and would have established an important new principle. But heavy lobbying by highway and oil interests, and political stumbling by the plan's supporters, have so far prevented its coming to a vote, as of this writing.

If approved, the funds would allow seven rapid-transit lines to be built along with fifty-nine stations, plus a coordinated bus network. Not only the combined lines would connect points around St. Louis, but two of them would cross the Mississippi River into East St. Louis in Illinois. St. Louis is considering meeting some of the costs by using either a pay-as-you-go sales tax like Atlanta's or a special tax on property, income, gas, or motor-vehicle licenses.

In St. Paul–Minneapolis, the Twin Cities Area Metropolitan Transit Commission has announced that plans for a new transit system are under consideration to be operational in the early 1980s. By 1973 the commission will decide whether the transit system will be conventional rail or a fixed-guideway system—i.e., monorail or troughlike, as in TACV. Financing is expected to be considered during the 1975 legislative session.

So, at this writing, are the mass-transit plans for Pittsburgh formulated by Port Authority Transit (PAT) of Allegheny County. PAT would like to tear up Penn Central tracks and build two busways and an 11.5-mile elevated "Skybus" line for rubber-tired electrically propelled buses; but citizens' groups—prorail taxpayers' organizations, railway labor locals, and environmentalists —have protested the bus approach, urging instead the use of fast steel wheels on steel tracks. Most want a Lindenwold-type system. Nevertheless, UMTA, in September 1971, awarded $60 million to PAT to help fund the more expensive busway system and Skybus.

A clue to Pittsburgh's mass-transportation future may lie partly in the November 1971 election results. Then, one county commissioner who ran for reelection as an outspoken critic of Skybus received more votes than the two other elected candidates. However, that vote may have been more a reflection of resistance to taxes and opposition to change than of voter sentiment for rail transportation.

But all over America the tide is running in favor of rail transit, even though there are occasional setbacks. For example, in 1971 the New York State Legislature—with only one negative vote in the Senate and Assembly combined—authorized the Niagara Frontier Transit Authority in Buffalo to spend $86 million to build a "duo-rail" system. But the authorization hinged on voter approval of the 1971 New York transportation bond issue, which was defeated (more of that later in this chapter). The rest of the funds, more than $170 million, was to come from the federal government's UMTA.

Even though its financing is problematical at this writing, the Buffalo project is worth a look. Trains would start at the now empty Buffalo terminal of the old Delaware, Lackawanna & Western Railroad (now the Erie Lackawanna) and would go 12.5 miles to Amherst, New York, with stops at the south and north campuses of the ever-expanding State University of New York at Buffalo. At least 3.9 miles would be subway, 7.3 miles elevated, and only 1.3 miles on the surface. Also planned are a track to North Tonawanda (phase 2) and, even further into the future, a third line which would take a more northwesterly direction through the city.

Houston, Texas, is typical of fast-growing western and southwestern cities which have depended solely on automobiles and freeways to bring in commuters from their sprawling suburbs. Indeed, Houston is about the last city one might expect to be a candidate for mass rail transit. But congestion and pollution are great mind-changers, and in April 1970 Houston approved a $796,000 study of rapid transit, including—according to Public Service Director Thomas B. Tyson—a look at the most advanced rail transportation, since "there will be a need for rail mass transit as a major part of our system."

Motivating the 1970 study were the returns from a 1969 study which showed that present freeways, streets, and parking areas would be overstrained by 1975 and completely inadequate by 1990—even though one 6-mile stretch of highway is now nineteen lanes across! Houston's 2.2-million population is expected nearly to double by 1990.

Washington, D.C., can see the light at the end of the mass-transit tunnel but has had bad trouble reaching it. UMTA made a study in 1971 of commuter traffic in the District and recommended 95 miles of rail service extending—on already existing tracks—in three directions from downtown Union Station. One line would extend to Baltimore by way of Bowie, Maryland; another northwest to Gaithersburg, Maryland; a third south to Alexandria and Quantico, Virginia. The existing tracks are B&O, Penn Central, and the Richmond, Fredericksburg & Potomac. This new service would supplement as well as tie in—at Union Station—with the 98-mile Metro Subway System now being built. The Gaithersburg line would connect with the subway system again at Silver Spring, Maryland.

UMTA estimates that the 95-mile commuter system would cost about $15 million, but this would be reduced by about a third if refurbished rather than new equipment were used. The projected daily passengers would number 14,000.

Hardly anyone seriously questions the need for this system, but its realization is impeded by labor work rules, technical problems, safety-inspection requirements associated with running the trains to Union Station—and, not surprisingly, by a money problem: the study predicts a $300,000 annual operating deficit. *Passenger Train Journal,* however, points out that this loss should be measured against the $50-million-per-mile cost of building an urban expressway which would handle much less traffic. Washington's Metro Subway System, with 550 new cars and lines radiating from the heart of the city to seven suburbs, is scheduled to start partial operations on July 4, 1974, and be completed by 1980. It will have cost over $2 billion. (See Chapter VI.)

In Boston, the Massachusetts Bay Transportation Authority (MBTA) is sparking a local rail revival by converting former railroad lines to rapid transit. One such extension took place the first week in September 1971 when the South Shore Rapid Transit Extension, running from the heart of Boston for 6 miles to Quincy, was completed along the old New Haven Railroad track. In its first three weeks it reached a level of passenger usage that the estimates had said it would reach by the end of its first year. In the future this line will be extended another 6 miles to Weymouth. Other transit lines now extend from Boston on tracks of the old

Boston & Maine, the Boston & Albany, and another branch of the New Haven.

MBTA's success with transit service, according to *Railway Age* Magazine, was due in part to its providing more uninterrupted rides, provision of adequate parking at suburban stations, coordination of feeder bus lines, and generally better service. Noteworthy also is MBTA's use, on some lines, of continuous, or non–clickety-clack, welded rail on concrete ties and of modern controls such as cab signals, automatic train controls (ATC), and automatic train operation (ATO), all standard on Lindenwold and BART. Most advanced is the South Shore Extension, which is like Lindenwold and BART in having its operations centered in one place, in downtown Boston. Eventually the complete MBTA system will be centrally controlled.

MBTA has added seventy-six all-aluminum Pullman-Standard cars (cost $13 million), each propelled by four Westinghouse Tra-pak traction motors (100 hp each). These new cars have a maximum speed of 70 mph, three double doors per side, and a brushed aluminum finish said to be the first ever used on a transit car in the United States. (The country's first aluminum streetcar appeared December 2, 1926; it ran for the Cleveland Railway Company. But aluminum subway cars dated back to October 27, 1904, when the Interborough Rapid Transit Company of New York City introduced three hundred of them. The first subway run was in Boston, September 1, 1897.)

MBTA's cars are fluorescent-lighted and air-conditioned, with black vinyl seat covers, and are colorfully decorated for commuters who look up from their papers.

Of course, not all Yankees are on the rail bandwagon. According to *Passenger Train Journal,* Dr. Paul Cherington, a former DOT official and a trustee of the Boston & Maine Railroad, proposed in 1971 that the B&M abandon its commuter line between Boston and Gloucester and that it be replaced by a two-lane "reversible" highway—that is, going with the traffic flow. He would have restricted it to express buses, and to automobile drivers who had bought monthly passes at $120 each—an idea whose time seems to have come and gone.

Honolulu, harassed by increasingly sticky traffic jams, has already spent $1.4 million studying a proposed 18-mile subway/ elevated rail system. Detroit, Kansas City, Denver, Miami, and other cities are studying or planning new rapid-transit systems involving trains. (Miami's will be a 59-mile elevated system with fast rail cars on rubber-tired wheels.)

We would like to be able to report that Los Angeles, birthplace of the word "smog," was well on its way to having a smooth, clean, quiet rail system to unclot those freeways, but at this writing, although there is some planning under way, the most relevant word about the Los Angeles situation comes from an Australian, M. M. Summers, Secretary of the Commonwealth Department of Shipping and Transport, writing in the June 1971 issue of *Modern Railroads*:

> Overseas experience argues against building our [Australian] cities around motor transport. Thirty years ago Los Angeles virtually decided to seek a solution for city transport in the motor car. Its elaborate system of freeways is now complete and planners concede that a city cannot be built around the motor car.
>
> Nowhere is the search more desperate for a solution to the problem of rapid transit for commuters. Yet 30 years ago Los Angeles had some 1500 miles of railways serving the city and dormitory area. Today virtually none of this exists. Planners now say frankly that if they had the 1500 miles of railway today, the city would have one of the finest suburban commuter systems in the world.

And that clears the track for our consideration of the American city with the granddaddy of commuter problems: New York. One might expect New York to be farther advanced in rapid rail transit than any city in the country, if not the world, because of its enormous population, small size, and early adoption of rail transit. It hasn't worked out that way, though, and since World War II, New York transportation has limped along from one crisis to another, too busy reacting to do much foresighted acting or innovating.

Volumes could be, and have been, written about traffic and transit in and around New York. Our aim here is to offer a fast once-over, and we begin with one basic statistic: Each day between 4 and 5 million people (the population of New Hampshire is 740,000) commute from the suburbs to work in Manhattan, mainly in a small (8.6 square miles) central business district.

Only mass transportation—bus and rail—can move such great numbers into and within so small a space, and 79 percent of New York commuters depend on it. Rails—including regular trains and subways—carry about three-fourths of the passengers into and within the city.

Commuter trains and intracity rapid transit are closely related in any city, for after commuters enter by the former they have to be spread around by the latter. In New York a number of agencies get into the act. Within the city, the key one is the Metropolitan Transit Authority (MTA), a state agency created in 1968 by Governor Nelson Rockefeller and the Legislature to revitalize New York's deteriorating transportation facilities. Dr. William J. Ronan was appointed chairman, a position he holds at this writing.

This superagency was given control—a questionable word!—over: the nation's largest passenger railroad (in terms of passengers carried), the Long Island Rail Road, which the state bought from Penn Central in 1965; the 70-year-old New York City subway system, the world's largest; Staten Island Rapid Transit; Penn Central's Hudson and Harlem divisions (subject to court action not completed at this writing); Erie Lackawanna's commuter service in New York State; the New Haven Railroad (the states of New York and Connecticut took over that line from Penn Central in 1971 for $11 million and each state now operates the portion of it that runs within its boundaries); two airports (Republic and

Stewart); the Triborough Bridge and Tunnel Authority (includes the Triborough, Whitestone, Throgs Neck, Henry Hudson, Queens Midtown, and Verrazano-Narrows bridges, not to mention the Cross Bay Parkway, Marine Parkway, and Brooklyn–Battery Tunnel); Transportation Centers (air, rail, bus, interchanges); and a bus service that deploys 4,200 buses.

Each day MTA with its 56,000 employees moves more than 8 million riders (the combined population of Denmark and Ireland is 7.8 million), and, again according to MTA figures, it moves more than 2½ billion persons a year. Admittedly, these statistics are confusing. What they refer to is rides rather than riders. Fantastic numbers in any case.

If the transit situation in New York sometimes seems fouled up, try to picture it without an overall coordinating agency. MTA has brought more efficiency to its agencies and some relief to the individual commuter, most noticeably on the Long Island Rail Road (LIRR). In 1968, the MTA ordered 620 brand-new Budd Company passenger cars at a cost of $132 million, the largest single order ever placed for passenger cars. They were to replace the aged stock then fitfully rolling on the LIRR, known unaffectionately as "cattle cars."

A word about maintenance: A New York law says all maintenance costs, whether preventive or for repair, must be paid out of fares—which puts the MTA in a bind. On one side, politicians try to hold fares down; on the other, labor wants higher wages. Thus funds for maintenance are squeezed. An early-retirement plan for workers dealt the repair shops a blow from which they still have not recovered. So New York's trains and subways too often ride with faulty equipment, such as inoperative doors, malfunctioning switches, and wheels with a regrettable tendency to lock. This may compound the maintenance-cost problem by causing permanent damage to cars and tracks.

Those Budd cars, called "Metropolitans" and designated M-1, are now in use and are in pretty dramatic contrast to the sooty, green-brown MU (multiple-unit) cars they replaced. They are larger, are of stainless steel construction, and have a wide blue band streaming the length below the windows. The sculptured ends of the cars add to their speedy look.

Each M-1 Metropolitan is powered by four 150-hp GE electric motors in paired car-units that run over a third rail at speeds of up to 100 mph. Most of the latest operating equipment is aboard: an automatic train-control system (the automatic train control maintains uniform speed levels but does not include automatic operation at station stops the way the ATO system of BART and Lindenwold does); a seven-aspect cab signaling system; a combination of dynamic and wheel-tread air brakes; a variable train radio and PA system (can notify people at the station as well as aboard when a train is late), and a wheel-slip-detection system.

Railroad critic William D. Middleton, writing in *Trains* (January '71), said the "M-1 car design . . . represents what must be regarded as the most advanced commuter car ever built." One assumes he meant to exclude the cars of BART and Lindenwold, regarding them as rapid-transit rather than commuter trains.

Inside, the cars are good-looking and comfortable, with contoured seats in a 3-2 arrangement, diffused fluorescent lighting, tinted double safety-glass windows. thermostatic heating-cooling, chemical toilets, and adequate luggage racks. Of each two-car pair, one is designed as a smoker, the other a nonsmoker—the floors of the former being rubber-tiled; of the latter, carpeted. There are no vestibules, and the two sliding double doors per side are located at the quarter points of each car.

The Metropolitans were put into service so fast that for a time they—and their passengers—were plagued by equipment failures, causing overcrowding and schedule delays. A wildcat strike in late 1968 didn't help, nor did a slowdown that extended into mid-1969. But finally, by the fall of 1970, enough new cars had been added and equipment problems had been ironed out, and on-time performance approached 95 percent. By mid-1972 a total of 770

Metropolitans had been delivered. It went to show what could be done to bring rail travel into the twentieth century.

Poor labor relations, largely inherited from the past including rigid and irrational work rules, continue to haunt the LIRR. MTA has to contend with so many agreements with so many unions that negotiation seems almost continuous. Innovations such as automated ticketing are too sensitive an issue even to be discussed. Still, the improvement is exhilarating. Track and roadbed are being modified to handle 100-mph speeds, grade crossings are being eliminated, high-level platforms are being constructed (so passengers can step out without stepping down), electrification is being extended out into Suffolk County, and the control equipment is constantly being refined.

Looking farther down the track, the LIRR is considering going from its present Flatbush Avenue Terminal in Brooklyn right into lower Manhattan, so that a Long Island stockbroker can go to Wall Street without changing to a subway. This would require a costly new tunnel under the East River. Also on MTA's long-range agenda: a direct underground link between Penn Station and Grand Central.

Meanwhile, upriver, another East River tunnel nears completion at 63rd Street. This one will serve LIRR passengers and will also relieve pressure on existing subway lines, as it will carry both subway and train tracks—two above and two below in a two-story arrangement.

The LIRR tracks are not electrified to their outermost points, which means a rider must change trains going to and from those points, but electrification is being extended about seven miles eastward from Hicksville to Pinelawn and another four miles from Huntington to Northport. Further electrification is not contemplated because of enormous costs and a recurring power shortage in the New York area.

But the MTA has in mind a new combination gas-turbine/ electric car which, upon reaching the nonelectric portion of the

line, would—forgive the expression—take down its pantograph
and cut in its gas-turbines for the remaining two-thirds of the
trip, giving patrons a fast ride clear to Montauk, on the Island's
southeastern tip, or to Greenport, near Orient Point, on the north-
eastern tip, without the present need to change trains en route.

Testing of gas-turbine/electric cars goes back to 1966, when a
Budd GT-1 Turboliner logged nearly 18,000 miles. During a second phase, a rebuilt Turboliner, the GT-2, was tested to improve
electromechanical operations and increase fuel economy. At this
writing, extensive tests are being conducted on a GT-4. Results
indicate the gas-turbine/electric engine should be zipping passengers from Manhattan to Montauk before the end of the '70s.

We cannot say goodbye to the LIRR without mentioning one
new wrinkle which, though perhaps not consequential in itself,
dramatizes the potential advantages of rail over automobile commuting. At this writing, commuters on the LIRR's Port Jefferson
Line may take graduate courses leading to the Master's degree in
Business Administration (M.B.A.) during the seventy-six-minute
trip from Huntington Station to New York City. The courses are
offered by Adelphi University in a special converted parlor car the
university calls a "commuting classroom." The professors, commuters themselves, are from New York University. They sit in
swivel chairs and have voice amplifiers for lecturing, blackboards,
and an audiovisual system. Students can choose from among
courses offered on various days and on morning or evening runs.
The average time to earn the degree is two years. The Central
Railroad of New Jersey followed suit on its 6:30 A.M. Bay Head–
Newark run, whereon passengers were offered courses by the New
York University School of Continuing Education in such subjects
as Managerial Writing, Reading Improvement, Psychology, and
Investment. (The first recorded classroom-on-rails was begun in
July 1926 when Princeton University geologists inaugurated a
Summer School of Geology and Natural Resources of North Amer-
ica aboard a Pennsylvania-built Pullman, "The Princeton," a car

equipped with kitchen, a stateroom and office for two instructors, wash and toilet facilities, a shower bath, a library, a lecture section, and a regular Pullman section for twenty students. The idea was to take students across the United States and parts of Canada and let them learn about these countries' resources firsthand and also through instruction. The course was open to any student, American or foreign, who had taken at least one course in geology. It ended in 1934.)

What has MTA done for commuters on lines other than the LIRR? Well, 80 new General Electric high-speed self-propelled coaches went into service in 1971 on the Hudson and Harlem lines, along with a modernization program that included sprucing up stations and upgrading electrification and signaling systems. (Because of the pending court action mentioned earlier, 48 additional new cars sit idle in Queens awaiting the outcome.) The new GE cars are very similar to those on the LIRR, Budd being GE's subcontractor.

MTA began improving the Staten Island Rapid Transit system shortly after purchasing it from the B&O, but ran into so much vandalism (about seventy separate acts per month) that improvements were largely offset. Stations were defaced, cars not only damaged but sometimes made inoperative, and in some cases shopping carts and other objects were thrown onto the tracks. The result was more train delays, and more passengers' having to stand up because of fewer cars in service. But more frequent spot checks by local police, and more cooperation by schools and civic groups, were encouraged to counter the vandalism, and MTA was considering the use of frequent helicopter patrols, which had been effective in combating vandals on LIRR and Penn Central routes. Fear of vandals and more dangerous hoodlums undoubtedly deters some commuters from using mass transit in certain areas, and this is a hard problem for both the railroads and law-enforcement agencies.

On the New Haven line, MTA in mid-1971 started adding new GE cars—144 of them eventually—of a type called "The Cosmopolitan," at a cost of $59 million. These had to be specially designed to meet a rather peculiar requirement. On one part of the line, electric power comes from a third rail, while along another it comes from an overhead line, or catenary. So, though the cars do not differ noticeably from other new GE cars, they do have that two-way access to power. They have been criticized as uncomfortably cramped, and as unsafe because of inadequate provision for opening doors in an emergency.

Even a cursory look at New York City's commuter rail service would be incomplete without a glance at the Port Authority of New York and New Jersey—formerly the Port of New York Authority—hereinafter referred to as PA. It was founded in 1921 as a two-state body to "coordinate and develop terminal, transportation and other facilities of commerce" in and around the Port of New York. It has trade offices all over the world and a lobbying office in Washington.

Perhaps best known and least loved for its midtown Manhattan PA Bus Terminal, the agency has more impressive accomplishments to its credit and what some would call its discredit.

PA built the George Washington Bridge, Kennedy Airport, and most recently the controversial twin-towered, 110-story Manhattan office building known as the World Trade Center. Now in the planning stages: a new steamship passenger terminal in Manhattan, some airport additions, rapid rail access from Manhattan to Kennedy and Newark airports, and a modernization program for that Bus Terminal. But PA gets into our story because its subsidiary the Port Authority Trans-Hudson (PATH) Corporation has been moving people back and forth from New Jersey to Manhattan by rail, around the clock, since it was set up in 1962 to take over the bankrupt 54-year-old Hudson & Manhattan Railroad.

Over 70 percent of all passengers entering New York City from New Jersey by rail are carried by PATH trains. Each day the facility handles approximately 145,000 passengers along a 13.9-mile route, and to do this it has a fleet of modern rail cars including 1971–72 electric cars manufactured by Hawker Siddeley Canada. These lightweight aluminum cars have air conditioning, two double doors per side, two-way communication, and a public-address system.

Before going on to PA's perhaps more significant recent activities, we take the reader to the new PATH terminal under the World Trade Center on lower Manhattan's West Side, where train passengers transfer almost painlessly to subways and buses. Opened in 1971 to replace the 62-year-old (and looking every day of it) Hudson Terminal, it is America's first air-conditioned subway station and copes with about 85,000 riders a day, a number expected to reach 100,000 by 1975. (Some PATH riders go to the 33rd Street station.)

Another unusual feature of the terminal, bound to appeal to nerve-frazzled commuters, is its relative quiet. Great effort was made to lessen train vibrations by mounting rails and ties on neoprene pads. Sound-absorbing materials were applied to the undersides, walls, and ceilings of platforms. Entering trains have their wheels automatically sprayed with water and oil from nozzles to eliminate high-frequency squeal. "As part of our anti-noise-pollution effort we have tried to do everything possible to give commuters a safe and quiet ride," said Richard Schulman, PATH's project engineer.

The terminal is brightly lighted, in marked contrast to its predecessor's cavernous gloom. It has high-speed escalators, marble columns and terrazzo floors, tiled walls, and bill and coin change-making machines throughout. There are restaurants, snack bars, gift shops, clean (the day we were there, anyway) rest rooms, lockers, first-aid services, and—unfortunately necessary—police services. Closed-circuit television monitoring is used for both station security and passenger protection, as well as for public information. Like those of Lindenwold, the PATH terminal officials can view a caller on a one-way TV screen.

PATH is involved in another major construction program: the large, coordinated rail-bus Transportation Center at Journal Square in Jersey City, due to be completed in late 1973. It will have facilities for a PATH Operations Control Center and parking for six hundred autos.

Not everyone loves PA. New Jersey's then Governor William T. Cahill in 1971 criticized it for neglecting his state's transportation problems, saying it should do more about commuter rail systems and such projects as the New York–Newark Airport rail link. Others on both sides of the Hudson—though Governor Rockefeller was not one of them—urged putting more of PA's soaring surpluses into rail service instead of getting sidetracked into such things as building the ostentatious World Trade Center. Cahill said of PA's recently retired executive director, Austin J. Tobin, "He is running the PA as a business and it is not a business."

Tobin, reputed to be autocratic as an administrator, observed that PA is an organization without "recourse to taxation"—is a business—and for this reason could let funds go only to self-supporting projects such as the George Washington Bridge. He further maintained that mass transportation could never be a profitable venture. (The take-over of the Hudson & Manhattan was an exception, and according to a recent covenant, PA will in the future be barred from taking over deficit operations.)

But Cahill's attack and other pressures finally produced results: Tobin agreed to initiate studies on the possibility of building another rail tunnel under the Hudson for New Jersey commuter trains, installing a number of transportation systems, and buying Penn Station in Newark. It probably also influenced PA's decision to build two rapid rail airport-access lines. Meanwhile, the indefatigable Theodore W. Kheel has filed suit to force PA to undertake mass-transit projects, and New Jersey is exploring other ways to get PA to move much further in that direction. It was Tobin's idea that more UMTA funds should go to mass-transportation projects in New Jersey.

Tobin stepped down as PA's executive director and was temporarily succeeded by Matthias E. Lukens, and MTA's Dr. Ronan came in as vice-chairman, developments certain to put PA more solidly back of rail transit improvement. Meanwhile, both New York and New Jersey legislatures have approved, and the two governors have signed, legislation authorizing PA to undertake a $650 million mass transportation program including construction of important rail facilities including those airport-access lines mentioned earlier and described later.

The relationship between New York City and New Jersey is a complex one, and the New Jersey Department of Transportation is a third organization that moves people into New York by rail, though it does so indirectly by owning the cars that are operated and maintained by two private lines, Penn Central and Erie Lackawanna (EL), on their runs between the city and northern New Jersey. Between 1967 and 1970 the state bought 35 modern cars from the St. Louis Car Division of General Steel Industries, and these, called "Jersey Arrows," run under Penn Central's banner.

The state also owns 105 fancy aluminum Pullman-Standard cars and 23 GE locomotives built in 1970 and 1971 and run by EL. These cars operate by push-pull diesels at 75-mph speeds and are convertible to 100-mph electric MU (multiple-unit) operation should the push-pull operation ever be abandoned.

At this writing the New Jersey DOT plans to purchase cars for the bankrupt Central Railroad of New Jersey and for the New York and Long Branch Line (a line running along the New Jersey coast south to Bay Head, New Jersey).

Not to paint a rosier picture than the facts warrant, we note that New Jersey is still highway-minded. Of a $640-million transportation bond issue approved by voters in 1968, only $200 million was allocated for mass transportation, and of this amount not all went to improving rail service, though the state did take out $26.1 million of it to pay for the EL cars ($18.5 million) and engines ($7.6 million) mentioned above. By mid-1972 funds allocated for mass transit had not been spent, although they had been earmarked for various projects. The financial difficulties of Penn Central and the Central Railroad of New Jersey were more to blame than a lack of interest on the part of the state. Nevertheless, some critics charged that the money could have been put into some imaginative rail scheme.

In 1971 the New Jersey Citizens Highway Committee did a survey of New Jersey Legislature candidates, and of the 130 who responded, almost every one expressed dissatisfaction with the amount the state was appropriating for transportation and favored larger outlays for highways. A clear majority favored applying highway-user taxes to highway construction, despite the state's Clean Air Council's warning that New Jersey was sitting on an "air pollution bomb" because of receiving 3,260 tons of automobile-emitted pollutants each year. At the last reading, New Jersey, the nation's most urbanized state, averaged 400 vehicles per square mile (the nation's highest), and its crowded Hudson County had 3,961 vehicles per square mile.

In November 1972 New Jersey voters turned down a $650-million transportation bond issue which environmentalists had opposed on the ground that too much of the money was earmarked for highways and too little for mass transit, including rails. The year before, New Yorkers voted down a $2.5-billion transportation bond issue which had been opposed for the same reason. The word seemed to be getting around.

––––––––––

Before we leave the commuter, a word about two significant links that are developing between rail commutation and aviation.

First, as noted earlier, and as we will explain more fully in a moment, rail lines are being built or planned to connect several inner cities with their remote airports: and second, the aerospace industry is getting into the building of new high-speed rail cars, principally for commuter lines. They can use the profits, because the industry, from Boeing to Lockheed, is depressed. It is a heartening development for the railroad passenger, because the competition with existing rail-car builders should result in better cars.

Not only did United Aircraft build the Turbos: the Rohr Corporation built the BART cars, and Hawker Siddeley Canada, which built the new PATH cars, is a direct descendant of Hawker Aircraft. The Vertol Division of Boeing has been awarded a $10.5-million DOT contract to investigate, test, and evaluate new concepts in rapid-transit car design. Grumman Aerospace is constructing the tracked air-cushion research vehicle (TACRV—described in Chapter IX), while Vought Aeronautics has done a number of studies for DOT. Also, Vought bid on Washington's Metro and Boeing on the Southeastern Pennsylvania Transportation Authority's new electric cars. General Electric, though not an aerospace company, is an impressive Johnny-come-lately into the field of rail-car building.

"Make no mistake—this is an invasion," wrote Joe Asher, whom we quoted earlier, in Railway Age, adding that the "old-line builders are squirming as they watch aerospace companies" take more of their "tiny market." Asher quotes many different suppliers and users, and their attitudes range from anger and alarm to "Why worry?" Robert T. Pollock, general manager and chief executive officer of the Cleveland Transit System, said "a fresh look from outside would be good," and Michael Cafferty, chairman of the Chicago Transit Authority, said the "old-line car-builders will respond to the challenge."

Asher's view is that the established suppliers should realize that they do not have the market "by divine right"—a view shared by General Steel Industries' chairman Ashley Gray: "There are definitely things we can learn from aerospace people, and they can learn from us."

There are indeed in the rail-car-building field a number of technological problems that aerospace engineers may be able to solve. For example, trains cannot at present be stopped precisely at a predetermined spot in the station. Since car doors and station doors thus cannot be matched up, the rider cannot step into an enclosed station area. It is as if an automatic elevator could not be made to align exactly with each floor. Lindenwold, with ATO, consistently makes station stops within a few feet of a given location, while BART, also using ATO, can stop exactly on target— but only *if* the weather happens to be ideal. Should the tracks be slightly wet, the computer is unable to take this into consideration.

Naturally, not everyone welcomes aircraft builders into this new-to-them field. Pullman-Standard Company executive James Pontius has complained in *U.S. News and World Report* that DOT is "looking to the aerospace companies for answers we already have." In *Passenger Train Journal* another Pullman executive, G. L. Green, has expressed chagrin at the government's award of that $10.5-million contract to the Vertol Division of Boeing, because the "old-liners" themselves are a depressed industry: "I find it difficult to understand why Boeing Company as a hardware manufacturer should be subsidized to the extent of millions of dollars for something which many companies, including Pullman-Standard, are able and willing to do as part of any production contract."

If Boeing has received what seems like a lot of government money, that has been partly a response to public opinion. After the stunning defeat of Boeing's SST and the resultant layoffs of personnel, there was a widespread feeling that the aerospace industry ought to diversify by getting into faster, more efficient mass rail transportation. (Incidentally, Seattle, home of Boeing and the SST, twice has defeated transit bond issues.) The reasoning was that this would benefit far more people than the SST at less cost to the environment, yet would require the kind of technological know-how that the aircraft industry could supply. *The New York Times* editorialized:

"The conversion of aerospace industries and the retraining of engineers and other personnel may not be easy; indeed, it would probably be prohibitive without government subsidy."

———————————

Now about rail transportation as an adjunct to air travel. Many major U.S. cities are either studying, planning, or constructing various types of high-speed rail transit systems to get more people —travelers, visitors, and employees—to and from airports more quickly. And rail travel in general will surely benefit in indirect ways, principally because technical breakthroughs are certain to occur and in time can be applied to intercity and intracity trains. Also, it will expose many persons—particularly the young—to travel by rail for the first time. This, if the trains are as good as they ought to be, could convert them to rail travel in general.

A quick rundown of some city-to-airport rail plans:

Philadelphia. An airport-redevelopment plan was unveiled in June 1971 to link, by high-speed rail, the 30th Street Station (the main-line station serving the *Metroliner*) with the Philadelphia International Airport, 6 miles away. Such a line would feed into the city's subway system as well as the suburban rail network. At the airport a people-moving system will tie in with the trains.

Baltimore-Washington. A study by Gibbs & Hill, Inc., of New York, sponsored by DOT ($92,874), shows that car trips to Friendship International Airport by 1985 will be increased by a factor of 6 (to 77 million auto trips) and that it is imperative that a high-speed electric rail system be built to the airport from Union Station in Washington and Camden Station in Baltimore.

New York. The Port Authority of New York and New Jersey, as we mentioned earlier, plans to finance and construct high-speed rail access from downtown Manhattan to Kennedy International

Airport and to Newark Airport. The two projects will cost upwards of $410 million. Passengers who now go to Kennedy from downtown Manhattan via taxis and limousines in 75 minutes, depending on traffic, will be able to make the trip (from Penn Station) in about 16 minutes in comfortable "Metropolitans"— with wider seats, since the cars will have 2–2 seating instead of 3–2. Initially, trains will leave Penn Station at the rate of four per hour. The authority is coordinating the project with MTA, since part of the route to Kennedy will be over LIRR rights-of-way. It is predicted that by 1981 more than 43 million passengers will travel annually to Kennedy: in 1971, there were over 19 million. (Again to shade the rosy picture: One transportation expert at a 1971 Princeton University transportation seminar on rail access to JFK Airport hit the ceiling when he learned that the rail system in 1981 would cut down rubber-tire entrance to the airport by only 25 percent. He thought it "lunacy" to build, as is planned, elaborate roadways around the terminal and four-tier parking facilities for automobiles. He favored banning all but a few automobiles and, if necessary, expanding the rail service instead.)

If a fourth jetport is built 50 miles north of the city, as now planned, at the Stewart Air Force Base near Newburgh, New York, MTA will provide rail links using an EL line.

Chicago. DOT-sponsored studies have shown that rail service should be provided from the city 19 miles out to O'Hare Airport to accommodate the 30 million a year air travelers. It now takes sixty minutes by auto, would take less than half that by rail. If such a rail line were built, it would be by the Chicago Transit Authority. Should Chicago decide to build a large third airport to the south of the city, it would probably have a high-speed rail link with the city. Illinois Central Gulf has completed a feasibility study showing that it is within that line's capability.

Los Angeles. Here, a 150-mph tracked air-cushion vehicle (TACV: see Chapter IX for description) had been planned to start carrying air travelers from the San Fernando Valley area of

Los Angeles to Los Angeles International Airport in late 1972 or early 1973. However, not only is this *not* out of the planning stage, but its future is highly uncertain. The new railroad age is going to come hard to Los Angeles.

Dallas. LTV Aerospace Corporation is building a $31-million electric-guideway rail system that will carry passengers along a 12-mile route around the enormous Dallas–Fort Worth airport, and is promoting the addition of a guideway system between the airport and downtown Dallas.

Cleveland. The Transit System's airport line, already in operation, has been successful despite pessimistic predictions. It cuts the forty-minute auto trip in half. Travelers ride comfortably in 1968 to 1970 vintage Pullman-Standard cars in trains of up to four cars.

San Francisco. Studies are now being completed to extend BART 15 miles from the city to International Airport, cutting travel time to less than half.

Washington, D.C. One high-speed airport rail proposal received a temporary setback when Congress shelved the plan to build a 25-mile TACV line from downtown Washington to Dulles Airport. The line was schedule to be completed for the opening in 1972 of the U.S. International Transportation Exposition. One reason for its defeat was that Congress wanted further evaluation's of TACV's possible advantages over other rail systems.

There seems no doubt that in time a rail connection will be made. The present National Airport is overcrowded, it is a constant source of noise to Washington residents, and its airspace is overcongested. Dulles, on the other hand, is far enough away from Washington and has relatively little traffic.

––––––––––

And so something *is* being done to put more commuters back on the rails where they belong; not enough, and not fast enough, but something. Is there reason to be optimistic about the future?

Carlos C. Villarreal, administrator of UMTA, sounded so when he was quoted in *Modern Railroads* in April 1971: "I am convinced that commuters will leave their autos at a parking lot on the outskirts of the city or leave them at home if public transport can be made sufficiently attractive—and by attractive I mean the systems should be comfortable to ride. . . . They should have reliability, dependability and sufficient frequency . . ." He conceded it would be an enormous job to get people off the highways and into mass transit while our auto-production rate was outstripping our birthrate, and thought it might take five years to accomplish the turnaround.

But despite Villarreal's insight and his own splendid efforts, all-out commitment by the federal government is still lacking. Herbert J. Holloman, provost of Massachusetts Institute of Technology, is one who deplores the relatively minuscule amounts being spent on urban transportation and the low priority it is given: "A problem of this sort needs the kind of intellectual-educational support that a major social and urban problem affecting the whole of the fabric of society requires . . ."

This is not to say that the sum of $10 billion allocated for twelve years (1970–1982) is not an impressive amount, particularly when compared with past amounts. But it is inadequate even by UMTA's own estimate, for it placed the need at around $30 billion for a ten-year period. (Part of UMTA's desire for more funds is tied up with its estimate that 4,000 transit cars will be needed around the country during a three-and-a-half-year period ending around January 1975. At the time of the estimate—September 1971—1,200 of the cars were on order.)

On the other side—the receiving side—the American Transit Authority (ATA), representing companies that carry 85 percent of the nation's mass-transit riders, not surprisingly would like to see still greater disbursements made. While some local transit authorities have been lucky enough to receive some capital funds, all seem to be in agreement that there is very little funding available anywhere for operations, including maintenance. So it was no wonder that transit officials were furious when the Nixon Administration—while paying some lip service to mass transit (Vice President Agnew said, "We cannot eliminate the motor vehicle, but we can reduce the dependence on it by enhancing the attractiveness of other forms of transportation")—held back from that program $200 million from the $600 million obligated for fiscal 1971, the first year of the new mass-transit programs. Thirty-seven Senators, led by New Jersey's Clifford P. Case and Harrison A. Williams, wrote a joint letter to the President urging him to free all the funds. They wrote of the need for mass transit and declared that "without adequate support from the Federal Government it surely will fail in the vital job which only it can perform." Although it was predicted that as much as $1 billion—the amount requested by President Nixon's budget—would be spent during fiscal 1973, a sum equal to what was spent between 1965 and 1970 for transit projects, the ATA said this would not be enough. It estimated the need at more than two and a half times that amount.

But insufficient federal spending is not the only cause of the relatively low state of mass rail transportation. There still is no adequate, well-directed, well-coordinated effort by the rail industry or the government to persuade the public to go by train. More market research also would be valuable. This was emphasized by Science News writer Richard H. Gilluly, who said, "There have been few behavioral studies of the reasons people choose one form of transportation over another." There is now evidence that this is about to be remedied somewhat through UMTA research grants.

Meanwhile, on the state level, officials continue to allow highway habits to dominate their thinking, as is evidenced by many of the transportation bond issues, some of which, as we have already seen, are heavily stacked in favor of highway interests. Another indication of state attitudes can be found in a look at their transportation budgets. Virginia, for example, outlined its capital spending needs for transportation systems between 1974 and 1990. There, for every dollar spent on mass transportation, $26 would be spent on highways—and 10 cents on intercity railroads. "And this is a state," to quote *The Washington Post*, "in which more than 50 per cent of the citizens already live in three major urban areas—Washington, Richmond, and Norfolk–Newport News."

All in all, the situation over the country suggests that the friends of railroad passenger service need to step up the pressure.

"For hundreds of chronically frustrated Penn Central commuters it was a heady though harrowing experience: braving rain and snow, they piled out of a stalled local near Pelham the other morning, slogged a half-mile down the tracks through mud to the Mount Vernon station, watched three express trains whisk by, and finally leaped back onto the tracks en masse to stop and commandeer a fourth express which grudgingly deposited them at Grand Central 71 minutes late."
—*New York Times* editorial, October 24, 1972

"It was worse than usual, the Penn Central commuter recalled—the three-car train was broiling on that afternoon last August; it was crowded; neither water nor toilet facilities were available. So Manhattan editor Milton Machlin refused to pay the $3.55 fare to Dover Plains. 'I suddenly thought,' he said, 'that if you shipped animals under these conditions, you would unquestionably be arrested.' Actually, it was the recalcitrant Mr. Machlin who was arrested. Last week, a jury acquitted him of the 'theft of service' charge. A key question Mr. Machlin's attorney had asked the jury: 'The railroad failed to perform its part of the bargain, and what right does it have to prosecute a passenger who refuses to perform his half?'"
—*The New York Times*, November 19, 1972

Frightening Facts and Figures
about Automobiles and Airplanes

AUTOMOBILES

BEST ESTIMATES are that automobiles generate from 50 to 60 percent of the hydrocarbons, slightly over 40 percent of the nitrogen oxides, and about 80 percent of the carbon monoxide in our polluted air—though of course it varies somewhat from time to time and place to place. (Tiny amounts of dangerous asbestos fibers are released into the air when brakes are applied to a car, as are tiny rubber particles abraded from tires.)

Tetraethyl lead, a common gasoline additive which in its exhaust form has extremely toxic effects on the human body, has contributed to an increase in the lead content of the air of our cities of about 5 percent per year. It is estimated that roughly 225,000 tons of lead are spewed into the U.S. air every year from the tail pipes of automobiles, trucks, and buses. Dr. Henry A. Schroder of the Trace Elements Laboratory at Dartmouth College was quoted in the December 1971 issue of *Natural History* as saying that his group had "found enough lead in vegetation growing beside a secondary highway (up to 200 parts per million) to abort a cow subsisting on this vegetation. The concentration has trebled in six years." It is, therefore, not surprising that John R. Goldsmith, head of epidemiology for the California Department of Public Health, found blood lead levels in persons near a freeway to be much higher than those of persons living a mile away. Automobile engines will inevitably be weaned away from leaded gasolines, but the process will be complicated and costly, and we can therefore expect considerable foot-dragging.

———————

A U.S. Forest Service study found that millions of trees die annually from smog (mostly in the greater Los Angeles area and in the East, particularly along turnpike rights-of-way), and we are now losing millions of dollars annually from pollution-caused crop damage, particularly in Southern California and in the Northeast. Air pollution also eats away at nonliving matter—rubber, steel, and stone. Some of the buildings and statues it damages are historic and irreplaceable, and for others, repair and cleaning costs run into billions of dollars a year. This situation is further compounded by the recent discovery by scientists that air pollution causes rainwater acidity; this contaminates land, water, and man-made structures.

———————

That air pollution affects local weather patterns was made clear by studies showing a dramatic increase in rainfall over La Porte, Indiana, downwind from the smoky Chicago area. The long-term effect of air pollution on the earth's atmosphere is being studied, and though not all the facts are in, the theories so far are pessimistic.

At the end of 1971, the National Wildlife Federation ranked air pollution—most of it caused by the automobile—as still our number one environmental problem. Deaths attributed to lung cancer, emphysema, bronchitis, and other respiratory diseases show a steady increase.

Stringent auto pollutant-emission standards for the United States have been set, with a 1975 deadline, but auto manufacturers complain that it will be extremely difficult, if not impossible, to meet them, particularly for the levels of nitrogen oxides. One such complaint came from Edward N. Cole, president of GM, when in early 1972 he said the auto industry would lick the problem in a decade but not by 1975–76. (In mid-1973 the deadline was put off till 1976.)

In response to the claim that the 1975 requirements will eliminate 90 percent of our auto-caused air pollution, the February 1972 issue of *Environment* Magazine said, "Not so. There will still be many pre-1975 cars on the road; the number of cars and miles traveled per vehicle and the concentration of cars in cities and their environs are expected to continue rising; and the efficiency of the control devices is expected to deteriorate with age."

In that connection, a number of 1971 and 1972 model cars, all fitted with exhaust pollution controls, were tested in late 1971 by New York City's Department of Air Resources. Of the 372 vehicles tested, 60 percent emitted excessive carbon monoxide in spite of their exhaust controls. This was seen by the department as a step backward, because these new cars proved worse than older models with no exhaust controls.

Auto production, says *Fortune,* is confidently expected by Detroit to double by 1980. The AAA, the article went on, expects the number of automobiles on the road to reach 178 million by 1985. In 1970 there were 108 million.

Rock salt containing sodium and calcium chloride is spread on thousands of American roads in the winter by state or local road maintainers—about 6 million tons of it in 1970, an increase of 1,800 percent since 1940. The Massachusetts Department of Public Works alone spread 200,000 tons of salt, plus 61,000 tons of calcium chloride and 150,000 tons of sand, in that year. The salt seeps into underground water tables and runs into waterways, killing fish and wildlife, ruining private wells, and sometimes closing town water supplies. Roadside trees that might be strong enough to withstand auto exhausts slowly die of salt spray splashed into the air. Maples along residential streets are particularly susceptible. Their autumn leaves turn red prematurely as a sign of sickness.

There is evidence that some of the 217,000 U.S. gasoline stations dump waste oil into sewers via station drains, placing an added burden on water-treatment plants. An article in the January 1972 *Environmental Science and Technology* estimated that 500 million gallons of such waste annually goes into sewers, vacant lots, or the nearest waterway. So far, tax advantages to oil companies using virgin oil make recycling of reclaimed oil impractical.

The United States has one mile of road for each square mile of land, and 80 percent of the road surface is paved. U.S. highways, excluding parking lots, equal in land area the combined states of Connecticut, Delaware, Massachusetts, New Hampshire, Rhode Island, and Vermont.

For the last twenty years, we have built an average of 75,000 miles of new roads each year.

Parking lots now take up vast amounts of the land of our cities and it is not uncommon for cities to devote from 50 to 70 percent of their downtown land areas to the car or its supporting facilities.

Every mile of four-lane freeway takes 24 acres of land, and every interchange on such a freeway takes 80 acres.

A one-day census taken throughout the country in 1967 revealed that 1.3 million animals—from squirrels and rabbits to dogs and deer—were killed by automobiles on that day alone, 90 percent of them "wildlife species."

During a period of a little more than one year, according to a federal report, more than 27,000 dwellings were razed to make way for federally aided highway projects Close to 80,000 individuals lived in those dwellings, and it cost the taxpayer over $18 million to relocate them. Some sociologists claim that city expressways are a major cause of ghetto unrest because of the bitterness caused by loss of jobs, displacement of homes, and destruction of communities.

An article in the October 10, 1972, issue of *World* Magazine said Californians are moving to Australia in considerable numbers; one reason given is that highway construction has been uprooting 3,000 California families per year in recent years.

Some 183,000 miles of highways have been built in our national parks and forests, not to mention acres of parking lots, gas stations, and paved camping grounds to accommodate the new breed of camper in his motorized van or "home on wheels." The Council on Environmental Quality had this to say about highways built through our national parks:

Unlimited access to wilderness areas may transform such areas into simply another extension of our urban, industrialized civilization. The unending summer flow of automobiles into Yosemite National has changed one of nature's great wilderness areas into a crowded gathering place of lessened value to its visitors.

Auto congestion has become so bad in Yosemite National Park that cars are banned from some areas, and the Council on Environmental Quality has said:

Some of the more popular natural areas in our parklands have become clogged with traffic, noise, litter, smog, and most of the other elements of our technological society from which the visitors are trying to escape.

The Conservation Foundation says that locustlike masses of humanity descend on national parks partly because overpaving and a lack of green parks have made "back home" so unpleasant and boring. (Critic Lewis Mumford describes what too often happens when the motorist tries to find nature: "When he reaches his destination in a distant suburb, he finds that the countryside he sought has disappeared; beyond him, thanks to the motorway, lies only another suburb, just as dull as his own.")

Pavement turns marvelous life-giving soil into a dead surface. While the human population soars, needed resources are depleted by the cutting down of oxygen-producing plants (crops, orchards, and forests) in a highway's path and by the covering of vital food-producing soil. It takes five hundred years to create an inch of good topsoil, but only a few hours for it to be bulldozed and asphalted.

History records that many countries, notably in the Middle East, have declined because of land abuse. "Crops can be replanted. Stocks can reproduce. So can human beings. But the land is not like these. Once it is taken away, it is gone forever," said an elder Navajo councilman in 1967 at a tribal council.

There is a direct relationship between floods and the substitution of paving for trees and vegetation. Paving reduces the earth's "sponge" effect, not only adding to flood danger but reducing our water table at a time when the demand for water is increasing annually.

Although camping vehicles are soaring in number, there were 52,000 motels scattered along the nation's highways in 1972, and new Holiday Inns during one period were opening at the rate of one every seventy-two hours.

According to former Transportation Secretary John A. Volpe, "Every time the Census Bureau's clock ticks off a net gain of one in the population of the U.S., there are two motor vehicles added to the nation's roads." On another speech-making occasion, Volpe looked at his watch and said, "It's now 11:20 A.M. By this time tomorrow 160 people will have been killed in the U.S. in automobile accidents." "Everyone talks about the population explosion," said Lewis Mumford. "It might be observed that the car explosion is equally in need of birth control." The February 1970 issue of *Fortune* quoted one Detroit city planner, commenting on the problems of the auto: "If you're going to drive you'd better do it before 1975." Richard J. Sullivan, eloquent commissioner of New Jersey's State Department of Environmental Protection, quotes a friend as saying that since New Jersey's human population increases 25 percent a decade and its automobile population increases 40 percent a decade, by 2011 or so, "every fourth car that goes by will be driverless!"

Americans make up only 6 percent of the world's population, but we own—and drive and park—one-half of the world's passenger cars. In this country there is one car for every two persons, but statistically it averages out that less than two persons (1.2) ride in one car per trip.

Demographers estimate that there will be 230 million Americans by 1980, a gain of 3 million per year—like adding one city larger than Boston every year—and more than half of that increase will be in the three major corridor complexes: the Northeast, California, and the Great Lakes region. About 8 out of 10 Americans now live in cities. Within thirty years, if the trend continues, it will be 9 out of 10. Moving all these Americans around by automobile will be impossible, because a one-lane highway can handle only 2,000 cars an hour, a six-lane highway only 9,000.

Auto deaths in the one year of 1970 (55,300) exceeded all American deaths (44,249) in the Vietnam War from 1961 through 1970, and in 1973 highway deaths were predicted to reach more than 57,000. Each year an estimated 170,000 people are permanently maimed, and close to 3.5 million are injured. (Safety devices run up the price of new automobiles. U.S. Department of Labor figures show that in 1968 auto safety features cost the buyer an average of $53 per car and by 1972 they had increased to $143. DOT estimates the total extra cost by 1976 will be $615 per car.)

Automobiles account for about 85 percent of the noise pollution in a city, according to *The User's Guide to the Protection of the Environment*.

We have 3.2 million miles of paved highways. Just to build the nation's 41,000-mile Interstate system, according to DOT's pamphlet "American Lifelines," required enough concrete to build six sidewalks to the moon; enough sand, gravel, and crushed stone to build a mound fifty feet wide and nine feet high completely around the world; and enough tar and asphalt to pave 35 million home driveways. The steel required for bridges, overpasses, railings, and foundations took 30 million tons of iron ore, 18 million tons of coal and 6.5 million tons of limestone, plus astronomical amounts of slag, clay pipe, board lumber, explosives, and machinery. (General Motors' Charles Kettering boasted in the 1930s, "As a consumer of raw materials, the automobile has no equal in the history of mankind.")

To produce its 1968 models, Detroit used 19 million tons of steel, close to 2 million tons of rubber, over 1 million pounds of aluminum—and 54.7 percent of the year's total U.S. consumption of lead. In addition, it made heavy use of zinc and malleable iron.

Like most heavy eaters, the automobile industry has a waste

problem: how to get rid of discarded cars. We abandon about 1.4 million a year, but the average worth to the junk dealer, says a Bureau of Mines study, is only $55.94. Abandoned cars in New York City alone totaled 83,000 in 1971, an increase of 13,000 over three years earlier and 20 times the figure of ten years ago. The national total in 1972 was between 2.5 and 7.6 million. Disposing of these sad cadavers without despoiling the landscape is enormously costly.

More than two-thirds of our nation's energy comes from petroleum, of which daily consumption is 15 million barrels, and increasing. Our consumption of crude petroleum has increased 300 percent in the last forty years, while our population was growing by 63 percent.

The automobile accounts for 40 percent of our petroleum usage. (The rest of the world burns only 14 percent of the petroleum it uses in autos.) We consume over 93 billion gallons of gasoline a year, or 26 million gallons a day; or 18,000 gallons every minute. The average passenger car burns 700 gallons per year. A commercial airliner burns between 1,700 and 4,800 gallons in one hour, depending on its type and payload.

Our own petroleum reserve is put at 40 billion barrels—about a 30-to-35-year supply at our present consumption. William P. Tavoulareas, president of the Mobil Oil Corporation, says, "The U.S. is depleting its reserves of oil faster than they can be replaced." *New York Times* columnist Anthony Lewis wrote from Stockholm at the completion of the United Nations Environmental Conference in June 1972 that an oilman there had said, "it would take 'a new Kuwait' annually just to satisfy increased American use."

The United States is engaged in a world-wide search for new sources of oil—off the coast of western Africa, off southern Australia, in the North Sea, in northern Alaska, in the Everglades, and practically everywhere along this country's outer shelf. Other countries are as eager as we to discover oil. Yitzhak Rabin, Israeli Ambassador to the United States, complained about the lack of oil in Israel: "Moses traveled forty years in the desert and picked the only country in the Middle East with no oil."

More than eight thousand wells have been drilled off the Gulf of Mexico's shores, and around Los Angeles, oil companies have drilled in backyards, in parks, in streets, in harbors, and even under the Los Angeles city hall and police station. Under consideration is the controversial mining of oil-shale rock, much of it located in public lands, which would leave great scars similar to those of strip mining.

The biggest and most recent U.S. oil strike, on Alaska's North Slope at Prudhoe Bay, raised the problem of how to get the oil to market without irreparable damage to the environment, a problem over which the oil industry might have lost little sleep had it not been for U.S. conservationists.

But even getting the Alaskan North Slope oil will satisfy only about 5 percent of our projected annual demand. According to a Standard Oil Company advertisement, the Alaskan strike would give us just a three-year supply if we depended on it alone.

We now get about 23 percent of our oil from abroad—a cause of much concern to this country because of the payments and international politics involved. At present there is every indication that U.S. oil companies will have to continue to increase their payments to oil-producing countries as petroleum sources dry up, and therefore the price of gasoline to U.S. consumers will continue to rise.

Oil tankers continue to increase in size. Some being built are 1,280 feet long; others on the drawing boards will be 1,600 feet long. Oil spills become more frequent and more serious. Most occur in the vicinity of underwater vegetation (80 percent occur within ten miles of shore), so that beaches and most varieties of sea life are affected.

John F. O'Leary, former head of the U.S. Bureau of Mines and an energy economist with the Atomic Energy Commission, has called the present fuel situation—i.e., exponential increases in our demand on finite supplies—"a nightmare." He said we are running out of oil, atomic energy is too far off to help in the immediate future, and use of coal produces too many environmental problems. We must, he said, place even greater reliance on imported oil—*and use less.*

"*Lewis M. Branscomb, former director of the National Bureau of Standards, has a sure-fire way to solve the automobile pollution problem.*

"*He suggests 'a law that all automobile engine exhausts must be discharged into the passenger compartment. Then the owner would have the exclusive benefit (and cost) of the pollution, and he would soon either take up walking or pay what it takes for an automotive technology that produces nice smelling exhaust of no toxicity or no exhaust at all.'*"

—*Science & Government Report,* January 15, 1973

"*By driving 10 men with heart disease through heavy morning Los Angeles freeway traffic, a team of doctors has found 'compelling evidence' that small amounts of carbon monoxide from automobile exhaust aggravates their pre-existing cardiac condition for at least two hours thereafter.*"

The New York Times, November 20, 1972

"*It is the very popularity of the automobile that now seriously threatens its usefulness. In many of our cities, we are confronted by pollution, congestion, noise, delay, ugliness, and urban breakdown on a scale that has not been seen since the last days of imperial Rome.*"

—ENVIRONMENTAL PROTECTION AGENCY ADMINISTRATOR
WILLIAM D. RUCKELSHAUS, addressing the American
Automobile Association, fall 1971

"Pollution control systems for automobiles could add $860 to the price and operating costs of cars by 1976, according to a report presented to a convention of the Society of Automotive Engineers today."
—*The New York Times*, January 9, 1973

"The mandate for clean automobile engines will mean gasoline prices of $1 a gallon in three or four years, a top Transportation Department official flatly predicts. The 1973 models, he notes, gobble 20 percent more fuel than last year's cars, and the '76s (which by law will have to be 90 percent pollution-free) will need another 20 percent. To make the open road even more expensive, the growing U.S. dependence on foreign oil (imports are expected to swell at a $1 billion-a-year rate) plus the price increases exporting countries have already started to impose will make the reading on the gas pumps even more forbidding."
—*Newsweek*, January 8, 1973

"For a decade, the drive to clean America's air has been expanding the maze of pollution controls in U.S. autos. At high cost, manufacturers have installed devices like positive crankcase ventilation systems, evaporative control systems and air injector reactor systems.

"Currently, the first meaningful tests of this apparatus are being conducted on cars that were driven for many miles and months under real-life conditions. The findings are discouraging for those who dream of purer air in and around traffic-choked cities. In too many instances, it seems, the pollution-control mechanisms aren't doing much to control pollution.

"This unhappy conclusion is emerging from emission-inspection programs begun this year in two of the most pollution-plagued states, New Jersey and California; they are the first statewide checkups in the nation.

"Here in the Garden State's capital, officials are pained at finding an unexpectedly large 30 percent of 1970 models and 25 percent of 1971 models spewing out either carbon monoxide or unburned gasoline hydrocarbons—or both—exceeding New Jersey's relatively lenient ceilings.

"In smog-smitten California, where standards are tougher, 30 percent of all vehicles tested thus far are over the limit, while the failure rate for 1970s and 1971s alone is an astounding 41 percent."
—*The Wall Street Journal*, December 14, 1972

AIRPLANES

Airports contribute to oil spillage into nearby bodies of water. For example, New York's Bureau of Environmental Protection in January 1971 reported that vast quantities of jet fuel and oil from Kennedy Airport were being dumped into Jamaica Bay, creating large oil slicks.

Airports contribute to the making of our asphalt desert, and as planes become larger, so do airports, Kennedy International, for example, is now approximately 5,000 acres (7.8 square miles). The Dallas–Fort Worth Airport, our first jumbo jetport, due to open in the summer of 1973, will cover about 17,000 acres, or 26.5 square miles—an area larger than Manhattan Island.

Airports not only have increased in size but have just about doubled in number since 1950. Still they cannot keep pace with air-traffic increases or the larger planes. Francis R. Gerard, director of aeronautics for the New Jersey Department of Transportation, in March 1971 urged the building of 19 new airports within that state. New Jersey already had 35.

No one with good hearing and good sense wants to live near a jetport, because jets are so noisy and dirty. Taking off, they dump pollutants every second, adding to the pollution resulting from automobile congestion around airports. Those who live in a jet alley also worry that one of those planes always taking off or landing will crash on them.

But noise is the major reason people move, or want to move, away from airports. Noise travels fast through today's thin-walled houses. The AMA warns that "noise pollution can cause deafness, may produce ulcers and hypertension."

A UCLA engineering research team reports that in Inglewood, the town nearest the Los Angeles International Airport, the noise level at times reaches 90 decibels. Because decibel gradients are measured logarithmically rather than arithmetically, this is 10,000 times the hazardous-to-health limit of 50 decibels. A rule of thumb: every 6-decibel increase in sound represents roughly a doubling of volume.

(During the worldwide strike of airline pilots, protesting airplane hijackers, in summer 1972, residents of Fregene, a beach village near Fiumicino Airport—and also near Rome—rejoiced, according to an AP dispatch. "You can hear the birds today," said a local fisherman resident. "We have had very little peace since they built the airport 12 years ago.")

During summer 1971, airport noise became so unbearable for those living five hundred feet from a newly constructed runway at the Los Angeles International Airport that the city, bowing to angry complaints—and to $4 billion worth of lawsuits during the preceding ten years—agreed to buy about two thousand houses (plus some schools and shops) through condemnation proceedings. Some were substantial houses, ranging in price from $28,000 to $115,000. It cost the city over $200 million and the owners of those houses a lot of trouble.

———————

Gladwin Hill, writing in *The New York Times* in September 1972, said that "about 1 out of every 10 persons in the country lives close enough to airports to be bothered by plane noise and the number of airports and the amount of air traffic are expected to multiply in the years ahead."

A California law passed in 1972 requires jetports to monitor every plane takeoff and landing. Airlines are subject to $1,000 fines if individual planes are too noisy. Should the cumulative amount of noise in one twenty-four-hour period be too much, then there are additional fines. The law also provides for a twelve-year phased reduction of airport noise, beginning December 1, 1972. The law may be tested in the courts, since it may conflict with federal interstate commerce laws. The airlines are reported to be apprehensive on the subject, and some airline officials warn that such a law would cripple Southern California's economy.

The University of California in August 1972 reported that children attending school near the Los Angeles airport not only ran the danger of suffering permanent hearing damage from jet aircraft noise but also were being harmed emotionally. And a two-year London study showed that residents near London's Heathrow Airport were being admitted to mental institutions at an increasing rate.

Many Federation Aviation Agency experts recommend that new cities of the future set aside 20,000 to 30,000 acres (31.2 to 47 square miles) of land as jetport sites to avoid local opposition. Many older communities no longer have unused land nearby, and as we have seen, when they want to go farther out to "virgin" land, the conservationists are waiting for them.

"Five primary grades at Fisk School may have to be relocated if large jet airplanes continue to fly over the school, according to Ewing School Board President Frank Viteritto.

"Viteritto said the school board is concerned that jets taking off from Mercer County Airport will continue to frighten children at the West Trenton elementary school.

"He said that when a 727 jetliner took off from the runway October 5, it flew so low over the school that children ducked, and some screamed."

—*The Trenton Evening Times*, October 17, 1972

BIBLIOGRAPHY

Alexander, Herbert C., *Financing the 1968 Election* (Lexington, Mass.: D. C. Heath, 1971)

America's Sound Transportation Review Organization, *The American Railroad Industry: A Prospectus* (Washington, D.C.: July 1970)

Ayres, Edward, *What's Good for GM* (Nashville: Aurora, 1970)

Barsley, Michael, *Orient Express: The Story of the World's Most Fabulous Train* (London: MacDonald, 1966)

Beebe, Lucius, *Mixed Train Daily* (Berkeley: Howell-Norton, 1961)

——, *Mr. Pullman's Elegant Palace Car* (New York: Doubleday, 1961)

——, and Clegg, Charles, *Hear the Train Blow: A Pictorial Epic of America in the Railroad Age* (New York: Dutton, 1952)

Behrend, George, *Grand European Expresses* (London: Allen and Unwin, 1962)

Benarde, Melvin A., *Our Precarious Habitat* (New York: Norton, 1970)

British and American TACV System Developments (The Mitre Corporation, September 1970)

Brown, Tom, *Oil on Ice* (San Francisco: Sierra Club, 1971)

Buchanan, Lamont, *Steel Trails and Iron Horses* (New York: Putnam, 1955)

The Budget of the United States Government, 1973 (Washington, D.C.: U.S. Government Printing Office, 1972)

The Budget of the United States Government, 1974 (Washington, D.C.: U.S. Government Printing Office, 1973)

Burby, John, *The Great American Motion Sickness, or Why You Can't Get There from Here* (Boston: Little, Brown, 1971)

Burt, Olive W., *The Story of American Railroads and How They Helped Build a Nation* (New York: John Day, 1969)

Carper, Robert S., *The Railroad in Transition* (New York: Barnes, 1968)

Clark, Ira G., *Then Came the Railroads* (Norman: University of Oklahoma Press, 1958)

Commoner, Barry, *The Closing Circle* (New York: Knopf, 1971)

Cullen, Donald E., *National Emergency Studies* (Geneva, N.Y.: Humphrey Press, 1968)

Daughen, Joseph R., and Binzen, Peter, *The Wreck of the Penn Central* (Boston: Little, Brown, 1971)

Davies, J. Clarence, III, *The Politics of Pollution* (New York: Pegasus, 1971)

De Bell, Garrett, *The Voter's Guide to Environmental Politics* (New York: Ballantine, 1970)

———, ed., *The Environmental Handbook* (New York: Ballantine, 1970)

Donovan, Frank P., Jr., *The Railroad in Literature* (Boston: Railway Locomotive Historical Society, 1940)

"DOT High Speed Ground Test Center" (A pamphlet) (1971)

Ellis, Hamilton, *The Pictorial Encyclopedia of Railways* (London: Hamlyn, 1968)

Environmental Quality—1970, The First Annual Report of the Council on Environmental Quality (Washington, D.C.: U.S. Government Printing Office, August 1970)

Environmnetal Quality—1971, The Second Annual Report of the Council on Environmental Quality (Washington, D.C.: U.S. Government Printing Office, August 1971)

Environmental Quality—1972, The Third Annual Report of the Council on Environmental Quality (Washington, D.C.: U.S. Government Printing Office, August 1972)

"Facts and Figures" (A pamphlet) (Tokyo: Japanese National Railways, 1970)

Falk, Richard A., *This Endangered Planet* (New York: Random House, 1971)

Faltermayer, Edmund K., *Redoing America* (New York: Harper and Row, 1968)

Fellmeth, Robert C., *The Interstate Commerce Omission* (The Ralph Nader Study Group Report) (New York: Grossman, 1970)

Final Report on Basic National Rail Passenger Service (Submitted by John A. Volpe, Secretary of Transportation) (Washington, D.C., January 28, 1971)

"Four Winds Private Train Tours, 1971–72" (A pamphlet) (New York)

Green, Mark J.; Fallows, James M.; and Zwick, David R., *Who Runs Congress* (Ralph Nader Congress Project) (New York: Bantam/ Grossman, 1972)

Hogg, Garry, *Orient Express* (New York: Walker, 1960)

Holdren, John, and Herrera, Philip, *Energy* (San Francisco: Sierra Club, 1971)

Howard, Ernest, *Wall Street Fifty Years After Erie* (Boston: Stratford, 1923)

Hyde, Philip, and Jett, Stephen C., *Navajo Wildlands* (New York: Sierra Club/Ballantine, 1967)

Japanese National Railways (Tokyo: Dai-Nippon Printing, 1968)

Jerome, John, *The Death of the Automobile* (New York: Norton, 1972)

Johnson, Arthur M., and Supple, Barry E., *Boston Capitalists and Western Railroads* (Cambridge: Harvard University Press, 1967)

Josephson, Matthew, *The Robber Barons* (New York: Harcourt, Brace and World, 1934)

Kane, Joseph Nathan, *The Pocket Book of Famous First Facts* (New York: Pocket Books, 1970)

Kelley, Ben, *The Pavers and the Paved* (New York: D. W. Brown, 1971)

Kratville, William W., *Steam, Steel and Limiteds* (Omaha: Barnhart Press, 1962)

Leavitt, Helen, *Superhighway—Superhoax* (New York: Doubleday, 1970)

Ley, Willy, *Engineers' Dreams* (New York: Viking, 1954)

Love, Sam, ed., *Earth Tool Kit* (Prepared by Environmental Action) (New York: Pocket Books, 1971)

Lyon, Peter, *To Hell in a Day Coach* (Philadelphia: Lippincott, 1968)

McWhirter, Norris D. and A. Ross, compilers, *Guinness Book of World Records* (New York: Bantam, 1971)

Mines, Samuel, *The Last Days of Mankind* (New York: Simon and Schuster, 1971)

Mitchell, John G., and Stallings, Constance L., eds., *Ecotactics: The Sierra Club Handbook for Environmental Activists* (New York: Pocket Books, 1970)

Morse, Frank P., *Cavalcade of the Rails* (New York: Dutton, 1940)

Mowbray, A. Q., *Road to Ruin* (Philadelphia: Lippincott, 1968)

Nader, Ralph, *Unsafe at Any Speed* (New York: Grossman, 1965)

"1970 Automobile Facts and Figures" (A pamphlet) (Detroit: Automobile Manufacturers Association)

Oakes Ames: A Memoir (Cambridge: Riverside Press, 1883)

O'Connor, Harvey, *The Empire of Oil* (New York: Monthly Review Press, 1955)

O'Connor, Richard, *The Oil Barons* (Boston: Little, Brown, 1971)

Passenger Train Service. Report of hearings before a subcommittee of the House Committee on Interstate and Foreign Commerce, November 1969

Phillips, Lance, *Yonder Comes the Train* (New York: A. S. Barnes, 1965)

Population and the American Future, The Report of the Commission on Population Growth and the American Future (Washington, D.C.: U.S. Government Printing Office, 1972)

Quiett, Glenn Chesney, *They Built the West* (New York: Appleton-Century, 1934)

Rathlesberger, James, ed., *Nixon and the Environment: The Politics of Devastation* (New York: The Village Voice, 1972)

Report of the New Jersey Clean Air Council on the Status of Air Pollution from Mobile Sources (1970 Annual Report) (Trenton, N.J.: 1970)

Ridgeway, James, *The Politics of Ecology* (New York: Dutton, 1970)

Schneider, Kenneth R., *Autokind vs. Mankind* (New York: Norton, 1971)

"Shin Kansen—The New Tokaido Line" (A pamphlet) (Tokyo: Japanese National Railways, 1968)

Stover, John F., *American Railroads* (Chicago: University of Chicago Press, 1961)

————, *The Life and Decline of the American Railroad* (New York: Oxford University Press, 1970)

Swatek, Paul, *The User's Guide to the Protection of the Environment*
New York: Ballantine, 1970)

"Tracked Air Cushion Research Vehicle/Guideway System" (A pamphlet) (New York: Grumman Aerospace Corporation)

Transpo 72 Official Program (DOT) (New York: Spencer Marketing Services, 1972)

Udall, Stewart L., *The Quiet Crisis* (New York: Holt, Rinehart and Winston, 1963)

"UMTA Approvals of Capital Grants and Loans and Technical Studies Grants" (An analysis) (Washington, D.C.: March 24, 1971)

U.S. Department of Commerce, *Statistical Abstract of the United States, 1971*

"U.S. Department of Transportation—Facts and Functions" (A pamphlet) (Washington, D.C.: U.S. Government Printing Office, 1971)

U.S. Department of Transportation, *Fourth Annual Report* (Fiscal Year 1970) (Washington, D.C.: U.S. Government Printing Office)

————, *Northeast Corridor Transportation Project Report* (Washington, D.C.: April 1970)

————, *Rail Passenger Statistics in the Northeast Corridor* (Washington, D.C., 1969)

————, *Recommendations for Northeast Corridor Transportation*, Vols. 1–3 (Washington, D.C.: May 1971)

————, *Third Annual Report* (Fiscal Year 1969) (Washington, D.C.: U.S. Government Printing)

————, *Transportation Research Opportunities for Universities* (Washington, D.C., 1972)

U.S. Interstate Commerce Commission, *Review of Preliminary Report on Basic National Rail Passenger System* (Washington, D.C., 1970)

Wenger, William, *Eisenbahnen der Welt* (Lausanne, Switzerland: Mondo-Verlag, 1969)

Among periodicals we found particularly helpful, in addition to those cited in the book itself, are the following:

Audubon
Better Homes and Gardens
The Concrete Opposition (Highway Action Coalition)
Congressional Record
Dow Metal Product News

Environmental Action
Environmental Report
Gourmet
Holiday
Industrial Research
Island Ad-vantages (Stonington, Maine)
The Lamp (Standard Oil Co., New Jersey)
National Geographic
National Journal
National Wildlife
Newsweek
The New Yorker
Not Man Apart (Friends of the Earth)
Philadelphia Bulletin
Philadelphia Inquirer
Population Bulletin
Princeton Engineer
Reader's Digest
Research Trends (Cornell Aeronautical Laboratory, Inc.)
Sierra Club Bulletin
Sierra Club National News Report
The Smilodon (Department of Geological and Geophysical Sciences, Princeton University)
TVASNAC "Quotes" (Town-Village Aircraft Safety and Noise Abatement Committee, Hempstead, Long Island)
University: A Princeton Quarterly
Washington Science Trends

ACKNOWLEDGMENTS

THIS BOOK originated as an article in the Winter 1970–71 issue of *University: A Princeton Quarterly*. We are indebted to Peter Schwed and Daniel Green of Simon and Schuster for encouraging and helping us to develop that article into this book.

We owe thanks also to Edwin C. Hutter, a dedicated student of railroads, who not only gave us access to his extensive library of clippings, articles, reports, and studies, but encouraged us throughout our effort. Many others contributed facts, ideas, encouragement, advice, and criticism—among them Cleveland S. White, Gary Soucie, Robert Waldrop, Owen P. Curtis, Eleanor Lee Templeman, William T. Sutphin, Marshall Sittig, Patricia A. Taylor, The Honorable William H. Maness, Gar Kagnowich (executive assistant to Senator Clifford P. Case), Dorothy S. Tenenbaum (legislative assistant to Senator Lee Metcalf), and Professors Marcus P. Knowlton, Francis C. Moon, Paul M. Lion, Masakazu Konishi, Ahmet S. Cakmak, Ralph H. Fox, and Richard A. Lester.

Staff members of many organizations were extremely helpful, including especially those of the Port Authority of New York and New Jersey, New Jersey Department of Transportation, Association of American Railroads, Bay Area Rapid Transit (California), Port Authority Transit Corporation (Lindenwold), Santa Fe Railway, U.S. Department of Transportation (including the Federal Railroad Administration, Urban Mass Transportation, and the Alaska Railroad), Four Winds Travel, Inc., National Railway and Labor Conference Board, Metropolitan Transportation Authority, Louis T. Klauder and Associates, Japanese National Railways, French National Railroads (SNCF), White

Pass and Yukon Route, Penn Central, National Railroad Passenger Corporation (Amtrak), National Association of Railroad Passengers, American Transit Association, Council on Environmental Quality, and Auto-Train Corporation.

For reading and criticizing the manuscript at various stages we would thank Laurie Chauncey, Donald D. Crane, Suzanne Fremon, Janet Gemmell, Otto Janssen, Ann McCleery, and Margot Southerland.

For her helpful copy editing, our thanks to Lynn Chalmers.

For typing above and beyond the call of duty, Camille Biros, Frances Conover, Lucy Schon, and Margot Southerland.

Index